The Political Economy of Defense Contracting

The Political Economy of Defense Contracting

KENNETH R. MAYER

YALE UNIVERSITY PRESS

NEW HAVEN AND LONDON

Set in Times Roman and Futura types by Keystone Typesetting, Inc.,
Orwigsburg, Pennsylvania.
Printed in the United States of America by BookCrafters, Inc.,
Chelsea, Michigan.

Library of Congress Cataloging-in-Publication Data

Mayer, Kenneth R., 1960–
The political economy of defense contracting / Kenneth R. Mayer.
p. cm.
Revision of the author's thesis (Ph.D.—Yale University, 1988)
Includes bibliographical references and index.
ISBN 0-300-04524-7
1. United States—Armed Forces—Procurement. 2. Patronage, Political—
United States. 3. United States. Congress. I. Title.
UC263.M35   1991
355.6′211′0973—dc20   91-15358 CIP

The paper in this book meets the guidelines for permanence and durability of
the Committee on Production Guidelines for Book Longevity of the Council
on Library Resources.

10 9 8 7 6 5 4 3 2 1

To Marty and Judy

CONTENTS

Few issues of the past decade have attracted more attention than defense procurement, and few issues have generated as much criticism of Congress. Congress stands accused of selling out both national defense and the public trust, as legislators appear to show more concern about the economic benefits produced by defense contracts—or the PAC money produced by defense contractors—than about whether weapons actually do what they are supposed to. The military and defense contractors encourage this interpretation by intentionally focusing on the issue of jobs when they present their programs to Congress. Yet political scientists have been unable to find conclusive evidence that such practices are as widespread as is believed, or that they make much difference.

This book represents an attempt to arrive at a more complete explanation of how politics affects defense contracting decisions. My major contention is that political theories of defense contracting vastly overstate the influence of parochialism on congressional decision making. This conclusion is based on analysis of several measures of contracting activity, such as accurate data on the distribution of subcontracts for several major weapons systems, which have never been available before. Using it, one can eliminate the most vexing obstacle to effective work in the political economy of defense: finding out exactly where defense prime contract work is performed and whether such allocation makes any difference in shaping congressional attitudes about specific programs. Without this kind of information, it is impossible to determine whether defense contracts are spread around the country in order to build support in Congress or whether members will even respond when work is awarded to their districts (the answer to both questions that immediately comes to mind—"of course"—is often wrong).

The book proceeds as follows: Chapter 1 discusses the popular notions of how politics shapes defense contracting decisions and illustrates the problems involved in journalistic approaches that assume politics is everywhere. Chapter 2 is a detailed description of the various players in the contracting process; focusing on Congress and defense contractors, it outlines the relationship between the congressional budget cycle and the procurement process. Chapter 3 is an overview of the weapons acquisition process itself: how the military services conceive, develop, and produce weapons.

Each of the remaining chapters deals with one of the popularly held notions of how congressional politics affects defense contracting decisions. Chapter 4 examines campaign contributions by defense contractors with a view toward determining if members change their votes on the basis of how money is distributed (and whether defense contractors change their contribution patterns according to how members vote). Chapter 5 addresses the critical question of whether members vote for weapons on the basis of district-level economic considerations; the analysis uses data on subcontract distribution for two nuclear aircraft carriers to see if a congressional vote to cancel the contracts was in any way dependent on the economic consequences. Chapter 6 looks at the nature of congressional influence in the procurement process and concludes that although members have very little say in determining where contracts are awarded, prime contractors do spread subcontracts around the country as widely as they can. Chapter 7 looks for evidence of an electoral cycle in defense contract awards. Throughout, an attempt is made to subject to rigorous empirical testing the various hypotheses generated by the political model of the contracting process.

The picture that emerges is one of a contracting process that is, at one level, consumed by political activity that ultimately makes very little difference in either the selection of which weapons the United States buys or indeed, the setting of the overall level of defense spending. At the same time, though, everyone involved in the process acts as though politics really matters. Defense contractors find political activity (subcontract targeting, campaign contributions) to be a reasonably priced insurance policy, one that they are afraid of doing without. Members of Congress make use of the substantial political benefits that defense contracts can generate, but the contracting decisions that the Pentagon makes would be much the same even if no such benefits existed. The politics of defense contracting involves a great deal of smoke, but very little fire.

ACKNOWLEDGMENTS

This book is a revised version of my Ph.D. dissertation. Bruce Russett and Ed Tufte, my advisers at Yale, supervised the dissertation over a four-year period with persistence and wisdom. My friends and colleagues at the Naval Air Systems Command were a source of much valuable insight into the contracting process; my year there gave me the unique opportunity to view the process from the inside. I conducted much of the early research for this project while working as a research assistant at the Brookings Institution. Both then and later, David and Samuel Menefee-Libey, Joe White, Jim Lindsay, and Samuel Kernell provided extensive comment, criticism, and direction. I completed the dissertation as a John M. Olin Dissertation fellow at Harvard University's Center for International Affairs, a privilege made greater by my colleagues there and by Samuel P. Huntington, the center's director, who has succeeded in creating a stimulating research environment.

In making the transition from dissertation to book, I benefited from the insight of Rob McCalla, Dave Tarr, Robert Higgs, Charlotte Twight, and Tom Glennan and Paul Hill of the RAND Corporation. Most of the time I was smart enough to take their advice.

A few people deserve special mention. Michael Berger gave me invaluable suggestions and comment over a six-year period and never failed to provoke ideas when I encountered what appeared to be dead ends. Christopher Thorn, my research assistant, collected nearly all of the data on PAC activity, putting himself and his hard disk through many hours of painstaking work. I would never have completed revisions during my first year of teaching without his help.

Various members of Congress, officials in the Department of Defense, defense industry personnel, and people working on defense issues in the nonprofit domain consented to interviews or provided critical data.

In most cases, I promised anonymity. Without them, this study would not have been possible.

Finally, I thank my family, especially my parents, and my wife, Susan, for her constant admonitions to "write, write, write" and her reminders of how life would be when I finished.

AH-64A	Apache attack helicopter
ATF	Advanced Tactical Fighter
CAS	Close Air Support
CBO	Congressional Budget Office
CVN	Navy designation of nuclear-powered aircraft carriers
DAB	Defense Acquisition Board
DIVAD	Division Air Defense Gun (Sergeant York), an army short-range antiaircraft gun system
DOD	Department of Defense
DSARC	Defense Systems Acquisition Review Council
FAR	Federal Acquisition Regulation
FSD	Full-scale development
FY	Fiscal year
GAO	General Accounting Office
HASC	House Armed Services Committee
HADS	House Appropriations Committee, Subcommittee on Defense
MLRS	Multiple Launch Rocket System
MRC	Military Reform Caucus
NATF	Navy version of the Advanced Tactical Fighter
NSI	National Security Index

OMB	Office of Management and Budget
OSD	Office of the Secretary of Defense
PAC	Political Action Committee
RFP	Request for proposal
SASC	Senate Armed Services Committee
SADS	Senate Appropriations Committee, Subcommittee on Defense
SDI	Strategic Defense Initiative
TADS/PNVS	Target Acquisition Designation Sight/Pilot Night Vision Sensor; fire control package for AH-64A Apache attack helicopter
TFX	Tactical Fighter Experimental; early name for F-111 fighter/bomber
TPP	Total package procurement

The Political Economy of Defense Contracting

Four Myths about the Politics of Defense Contracting

Each year since 1980, the Pentagon has awarded about $120 billion in defense contracts to develop and buy weapons. That figure—equivalent to six months' worth of South Korea's gross national product—makes defense procurement the largest discretionary class of government spending by a wide margin. Defense procurement absorbs an enormous absolute fraction of our national wealth, a level of commitment that cannot be sustained without public confidence in the institutions and individuals that make up the system. Even before Eastern Europe and the Soviet Union made remarkable moves toward democracy, the post-1980 public consensus favoring higher defense budgets, which Ronald Reagan parlayed into the largest peacetime military buildup in U.S. history, had begun to crumble in the face of images of procurement waste and fraud, including outrage over $435 hammers and $7,000 coffeepots. The breakdown of public support for defense spending was no doubt hastened by the widespread impression that the procurement troika—defense contractors, members of Congress, and the Pentagon—were too friendly with each other. The ambition of defense contractors to secure more defense work, Congress's desire to preserve the jobs produced by defense contracts, and the military's perceived need to protect its pet weapons at all costs—even if they do not work—appeared to produce procurement decisions based more on political expediency than national interest.

An understanding of the domestic political and economic factors that drive defense procurement will be critical to any effort to reduce the defense budget in the next decade. Now that the Warsaw Pact has ceased to exist and the Soviet Union no longer poses the threat it once did, American policymakers are being forced to find ways to reduce defense spending. Already the first budget skirmishes have been contentious. In the fiscal year (FY) 1990 budget cycle, Congress overrode Secretary of Defense Richard Cheney's decision to cancel the navy's F-14 fighter and the Marine Corps' V-22 tilt-rotor aircraft. Congress is poised to make deep cuts in future budget requests, and fights between the Department of Defense (DOD) and Congress are likely over the B-2 bomber, modernization of intercontinental ballistic missiles, and the fate of expensive weapons now in development. Supporters of defense spending point to the Persian Gulf War as justification for increased budgets, but the war has not altered the Pentagon's plans to reduce spending significantly by 1995.[1]

These fights will only become worse if the budget is to shrink to levels recommended by some members of the defense community, such as William Kaufmann of the Brookings Institution, who believes that the budget can be reduced by as much as 50 percent in the 1990s.[2] If that is to occur, and if there is to be a significant peace dividend available for domestic needs, members of Congress will have to learn to do without major defense contracts and military bases. Many observers claim that such congressional self-denial is impossible, arguing that politics, a code word for Congress's desire to protect local economic benefits, will prevent such a reduction. So strong is the attraction of the jobs produced by defense spending that Congress will not allow severe budget cuts; to do so would be political suicide.

Yet this popularly accepted notion of how domestic political considerations affect defense spending is a gross oversimplification. Pork barrel politics, a staple of theories explaining large defense budgets, simply cannot serve as a complete explanation of how Congress acts on defense. Why were many members of Congress—especially those who objected when Cheney canceled the F-14—elated when former secretary of defense Caspar Weinberger canceled the Sergeant York division air defense gun (DIVAD) in 1985? Why was the New York congressional delegation successful in saving the F-14 in 1989, when it was unable to rescue the T-46 trainer from cancellation in 1986? Why did Congress in effect force the army to cancel its Cheyenne attack helicopter and Main Battle Tank? If Congress is concerned only about jobs, why did it cut Reagan's defense budget requests every year? The quest for economic benefits and jobs by itself cannot explain these outcomes. Clearly we need a more sophisticated understanding of how politics controls the procurement process.

The belief that the defense budget is driven by domestic political necessity is based on a number of mistaken notions—popular myths—of how Congress and the military deal with each other. These myths, which are uncritically accepted as fact, can be grouped into four categories:

—Congress supports major weapons systems because defense contracts produce jobs in many congressional districts and states. It will not cancel weapons because doing so sacrifices economic benefits;

—Congress supports major weapons systems according to how campaign contributions from defense contractors are distributed;

—the Pentagon awards defense contracts to particular companies in order to win the support of influential legislators, hoping that the creation or safeguarding of jobs in their state or district will overcome opposition;

—members of Congress can demand that the Pentagon award a contract to pet firms in their districts or states.

The number of cases set forth as proof of these statements is huge. Systems as diverse as the B-1 bomber, the MX missile, and the V-22 tiltrotor aircraft are said to have survived only because they produce so many jobs. Lockheed is said to have won the C-5 cargo transport because it agreed to build the plane in Senator Richard Russell's home state of Georgia; Northrop won the B-2 contract because it had been cheated out of F-20 fighter sales; General Dynamics won the F-111 contract over Boeing because of its connections to the White House. Nearly every journalistic study of defense contracting has confirmed the importance of pork barrel politics and would undoubtedly view conclusions to the contrary as hopelessly naive. Public interest lobbying groups are quick to argue that, as Common Cause puts it, "very few legislators, even defense critics and fiscal conservatives, will oppose costly, destabilizing, or faulty weapons systems when his or her [sic] district stands to benefit from defense contracts."[3] Even people active in the defense community claim that politics is paramount: former Office of Management and Budget (OMB) official Richard Stubbing claims, "Often it is raw politics, not military considerations, which ultimately determines the winner [of a contract]."[4] At the same time, scholarly treatments of the procurement process have concluded that defense contracting is unaffected by political or pork barrel considerations. Political scientists have tried to move beyond anecdotal evidence by analyzing, for example, whether DOD targets contracts into the districts or states of influential legislators—especially those on the Armed Services committees and relevant Appropriations subcommittees. This research track has produced uniformly negative results, which leads to unconvincing explanations of why Congress has no influence on how DOD distributes defense benefits. Economic analyses have come to the same conclusion, producing a clear picture of an entirely apolitical contracting structure.

Why are we faced with two such divergent views of the procurement process? How can some people see politics everywhere, while others cannot find it at all? First, consider the arguments made by those who see pervasive politics. Some of the problems with this line of reasoning can be grouped into three broad categories:

Generalizations from anecdotes. It is always possible to find some members of Congress whose support for a weapon system correlates with their district or state level benefit. Examples are often taken as proof of a causal relationship that holds for the entire institution. Critics of the B-1B made much of Senator Alan Cranston's (D-Cal.) support of the aircraft, a position at odds with his consistent opposition to strategic nuclear systems (the same is true of Senator Howard Metzenbaum [D-Ohio], in whose state the B-1's engines were built). Since Rockwell International would build the plane in southern California, Cranston's support was taken as clear evidence that the economic benefits from defense contracts can co-opt even doves.[5] Although Cranston may have been concerned about jobs, few pork barrel expositors go on to note that Cranston is a leading opponent of the B-2 bomber, which stands to bring about twice as much money into California at a time when the state's defense industry is in the midst of a serious slump.

Anecdotal explanations as a rule also tend to ignore examples that run counter to the expected role of pork barrel influence. Congress did not vote to extend B-1B production after 1986, even though the end of the program effectively put Rockwell out of the combat aircraft business; John Glenn (D-Ohio) introduced legislation to keep production open but did not come close to succeeding. Local economic impact worked against MX basing proposals and the proposed Staten Island Naval Base, with the affected constituencies opposing the projects despite the large economic benefits each would have provided.[6] It is, furthermore, a mistake to conclude that Congress as an institution bases its weapons procurement decisions on economic impact simply because one or two members are found to do so. James Lindsay found that none of the votes ever recorded on the B-1 bomber would have changed even if every member with contracts in his or her district or state had voted on the basis of economic interests.[7]

Some research uses misleading analytical methods to support the argument that contract awards are made according to the power of certain key members of Congress. A study of contract award patterns for the Strategic Defense Initiative (SDI) noted that 92 percent of the prime contracts awarded in FY 1985 went to states represented on Senate military committees.[8] The implication is either that Senate committee members encouraged those awards or that the Pentagon distributed the contracts to win their support. However, the statistics by themselves say little. Of the $4.3 billion in SDI contracts awarded to those states in FY 1985, $3.7 billion, or 86 percent, went to California, New Mexico, Massachusetts, and Alabama. California and Massachusetts top the list of states doing defense work, so their presence here is expected. Los Alamos, one of the largest recipients of SDI contracts, is a major high-energy physics research center located in New Mexico. And Alabama is home to the Army Ballistic Missile Defense Command, which oversees many SDI contracts. The geographic location of contractors and research facilities that are able to perform SDI work, not committee memberships, explains why SDI contracts are distributed as they are.

Anecdotal evidence can be useful in highlighting events or patterns of potential interest. Their use, however, can lead to the fundamental empirical error of confusing correlation with causation.

Generation of nonfalsifiable political explanations. Given a particular example of congressional or Pentagon action on a defense contract, it is always possible to explain the action as the insidious result of illegitimate political pressures. Critics claim that Congress, against the DOD's wishes, voted to fund the V-22 because it produces jobs (indeed, the argument is made even by some supporters of the aircraft). However, Congress did not consider the V-22 in a vacuum. The tilt-rotor aircraft competed for funding with the two existing helicopters it was designed to replace, the CH-60 and CH-53 (both built by Sikorsky). The need for the V-22 mission was accepted; the controversy was over what mix of systems could meet the need at lowest cost. Where was Sikorsky during this debate? Perhaps it was staying out of the fight, but it stood to lose hundreds of millions of dollars in contracts if the V-22 survived. One can easily imagine the headlines if Congress had been unable to save the V-22: "Sikorsky Lobbying and PAC Money Save Endangered Programs."

Political explanations frequently neglect the effects of these cross-pressures. For example, the outcomes of both of the issues discussed in chapter 3 (the army's attempt to establish a second source for the M-1 tank engine and Boeing's nearly successful effort to substitute 747s for C-5B transports), are explained as the direct result of the political power (and Political Action Committee [PAC] money) of the winning side. On both issues, though, powerful forces were aligned on both sides: AVCO Corporation against United Technologies on the M-1 engine; Boeing, the commercial airlines, and banks against Lockheed on the C-5B/747. In either case, the same story—albeit with switched names—would suffice to explain any of the results.

One account of the T-46 air force trainer aircraft (a case more fully discussed in chapter 7) savages the New York delegation for trying to protect a plane that was behind schedule, overpriced, built with defective parts, and poorly managed by the contractor. Yet rather than find virtue in the fact that Congress ultimately scrapped the program, Robert Higgs calls the case "a monument to congressional parochialism." He also criticizes key T-46 opponent Senator Robert Dole (R-Kan.), who represented the state where the T-46's major competition was built, as "acting on this occasion as the senator from Cessna."[9] Congress, it seems, is criticized for building systems and also for not building systems.

In cases such as these, political explanations suffice no matter what the outcome may be. As such, theories of political influence might be of value in describing events, but they cannot serve as useful explanations.

Confusing spectacle with substance. There is no doubt that politics—here defined as the process of deciding how scarce resources should be distributed—consumes the defense budget and contracting processes. Competing players jockey for position, push their own agendas, seek to advance their own interests, and use whatever resources they have to persuade other decision makers. Some contracts are awarded for political reasons. A notable recent example is the awarding of a small business set-aside contract for engines to the corrupt WEDTECH Corporation, granted to the company over the army's objections after the company enlisted the support of powerful Washington officials, including presidential adviser Ed Meese. Once the White House became involved, the army succumbed to substantial political pressure and gave the contract to WEDTECH, even though it doubted the company could do the work.[10] Congressional politics intrudes as well on parts of the process. Yet politically motivated awards, especially ones involving big-ticket weapons programs, are too rare to permit generalizations.

It is the major contention of this book that nearly all of the political activity surrounding major defense contracts is largely for show and has little substantive impact on the process. Indeed, it is in every member's interest to maintain the illusion that the contracting award process is political. Legislators like to give the impression that they hold sway with the Pentagon—a myth once reinforced by the practice (since discontinued) of having congressmen announce contract awards to local companies. The making of such announcements gave them the opportunity to take the credit when local companies were awarded contracts and allowed them to deflect criticism when "their" contractors lost. In the latter case members could claim the contract was rigged or call for investigations or otherwise express outrage that their constituents have been cheated. Members whose districts stand to lose major contracts will naturally fight to preserve them, yet the efforts are largely symbolic and will fail if the only argument in favor of a program is jobs. Moreover, the success or failure of the attempt to save the contract can be less important than the fact that the member made the effort. Such performances, however, naturally give the impression that winning a contract is as much a matter of political pull as technical merit.

Another reason behind this impression that politics drives weapons procurement is that other aspects of defense policy have blatant political roots. No one disputes that military bases are a classic example of pork barrel politics, and members will fight furiously to protect local installations that have no conceivable national security justification (in 1989, for example, the Utah delegation tried to preserve Fort Douglas, arguing that it was essential to defense; the base was originally established in the mid-nineteenth century to protect Pony Express mail routes). As I note in chapter 5, the Pentagon periodically tries to close bases in the districts of outspoken defense opponents. It is a short leap to conclude that this activity extends to defense contracts, even though such is rarely the case.

These criticisms of political explanations of defense contracting decisions are not meant to signify unqualified acceptance of the political science literature, which cannot find any evidence of political influence. It would be foolish to argue that politics never intrudes on the process, that no one ever votes on the basis of local economic benefit, or that DOD has never steered a contract toward a particular firm for political expediency. That politics influences defense contracting is a given; what matters is the kind of influence exerted. Both the popular and scholarly literatures are wrong in concluding that political influences are absent or pervasive. The full story of the politics of defense contracting is much more complex and subtle than either brute force explanation allows.

The picture that emerges from this investigation shows that domestic political and economic considerations do shape contracting decisions, but in ways that are more subtle than defense critics will admit. These political and economic effects can be grouped into four substantive categories:

Congressional Response to Local Economic Benefits. Members of Congress do not, as a rule, vote for (or against) a particular weapon on the basis of the amount of work to be performed in their state or district. Once other considerations are taken into account—predisposition to support defense spending in general, personal characteristics, and political party—spending has very little effect on a member's vote. Although some members, under some circumstances, will use economic impacts as their decisions rule, their votes will almost never be decisive (in the aircraft carrier vote examined in chapter 4, a number of conservative Republicans voted against the ships). Local economic interest may get a member's attention and put an issue on the congressional agenda, but it will not determine outcomes.

Congressional Response to Defense Contractor Lobbying. Defense contractors spend millions of dollars on campaign contributions and congressional lobbying, unexceptional behavior given their reliance on government contracts. Contractors invest heavily in PAC activity and make their heaviest campaign contributions to influential members of the Armed Services committees and Defense Appropriations subcommittees. These contributions do not appear to purchase votes; careful analysis shows that nearly all defense contractor PAC money flows to members who are predisposed to support defense programs—their voting behavior would have been the same even if contributions had stopped. This contribution pattern suggests that contractors are not as smart as critics argue. From a rational choice perspective, contractors would be better off giving to defense moderates and fence sitters: giving money to hawks is preaching to the converted.

Politicized Defense Contract Distributions. The Pentagon is sharply limited in the extent to which it can distribute prime contracts politically. Prime contractors, however, face no such constraints and purposely spread subcontracts for large defense programs over as wide a geographic area as practicable, commonly including more than 45 states and 250 congressional districts. The idea is to give as many members as possible some sort of economic stake in a program. Even though a wide distribution of subcontracts will not guarantee a program's survival, having a broad economic distribution can place a weapon system on the congressional agenda—a position it might not otherwise occupy.

Even though individual members of Congress hold little sway over the Pentagon in selecting contractors—they cannot, for example, make a few phone calls and change the outcome of a source competition—they can compel the Pentagon to act by inserting appropriate language in authorization or appropriation legislation. All members, though, benefit from the illusion that the contracting process is political because it provides many opportunities for them to claim credit.

Politicized Timing of Contract Awards. In perhaps the most blatant example of political manipulation of the procurement process (in an area in which few have suspected significant political effects), contract awards are accelerated in the two months immediately before elections, as an extra $3 billion to $4 billion of contracts are awarded. This stimulates the economy and provides legislators and presidents with major credit-claiming opportunities. Even so, there is no evidence that overall spending levels are higher in election years. The phenomenon involves a careful orchestration of the exact date on which to award a contract already in the pipeline.

The issues presented here are critically important to our understanding of defense policy in general. The weapons bought by the military, funded by the Congress, and built by the contractors are, in a very real sense, the instruments of U.S. military policy. Decisions about what types of weapons we buy, and what we will give up to get them, go to the heart of military effectiveness. Weapons that are unreliable, ineffective, or bought for the wrong reasons will enfeeble the best-trained military force. Whether the infiltration of politics into the procurement process might so weaken the military is an open question but surely one worth investigating. What we find is that political considerations can force an issue onto the congressional agenda and can help shape the contours of debate. Affecting process, though, is not the same as affecting outcomes. While sparks may fly on the floor of the House over an attempt to cancel a weapons system, the decision to continue production or end it is usually more a matter of strategy and ideology than jobs or pork.

CHAPTER I. FOUR MYTHS ABOUT THE POLITICS OF DEFENSE CONTRACTING

1. Michael R. Gordon, "Despite War, Pentagon Plans Big Cuts," *New York Times,* February 3, 1991, 14; Stephen Alexis Cain, *Analysis of the FY 1992–93 Defense Budget Request* (Washington, D.C.: Defense Budget Project, February 7, 1991).

2. William W. Kaufmann, *Glasnost, Perestroika, and U.S. Defense Spending* (Washington, D.C.: Brookings Institution, 1990).

3. Philip J. Simon, *Top Guns: A Common Cause Guide to Defense Lobbying* (Washington, D.C.: Common Cause, 1987), 31.

4. Richard Stubbing, *The Defense Game* (New York: Harper and Row, 1986), 165.

5. See Fen Hempson, *Unguided Missiles: How America Buys Its Weapons* (New York: W. W. Norton, 1989), 72–73.

6. On the B-1B and MX, see James M. Lindsay, *Congress and Nuclear Weapons, 1968–1987* (Ph.D. diss., Yale University, 1988), 224–25.

7. James M. Lindsay, "Parochialism, Policy, and Constituency Constraints: Congressional Voting on Strategic Weapons Systems," *American Journal of Political Science* 34, no. 4 (November 1990): 949.

8. Council on Economic Priorities, *Star Wars: The Economic Fallout* (Cambridge: Ballinger Publishing, 1988), 97.

9. Both citations are from Robert Higgs, "Beware the Pork Hawk," *Reason* (June 1989): 33.

10. For a comprehensive discussion of the corrupt machinations of WEDTECH, see William Sternberg and Matthew C. Harrison, Jr., *Feeding Frenzy: The Inside Story of WEDTECH* (New York: Henry Holt, 1989).

The Political Economy of Defense Contracting

When people speak of the politics of defense spending, they are usually referring to Congress's role in the process: its refusal to close unnecessary bases or obsolete production lines, its ability to extract political favors in return for votes on defense issues, or the fact that defense contractors often seem to get their way through campaign contributions rather than through the merits of their programs.

Congress plays the key political role in the defense contracting process because it controls the purse strings; the Pentagon's job of steering weapons programs through Congress and securing approval for funding requests is complicated and difficult. The universe of congressional players is large, and the military must repeatedly develop and maintain supporting coalitions among most of the 535 members of the House and Senate. At many points in the budget cycle members may attempt to curtail or kill funding for specific programs. This political fact of life affects the ways in which the defense budget is presented and shapes the behavior of everyone involved in the process. In the past, DOD had only to gain the support of the relevant committee chairs and senior membership in order to secure approval; the number of bargains and the amount of lobbying needed was limited. Now, the bargaining environment is much larger and requires new strategies capable of influencing an increasing number of members.

The Pentagon and defense contractors are far from powerless when it comes to dealing with Congress, however. In response to congressional attention to defense matters, DOD has developed and refined a number of strategies designed to smooth the defense budget's path through the legislature. Some strategies take advantage of the military's near monopoly on quality information; the debate over the B-2 Stealth Bomber is filled with examples of unsuccessful attempts to extract budget and cost data from the air force. Other strategies capitalize on the fact that members of Congress are believed to be acutely aware of the local economic benefits that defense dollars create. By stressing the economic consequences of budget cuts DOD tries to create support for its programs among members who benefit from the resulting largess. Defense contractors make the same sort of effort through the use of direct lobbying, campaign contributions, and strategically targeted subcontracts.

Congress, the Budget Process, and Procurement Activity

Each year, the president sends his defense budget request to Congress as part of his annual federal government budget package. The request sets out the amounts of money DOD proposes to spend on each of its thousands of separate programs, or line items. Congress can approve the budget as is or make any changes it deems necessary to any of the different line items. The possibility that Congress will eliminate or cut back money the military wants is a very serious threat.

Congress considers the defense budget in three steps. First, the House and Senate Budget committees set a defense spending ceiling, as part of an overall budget resolution setting forth limits on total government spending. Next, the House and Senate Armed Services committees authorize specific programs, a task that gives DOD the necessary legal authority to spend funds. Finally, the chambers' Appropriations committees, aided by the Defense subcommittees, appropriate the amounts that can be spent for each program. During each phase, the committee decisions are subjected to votes on the floors of both chambers.

In the past, Congress generally approved the president's defense budget and programmatic requests without major substantive changes. In the 1950s and 1960s, Congress deferred to military judgment and expertise on defense issues and was sufficiently disengaged from national security policy making that it examined very little of the budget in detail.[1] As one observer put it, "[Congress] routinely disposed of defense authorization and appropriations bills with little debate and few floor amendments."[2] Between 1961 and 1967, according to Lindsay's figures, the House and Senate spent a combined total of sixteen days debating defense authorization bills.[3] By the 1980s, however, congressional attention to and scrutiny of the defense budget had exploded. Because of the increased levels of congressional involvement, defense officials who solicit and maintain support for their weapons programs have found their jobs becoming more difficult and time-consuming.

The growth in congressional attention stems from several factors. Line-item authorizations, introduced in 1961, gave the Armed Services committees direct authority over individual programs, something they had never had before. Congressional reforms during the 1970s decentralized the power of the committees and eliminated barriers that had prevented most members from having much say on defense issues. Furthermore, in the aftermath of the Vietnam War and the dismal early performance of the highly touted F-111 and C-5A programs, Congress became more willing to challenge the military's judgment on weapons procurement issues.[4] Finally, public attention to defense issues, particularly procurement, has increased a great deal because of the Reagan defense buildup and the spare parts and corruption scandals of the 1980s. Taken together, these developments rapidly augmented the number of challenges that members could mount against defense programs.

The most significant factor in the increase in congressional attention to defense issues was the introduction of line-item authorization to the defense budget in 1961.[5] For the first time, DOD could spend money only if it had been specifically appropriated and authorized for individual aircraft, missile, or shipbuilding programs.[6] The amount of effort and attention the military had to devote to Congress immediately doubled because it was forced to solicit program approval from two committees in each chamber instead of one.

Before the advent of line-item authorizations, the House and Senate Armed Services committees had little control over most military programs. In contrast to the programmatic instructions contained in Appropriations bills, Authorization bills contained only general policy instructions. The allowable limits on air force aircraft procurement, for example, were set in the Army and Air Force Authorization and Composition Act of 1950. It authorized the air force to procure "24,000 serviceable aircraft or 225,000 airframe tons of aggregate serviceable aircraft, whichever amount the Air Force may determine is more appropriate to fulfill the requirements of the Air Force."[7] These ceilings were meaningless since the air force has never operated more than 9,500 planes.[8] The Appropriations Committee set program limits, specifying the number of fighter planes of a particular type the air force could buy and how much it could pay for them. With their new authority to review line items, the Armed Services committees expanded their power to set program budget levels and direction.

Almost immediately, the Authorization and Appropriations committees began to compete for control over the defense budget, a rivalry that has grown more fierce with time. The committees now occasionally ignore each other's work and carry out two complete and independent budget reviews. The Appropriations Committee has developed the habit of appropriating funds over and above the authorized limits and sometimes adds completely new programs: $3 billion worth in the House in 1984, and $6.5 billion in the Senate during 1985.[9] Members on Appropriations complain that their colleagues on Armed Services should attend to policy oversight and leave nuts and bolts questions of funding and program-level directions alone. Since the Armed Services committees originally sought line-item authorization because their policy oversight mission gave them too little leverage over DOD, a comfortable resolution of the jurisdictional battle is unlikely to come anytime soon.[10]

A second reason for the explosion of congressional oversight is the increase in the public visibility of defense issues, coincident with changes in the structure and norms of Congress. Until the early 1970s, autocratic senior committee chairmen controlled debate and limited subcommittee and floor activity on defense issues. Lindsay describes the institutional arrangement as one in which "the senior members of the defense committees generally could command the support of Congress for their positions on defense matters."[11]

Reforms adopted in the 1970s decentralized power and opened up debate in all policy areas, including defense. These reforms restricted the authority of committee chairmen, and the entire committee assumed the chair's erstwhile power to determine subcommittee jurisdiction and membership. The number of subcommittees on the defense committees grew, and junior members for the first time could serve as subcommittee chairs.[12] Norms that prohibited junior members from taking an active role in committee deliberations weakened, and those without seniority took advantage of the opportunity to speak out.

One indicator of how much the defense budget process has changed is the number of amendments offered to the budgets reported from the Armed Services and Appropriations committees. Once, few members challenged the committee by trying to amend the reported bill during floor debate. Now, it is accepted practice for members who do not sit on the military committees—as well as for those who do but are unable to get their way during markup—to offer floor amendments challenging the Armed Services committees' action.[13] These amendments vary from the trivial to the budget busting: some call on the military to increase funding for military bands or give permission for the Air Force Singing Sergeants to make a commercial recording with the Cincinnati Philharmonic; others attempt to stop huge programs like aircraft carriers or the B-1 bomber. The rise in floor amendments since the 1960s (table 2–1) has been tremendous. The number offered in the House in 1986 alone (116) is more than twice that offered during the entire period 1961 to 1969 (55).[14]

Another factor in the increasing visibility of defense issues was the presidential election of 1980, in which Ronald Reagan continually thumped Jimmy Carter about the decline in U.S. military power during what he called the "decade of neglect." Defense became a salient public issue, and a large majority in the public were in favor of increasing the defense budget. Defense spending rose very quickly after 1980, increasing 53 percent in constant dollars between 1980 and 1985, including increases of 12.5 percent in 1981 and 11.6 percent in 1982.[15] Congressional interest in the issue, particularly among Democrats, was piqued by Secretary of Defense Weinberger's disdain for Congress. Weinberger steadfastly refused to compromise on his Pentagon budget requests and evaded any questions about which low-priority programs could be cut for fiscal reasons.[16] Many legislators thought the Pentagon lacked discipline and was more interested in spending as much money as possible than in managing its resources wisely; they grumbled about contractor inefficiencies, poor quality, and the lack of effective supervision.[17]

Table 2-1

Line Item Changes and Floor Amendments to DOD Authorization Acts

Number of Programs Adjusted during House Authorization and Appropriations[a]

Year	Authorization	Appropriation
1970	180	650
1976	222	1032
1982	339	1119
1985	1315	1848

Number of Floor Amendments Offered to Authorization Bill[b]

Year	House	Senate
1961	2	0
1968	7	8
1975	15	28
1980	26	24
1985	140	108
1986	116	83

[a]Gansler, *Affording Defense*, 111, citing internal staff report of the House Armed Services Committee to the Senate Armed Services Committee, October 16, 1985, 592.

[b]Lindsay, "Congress and Defense Policy," 374.

For evidence of mismanagement, defense critics looked to a series of spectacular spare parts scandals discovered in 1983, when investigators found that the military was buying everyday items, some commercially available for pennies, for what seemed to be impossibly high prices. An avalanche of stories about $436 hammers, $10,000 hexagonal wrenches, $600 toilet seats, and $1,100 plastic stool caps followed.[18] The Pentagon and the contractors responded that the prices resulted from the peculiar way in which defense contractors allocated fixed overhead costs, a practice that artificially inflates the cost of small items; they argued further that some costs reflected stringent military quality requirements. Yet the arguments, even when occasionally correct, convinced no one, and DOD could not contain the rising outrage. The overwhelming perception was that procurement practices were simply out of control, and members of the House and Senate lined up to propose bills modifying the military's purchasing methods.[19]

Individual members now found themselves with opportunities to generate a great deal of publicity for themselves, as they now had both new avenues of influence over defense policy and an issue important to their constituents. Senator Charles Grassley (R-Iowa) was a key spokesman for congressional outrage. He used the scandal and his self-proclaimed position as treasury guard dog to become the first Iowa senator in twenty years to win reelection.

The spare parts episode opened up the defense issue in Congress to an unprecedented degree. More and more committees tried to muscle in on the new hot issue, using Congress's oversight authority to justify looking at the defense budget. As one observer put it, "A whole lot of people who didn't get to play before on defense issues have a whole lot of room to run; the defense oversight committees, those baronies, are no longer the only game in town."[20] By 1985, DOD officials were testifying before one hundred House and Senate committees, subcommittees, and task forces each year.[21]

Issues of Congressional Concern

Most members of Congress view the defense budget in terms of the individual programs it contains. Some policy oversight takes place, but members generally find it easier to think about line items than strategy. Instead of discussing the nature of U.S. military naval commitments overseas or the relative advantages of airlift, fast-sealift, and equipment prepositioning to readiness in the European theater, members argue over how many F-14s the navy will buy and how much they will cost and whether overseas military commissaries serve enough U.S.–produced beef, lamb, and pork to service personnel.[22]

Congressmen and senators operate in a political environment that discourages them from paying attention to policy oversight. Few can devote the time and effort necessary to become policy experts. "Policy oversight does not enhance a legislator's credit-taking posture; it does not garner him electoral votes; nor can it be tied directly to control over executive action. The impact of policy oversight is too general and diffuse, both on a legislator's career advancement and on those objectives he holds for public policy."[23] A member's time and attention are better devoted to issues on which he or she can have some discernible impact and which are accessible to constituents.

More important, when members try to influence defense policy, they find that about the only way they can obtain results is to review specific programs. Most defense strategies are implemented at the tactical level through specific weapons systems: the navy's forward-based naval strategy relies on large aircraft carriers, the air force's conception of strategic deterrence upon advanced penetrating bombers. Although there are exceptions, members who try to influence military attitudes and policies dealing with, for example, the arms control implications of chemical weapons or the effects of ballistic missile defense on strategic stability will fail. They will have more—albeit probably still limited—success if they attack funding for Bigeye or specific SDI programs.

Even at the programmatic level, Congress must repeatedly resort to drastic action to accomplish anything. During the 1989 budget cycle, the House Appropriations Defense Subcommittee (HADS) took the unprecedented step of eliminating all funding for the air force's Advanced Tactical Fighter (ATF) program, the follow-on to the F-15 air superiority fighter. The committee was unhappy with air force program management and worried about overly optimistic technical goals and funding assumptions. The committee action, described as a ten-megaton warning shot across the air force's bow,[24] was designed to "sound an alert that could not be ignored."[25] The action was more remarkable in that no one expected the funding action to last; subcommittee member C. W. Young (R-Fla.) explained that the money would probably be restored in House-Senate conference action.[26] The committee was simply trying to get the air force's attention and convince it that Congress was serious about addressing the program's problems.

Because policy oversight is difficult, time-consuming, and usually frustrating, members of Congress find it more profitable to focus on the narrower details of individual programs. Congress, in its thirst to have some impact on the defense process and in response to some clear shortcomings in the military's management of defense programs, will often specify in exacting detail how the services should manage each program, along with cost, schedule, testing, and performance goals. The services bitterly criticize these activities. They argue that micromanagement arrogates the power of program managers and makes it impossible to administer complex programs in the face of changing and inconsistent congressional direction. Critics of the military respond that Congress has to step in when the services fail to do their jobs efficiently or effectively. A frequently cited example is air force and navy management of the Joint Tactical Information Distribution System (JTIDS), an advanced communication system designed to link fighter aircraft, airborne early warning aircraft, ships, and ground-based controllers. Congress tried to force the services to establish common specifications since each service was developing a separate system. Fed up with numerous congressional restrictions on the program, one exasperated Pentagon official asked an Armed Services Committee staff member, "When the hell is your committee going to stop micromanaging our programs?" The staffer replied, "Just as soon as you start."[27]

Increasing attention at higher levels of detail makes the job of obtaining support for the defense budget in Congress more arduous than before. As the consensus in favor of high defense spending evaporated in the wake of the huge budget increases between 1981 and 1984 and the spare parts scandals, more members became willing to question the need for specific programs at more points in the budget process. In doing so, they complicated the task of DOD and defense contractors in their search for budget and program support. The new environment calls for updated strategies; the old-fashioned method of relying on committee chairmen and the leadership no longer works.

DOD and Congress: Strategies for Obtaining Budget Approval

All agencies, DOD included, engage in activities that increase the chances of their budget's passing Congress with a minimum of change or contention. The strategies that underlie these activities can be grouped in two broad categories: informational and distributive (or allocational). The first includes the ways in which agencies transmit information to Congress and the kinds of information members use when they evaluate budgets. The second deals with how agencies can distribute their re-sources strategically in such a way as to maximize congressional support.

INFORMATION-CENTERED STRATEGIES

Much of the literature on budgeting describes the kinds of information agencies deliver to Congress, how it ought to be presented, and how Congress obtains and evaluates its own information.[28] A major portion of the agency head's job entails persuasion; he or she must convince legislators—at least those on the authorizing and appropriating commit-tees—that the department provides a worthwhile, efficient, and popular service. Doing that job involves, in no small part, using information effectively. Program and budget information is provided in the formal setting of committee hearings and through informal personal contacts and private lobbying. Here, DOD has a large advantage in its dealings with Congress, since it can control the information that legislators see. The Pentagon is adept at slanting its presentations to display only those aspects of defense programs it wants to show.[29]

The most common and visible method of supplying information is the annual testimony at Authorization and Appropriations Committee hear-ings. Each year, DOD officials and service chiefs spend hundreds of hours before the military committees justifying department policies and budget requests and appealing for support. In 1985, for example, the House and Senate Appropriations and Armed Services committees held a total of 261 hearings, two-thirds of which dealt directly with budgeting issues, and received testimony from more than four hundred DOD and service officials.[30]

Budget hearings serve several useful purposes. They create a public record of both defense policy and congressional sentiment and can, at times, expose problems in the Pentagon. They provide information on the status of most DOD policies and programs and give defense officials an opportunity to make their case on budget issues. Despite the level of activity surrounding budget hearings, however, the hearings have little impact on congressional opinion. Members do take the hearings se-riously, but most important activity takes place during the complex process of putting the budget together within the Pentagon and in public revelations about defense policy. As Edward Luttwak put it, "Anything dramatic will have reached the public months before [the hearings] in the daily press, and much more will eventually appear."[31] Another observer noted that "in terms of the time expended and the volume of words spoken and recorded, hearings are the least efficient method of information transmittal."[32]

Congress is hampered by the fact that it is frequently denied timely and accurate information and cannot digest the voluminous amounts of data that the DOD provides to distract members from the real issues. The creation of institutions such as the Congressional Budget Office (CBO) and the Office of Technology Assessment, which are designed to give Congress independent assessments of defense information, has not eliminated the problems. The Defense Department carefully screens the information it presents to put the best possible face on all programs and issues. As J. Ronald Fox argued, "If a branch of the military believes the program to be essential to the service and/or to national defense, facts will be withheld from Congress as long as possible."[33] The Pentagon insists that it manages the defense budget with ruthless efficiency. Any incidents of shoddy quality, schedule delays, poor performance, or high prices are glossed over as minor glitches in an otherwise smooth operation. To be sure, defense officials cannot be expected to volunteer information cheerfully on all the problems their programs are having. But rarely is there even an admission that anything is wrong. In March 1985, General John A. Wickham, chief of staff of the army, told HADS that difficulties with the DIVAD air defense system were "simple problems and can be handled." He added that there were no major problems with either the gun or the radar.[34] His optimistic assessment was rebutted only five months later, when Secretary of Defense Weinberger canceled the DIVAD program because of repeated and intractable failures, including serious flaws in both the gun and radar systems. More recently, some members of Congress have expressed outrage over the B-1B bomber, charging the air force with knowingly concealing information about critical flaws in a number of areas.[35]

The services have also been known to keep information from top officials within DOD and even from their own leaders. In 1990, navy personnel working on the A-12 aircraft program failed to notify either Secretary of Defense Richard Cheney or top navy officials of serious problems with the aircraft, which was under development as a replacement for the aging A-6 planes of the carrier fleet. During a DOD review of aircraft programs, Cheney was given an optimistic assessment of program cost estimates, which a navy investigation concluded was "not supported by the facts available to [the program management team]"[36] (the investigation also noted that key navy officials had failed to notify their superiors about program difficulties).[37] Within weeks, the contractors reported delays, a large cost overrun (the Pentagon estimated that development costs, budgeted for $4.8 billion, would reach at least $7.5 billion), and technical problems dire enough for Cheney to call on the navy to "show cause" why the program should not be canceled. In January 1991, eight months after the optimistic reports, Cheney terminated the $57 billion program, the largest cancellation in DOD history.[38]

The Defense Department takes advantage of the fact that much of the information on weapons programs is highly technical, classified, or, in the case of programs still in development, uncertain. Classified, or special-access, programs—so-called black programs—are exempt from normal congressional review, and only a handful of members receive any cost or technical information (which they are unable to discuss with colleagues). The services may spend billions of dollars on black programs before Congress learns any details, and by then sunk costs are high enough to make cancellation nearly impossible. Often, according to critics like whistle-blower Thomas Amlie, programs are given special-access status specifically to elude any sort of oversight or accountability: "There are three reasons to have black programs. One, it deserves to be black. There may be five of those and [the B-2] isn't one of those. Two, you're doing something so dumb that you don't want anyone to know about it. Or three, you want to rip open the money bag at both ends and get out a big scoop shovel, because there's no accountability whatsoever."[39] A congressional staffer summarized the benefits of special-access programs: "You'd have to be crazy not to want a black program, because then you would have to run over to Congress and answer silly questions about schedule slippages and cost overruns."[40]

The best recent illustration of the political benefits (as well as the potential problems) of special-access programs is the ongoing struggle over the B-2 bomber. Even after the air force confirmed that the plane existed, it refused to divulge even the most basic details of the program;

only after Congress began demanding cooperation as a condition for continued funding did it accede.[41] No cost data of any kind were available until 1986, when the air force, following prolonged congressional pressure, grudgingly provided a summary report. Far from satisfying critics, it was characterized as "inadequate" by House Armed Services Committee (HASC) Chairman Les Aspin. Representative Duncan Hunter (R-Cal.), a strong Pentagon supporter, described the report as "less than a page long, highly classified, [and lacking] any substantial information."[42]

The air force finally unveiled the B-2 and released public cost estimates in November 1988. The cost of the 132-unit program was said to be $68 billion, or an astonishing $516 million per plane; this estimate soon rose to $530 million and has since increased to $860 million because of cutbacks in the number ordered. Range and payload figures were released several months later.[43] For the first time, the public and Congress had access to detailed information about the bomber, including information about potential development problems and the aircraft's strategic rationale. Congressional criticism began to mount, particularly over the plane's cost and ambitious production schedule. The air force wanted a production commitment before the first plane had even flown and intended to take delivery of 35 aircraft before flight testing had been completed. Some in the air force now think that keeping the program classified for so long may have been a mistake; the releasing of details earlier might have eased "sticker shock" and made the process of building a firm supporting coalition easier.

However, the B-2's critics confronted the fact that the air force had already spent over $22 billion on development and production before the first flight—a figure unknown until detailed budget and schedule information was declassified in June 1989.[44] In order to cancel the program, they would have had to justify walking away from a huge sunk investment and deal with the constituency that such a large expenditure had generated. According to John Pike of the Federation of American Scientists, the air force configured the B-2 program by "front-loading the program so that regardless of what the [flight] test results are, they'll already have spent so much money on it that it will be difficult to cancel."[45] Special-access status may not prevent controversy, and at times may even be counterproductive (the A-12's high classification is said to have prevented a "sense of [congressional] ownership"),[46] but it can delay close scrutiny until enough money has been spent to ensure the program's survival.

DOD LOBBYING OF CONGRESS. The Pentagon has other informational strategies besides control. The military services have crafted a comprehensive lobbying network that allows them to disseminate information rapidly throughout Congress. The extensive, regular contact between the Hill and the Pentagon gives the services immediate access on any issue that affects their interests.

The DOD, like all federal agencies, is prohibited from lobbying Congress, although loopholes and a lack of enforcement have rendered the relevant laws impotent. The older of the two applicable statutes, established in 1919, stipulates that no public money may be used "to influence in any manner a Member of Congress, to favor or oppose, by vote or otherwise, any legislation or appropriation by Congress" (18 U.S.C. 1913). The antilobbying prohibition was updated in the 1950s through a general provision included in the Treasury, Postal Service, and General Government Appropriation Act: "No part of any appropriation contained in this or any other Act, or of the funds available for expenditure by any corporation or agency, shall be used for publicity or propaganda purposes designed to support or defeat legislation pending before Congress."

Recognizing that government agencies could scarcely function without some advocacy contact with Congress, the statute of 1919 explicitly allows officials to take actions relating to "requests for legislation or appropriations which they deem necessary for the efficient conduct of the public business." The DOD may therefore ask Congress for appropriations but is limited—at least in theory—in the extent to which it can actively lobby members.

This means, in practice, that lobbying takes place under the guise of "legislative liaison," in which DOD responds to members' requests for information on legislation of interest. Alternatively, DOD can cover its activities under the "efficient conduct of the public business" exception to the antilobbying law. Annually DOD responds to more than one hundred thousand written congressional inquiries and some half a million telephone calls, not counting requests for information submitted during the course of budget hearings.[47] Defense officials also gain access to Congress through the intervention of sympathetic members, who can either request the relevant information (which they then pass on to their colleagues) or ask officials to come to the Hill and testify. To handle the volume of congressional requests, the military services have the only permanent liaison offices in the House and Senate office buildings.

It is difficult to get a good grasp of the size and scope of Pentagon lobbying efforts. Although the amount of money the services can spend on liaison activities cannot exceed ceilings set as part of each year's defense budget (it was $13.6 million in FY 1986), there are many ways of circumventing these constraints. Lobbying classified as "other legislative activities" is not subject to any financial limits. This category is broad, covering "personnel who spend at least 30 days a year on legislative activities, including coordinating and answering congressional inquiries, tracking legislation, performing legislative research, and preparing witness statements"; it has never been clear what is included and what is not.[48] Moreover, the department's internal control, accounting, and reporting procedures are so fuzzy that the General Accounting Office (GAO) has repeatedly been unable to determine if statutory limits have ever been exceeded.[49]

Despite the wide latitude permitted the military to conduct its liaison function and despite the fact that the antilobbying laws are never enforced, occasionally one service manages to step over the line far enough to become the subject of congressional and public opprobrium. A recent victim was the air force, which in 1982 helped one of its largest contractors lobby Congress during a heated dispute involving the C-5B transport aircraft.

In the early 1980s, the air force planned to augment its force of Lockheed C-5A aircraft with a new transport called the C-17, to be built by McDonnell Douglas. However, in January 1982, the secretary of defense, over the air force's objections, decided to scrap the C-17 and buy fifty updated C-5s, known as C-5Bs, instead.[50] This decision in itself was controversial, given the C-5A's status as a symbol of defense waste and mismanagement. At the time of the secretary's decision, Lockheed was refitting the entire C-5A fleet with new wings, since the original C-5A wing had cracked under the stress of full loads. Although the air force was unhappy, it accepted the decision and began to work out the arrangements with Lockheed.

The situation became more complicated in May 1982, when Senator Henry Jackson (D-Wash.) offered an amendment to the FY 1983 defense budget that substituted surplus Boeing 747s for the fifty C-5Bs. Boeing had offered to sell the 747s for one-half the price of the C-5B and argued that its proposal would save the government $6 billion over twenty years.[51] Such end-runs around the established procurement bureaucracy were unusual and rarely successful; both Lockheed and the air force were caught by surprise when the Senate voted to approve the amendment 60–39. Whatever doubts the air force had about the C-5 vanished when the program was threatened with budgetary extinction by the civilian 747.

After the Senate defeat, Lockheed and the air force, at the direction of Pentagon officials, began an unrestrained lobbying campaign in the House, which was scheduled to consider a version of Jackson's amendment. Officials from both the government and Lockheed met regularly in the Pentagon for strategy planning sessions. As part of the strategy, Lockheed compiled a computerized action plan (Congressional Contact Tally) that specified what steps were to be taken with each member; separate lists were maintained for the all-important military committees. The list chronicled the overt and often indelicate lobbying activities of air force officials, sympathetic House members, and Lockheed personnel. The lobbying effort itself was routine, a point C-5 supporters made clear by citing joint DOD-contractor lobbying efforts involving Boeing's efforts to sell the E-3A AWACS aircraft to Saudi Arabia and an air force-Rockwell effort on behalf of the B-1.[52] What made the campaign unusual—and what attracted the most attention—was that the air force was caught red-handed in what appeared to be a clear violation of the anti-lobbying laws: A source inside the Pentagon leaked a complete copy of the action list to the Project on Military Procurement, a nonprofit group associated with military reform, who in turn provided it to the press.[53]

According to the document, Lockheed and the air force arranged meetings between members of Congress and air force officials, subcontractors, and Lockheed personnel (the entry for Joseph Addabbo, chairman of HADS, read "[Deputy Secretary of Defense Frank] Carlucci one on one. [Secretary of the Air Force Verne] Orr one on one. AGAINST

C-5 in FY82 markup. More work to swing").[54] The air force assisted in the drafting of Dear Colleague letters, suggested questions for members to ask in hearings, and tried to enlist the support of nondefense committee chairmen.[55] During one congressional budget hearing the air force planted officers in the audience who were asked to testify by pro-Lockheed committee members. To no one's surprise, the officers proceeded to extol the virtues of the C-5 in spontaneous testimony.[56] Lockheed also arranged to fly a C-5A to Andrews Air Force Base and invited members of Congress to a demonstration of the plane's ability to quickly unload attack helicopters.

The air force was accused of using heavy-handed tactics as well. Norman Dicks (D-Wash.), a pro-Boeing congressman, charged that the air force was pressuring military contractors who also subcontracted for Boeing on the 747. Dicks claimed that these firms faced the threat of the Pentagon's taking away some of their defense contracts unless they supported the C-5B.[57] In one example, Fairchild Industries, a major defense contractor who also worked on the 747, sent Democratic congresswoman and HASC member Beverly Byron (D-Md.) a letter supporting the purchase of the 747s. One week later, Fairchild sent another letter that began, "We are delivering this letter at the direction of the Air Force" and went on to recant the first letter; further, it included pro-C-5 material provided by Lockheed.[58]

Although the air force denied coercing any contractors, the action plan indicated that the service was considering "ways to obtain support of DOD position from prime contractors and subcontractors like E-Systems, Vought, Northrop, and [Pratt & Whitney]," companies not involved in the C-5B.[59] Lockheed's chairman, Roy A. Anderson, worked to suppress support for Boeing among commercial airlines, who stood to benefit by selling their surplus 747s to the government. Anderson wrote to every airline that owned 747s, many of whom held DOD contracts for cargo and personnel transport, that the Boeing plan "could adversely impact airline revenues from government contracts."[60] Deputy Secretary of Defense Carlucci was reported to have done the same. Carlucci's tone was described by sources as "congenial but blunt . . . [he] simply says: 'We have a good relationship with your company, and we don't want anything to affect it. Now that's easy to understand, isn't it?' "[61] The threat, though unstated, was obvious: the government might penalize airlines supporting the 747 purchase by eliminating future transport contracts.

The air force/Lockheed lobbying was successful. On July 21, 1982, the House voted down the proposal to buy 747s instead of C-5Bs, on a 127–289 vote, and full C-5B funding was restored in House-Senate conference held several weeks later.

When the lobbying was exposed, members who supported the Boeing proposal were furious. Congressman Dicks, referring to the antilobbying statutes, called the campaign "an unprecedented abuse of a much abused law."[62] The air force responded that its activities were well within permissible bounds; for its part, Lockheed maintained that the effort was designed "to make sure that congressmen and their staffs have accurate information on the issues involved."[63]

The GAO, responding to a request from Congressman Jack Brooks (D-Tex.), chairman of the House Committee on Government Operations, investigated the incident and concluded unequivocally that "Air Force and OSD [Office of the Secretary of Defense] officials [violated] Federal antilobbying laws by expending appropriated funds in the aiding and supporting of contractors to perform lobbying activities."[64] Lockheed, according to the GAO, spent $496,000 on the lobbying campaign and intended to seek government reimbursement for those expenses.[65] Several congressmen responded angrily that the GAO could not produce any evidence to support its conclusion; their position was bolstered by the Investigations Subcommittee report on its hearings into the matter, which concluded that no laws were broken.[66] Samuel Stratton (D-N.Y.) had no patience with Dicks's protest, writing, "This is the first time I know of that any member of Congress representing the district of the losing contractor has cried 'foul' and 'illegal' because a conference committee of Congress refused to support his particular contractor."[67]

The C-5B/747 episode shows how persuasive DOD lobbying can be—it is an example, as a defense periodical put it, of "how the Pentagon lobbies when it's really mad."[68] And although the C-5 campaign represents an extreme example, it shows how politically effective the military and its allies can be when fully politically mobilized. It also illustrates the difficulty of controlling what many in Congress view as inappropriate interference in congressional affairs. Despite the apparent restrictions on lobbying efforts, the Pentagon actually faces few restraints. Even when defense officials act under the letter of the law they manage to get their point across: in 1981, a White House official recounted a speech he gave to a group of defense contractors: "I said: 'We're unable to request you to contact any specific member of Congress, due to a 1919 statute. But we hope you'll support the MX. I don't have to draw anybody any pictures. But you know there are groups out in the private sector that support it.' "[69]

CONTRACTOR LOBBYING OF CONGRESS. The extensive DOD lobbying organization is supplemented by a large network of defense contractor lobbyists. Defense contractors are unencumbered by the lobbying restrictions on federal agencies; as private actors, they must only register lobbyists with the Congress and avoid bribing members. Their corps of Washington-based lobbyists and their ability to provide millions of dollars for honoraria and PAC contributions give contractors a level and breadth of access on Capitol Hill that is perhaps unmatched by that of any other group.

Like many important indicators of defense activities, the size of the defense lobbying network is difficult to determine. Although lobbyists must register with the clerk of the House, the legal definition of the term is loose enough that "much of the Washington activities of the companies is not covered by existing legislation and is, accordingly, undisclosed."[70] Nevertheless, there are some unofficial sources that give the flavor of contractors' Washington activities (table 2–2).

Few of the contractor employees in Washington are there explicitly to lobby Congress; indeed, of the contractor employees listed in table 2–2, only about 5 percent are registered as lobbyists. These organizations perform many other services besides direct lobbying: they track legislation, work with PACs, collect information on future defense programs, and provide a base of operations for contractor personnel.[71]

Even though a Washington presence is important, defense contractors know the importance of mobilizing grass-roots support for their weapons, an effective strategy for getting Congress's attention: "The Washington office knows full well that many of its political activities ultimately aimed at influencing Federal decision making can only be furthered through grass-roots support."[72] Rockwell carried out such a campaign during the mid-1970s in an attempt to protect the B-1A bomber from

Table 2-2

Defense Contractor Washington Offices, 1986[a]

Company	Employees	Registered Lobbyists[b]
Boeing	80	11
General Dynamics	50	3
Grumman	32	1
Hughes Aircraft (GM)	60	0
Lockheed	50	3
McDonnell Douglas	60	1
Northrop	50	12
Raytheon	35	0
Rockwell	150	4
United Technologies	80[c]	0

[a]Philip J. Simon, *Top Guns: A Common Cause Guide to Defense Contractor Lobbying* (Washington, D.C.: Common Cause, 1987), 53–111.

[b]Does not include outside consultants retained as lobbyists.

[c]Includes all corporate divisions.

cancellation in 1977. In addition to a Washington-based lobbying effort carried out with the same air force assistance that Lockheed received on the C-5B, Rockwell worked diligently to mobilize support for the B-1 among communities, unions, and businesses throughout the United States.[73] The supposedly secret effort, dubbed Operation Common Sense, "included a massive letter-writing campaign by workers at Rockwell's 167 plants; solicitation of support from national organizations such as the Veterans of Foreign Wars and the American Legion; and the production of films and advertisements as well as prepared articles, columns, and editorials that willing editors could print in newspapers and magazines."[74] Not all of Rockwell's efforts were effective. Members of the House became suspicious when they received several hundred identical pro-B-1 letters from workers, one of whom wrote, "I've been asked to do this. Vote any way you want."[75]

A third major component of defense contractor lobbying—one that is perhaps more important than either Washington activities or grass-roots campaigns—is the distribution of campaign contributions from PACs. In

1987–88, the top fifty defense PACs donated more than $6.5 million to members of the House and Senate (see chapter 4). Of more interest are the activities of the largest defense contractors and those with the most active PACs. In the election cycle of 1985–86, the top ten defense contractors alone donated $2.9 million, with nearly half ($1.2 million) going to members of the defense committees.[76] The effects of these contributions are ambiguous; it is often impossible to sort out the chicken or egg aspect of the debate over PAC activity. Do contractor PACs distribute money with the implicit understanding that they expect favorable votes? or do they simply reward candidates who have similar issue positions? Critics claim that the money purchases votes. Others dispute this but have trouble devising convincing explanations of just what, exactly, the contractors expect for their money.

Contractor and Pentagon lobbying of Congress—the effective use of informational strategies—tells us a great deal about the power the agency has. The military has a number of advantages that are unavailable to any other executive department: a level of ideological support that transcends partisan divisions, a high level of secrecy, and an ability to quickly mobilize a large network of powerful political actors.

DISTRIBUTIVE STRATEGIES

The military can also deliver selective economic and political benefits to members of Congress. In doing so, the Pentagon can maintain access and give legislators their own stake in the military's programs.

This second set of congressional budgetary strategies involves the allocation of particularized local benefits to members of Congress, mostly in the form of pork barrel programs. Members' reelection prospects are heavily influenced by district or state economic conditions and perceptions of whether members are looking after their constituents. Therefore, many observers claim that a major concern in congressional procurement decision making is the location of the production site; as the C-5B/747 controversy showed, members do fight among themselves over this issue. According to some observers, members think less about a weapon's military value than about how many local jobs the ensuing defense contracts will provide; according to Aspin, this attitude is a consequence of the information made available by DOD: "Because of the nature of the information a congressman gets, the Armed Services Committee is typically less concerned about the question of how much we are buying in defense than the question of where we are buying it."[77] In theory, then, DOD should be able to improve congressional budget support by giving individual members stakes in agency programs by, for example, selectively awarding contracts either to a few influential members or to as many districts as possible.

Even the defense budget, though, is too small to satisfy every legislator's craving for pork. If the Pentagon is to use distributive strategies, heaping benefits on some parts of the country while skirting others, it must decide which areas will benefit. One possible rule is to channel contracts and bases to the districts of members who sit on the relevant appropriating or authorizing committees. There is nothing new about this idea. Richard Fenno noted twenty years ago that congressmen gravitate toward those committees that allow them to look after their constituents. In his study of the House Appropriations Committee, he wrote, "Far less apocalyptic than a desire to alter the economy, yet of far greater personal immediacy, is the unanimously held member belief that Committee membership will enhance one's ability to get projects for his constituents—thereby satisfying their need for service and his need for reelection."[78]

Alternatively, bureaucrats—officials in the military services and OSD—might make strategic decisions about whose support on the Hill is most valuable and direct their resources accordingly. For most programs, they would be members of the Authorization and Appropriations committees and subcommittees because "they make more decisions with a direct impact on bureaucrats' fortunes than nonmembers."[79]

A simple way of testing whether such decisions actually occur is to see if federal spending levels are especially high in the districts of members who are responsible for authorizing and appropriating money for different programs. Scholars have examined military prime contracts, defense employment, water projects, military construction, sewer and model cities grants, and combinations of different types of spending.[80] Committee-centered benefit distributions occur in some domestic programs, although Leonard Ritt concluded that "neither chairmen nor ranking minority members of exclusive committees have been able to translate their allegedly powerful positions into above average material benefits for their constituents."[81] Spending on public works, model cities and sewer grants, and military construction all favored committee members.

Past analyses of defense contracts have never found any relationship between membership on the military committees and higher levels of district defense contract awards. Committee members' districts receive no more contracts than nonmember districts, and local contracting levels remain unchanged when districts or states gain or lose seats on the military committees. Barry Rundquist's early work, the most comprehensive to date, concluded that defense contract distribution reflected district industrial and engineering capacity more than committee membership.[82]

What accounts for this result so at odds with prevailing notions of defense contracting? Some have questioned the notion that a congressman's vote can be swayed with a contract. This too runs counter to what is known as fact in public perception, but it is supported by studies that have found few strong links between the local economic effects of defense programs and members' approval of those programs. If these conclusions—namely, that there is in fact no payoff in allocating defense contracts to particular states or congressional districts—are correct, then the principal assumption underlying the distributive theory is violated.

Yet one must view with skepticism the entire literature on the distribution of defense contracts and constituency-interest voting on defense issues, since it has a serious problem. Until now, it has been impossible to measure with any precision the true distribution of defense contract benefits. Without knowing where the money and jobs go, it is difficult to determine what might drive the process of distributing them. The main flaw lies in the fact that prime contract data reveal nothing about the distribution of subcontracts, which compose over 50 percent of the dollar value of all prime contracts. This gap is crucial because the best available data indicate that the distribution of subcontracts appears to be very different from the distribution of prime contracts. One study of National Aeronautics and Space Administration prime contracts in the 1960s that involved the same type of advanced aerospace research, development, and production as that in defense contacts found that 60 percent of the value of the subcontracts awarded by prime contractors went to out-of-state firms.[83] A study of the defense industry in Utah reached a similar conclusion, finding that between 1960 and 1964, 86 percent of the dollar value of prime contracts awarded to Utah companies left the state through subcontracts.[84]

Although DOD publishes comprehensive defense prime contract data (which includes money expended in contractual agreements between the government and private firms), it has never collected detailed subcontract data, arguing that doing so takes too much effort and would be of little use.[85] Congress tried to establish a subcontract database in 1977, directing the secretary of defense to collect subcontract information from all firms receiving more than $500,000 in prime contracts. The department opposed the requirement, and industry compliance was poor.[86] A few preliminary reports were issued with incomplete data; Congress gave up and canceled the requirement in 1981.

Defense contractors as well are likely to fail to keep centralized and detailed records on the geographic dispersion of subcontractors and usually refuse to release them even if they have them, since they regard the data as proprietary. An important exception to this rule occurs when a program faces congressional resistance. In these cases, contractors may provide subcontracting information broken down by congressional district to members of Congress. The data are used to lobby members in the hope of perhaps swaying some votes with the jobs issue. Even these data, however, are almost never made public.

Because of this measurement problem, past work on the important questions of defense politics cannot be considered conclusive. We still know very little about where defense money is spent or how much attention Congress pays to that distribution. In chapters 5 and 6 I make use of subcontracting information for some major systems in an attempt to sort out these problems. These data have never before been subjected to rigorous analysis.

Relations among DOD, the defense industry, and Congress are extremely close. Indeed, the continuous contacts are so intimate that they are not infrequently taken as prima facie evidence of egregious conflicts of interest among all parties. Yet a number of key questions remain unanswered. It is not known with any certainty, for example, whether district level subcontracts and campaign donations and honoraria actually influence voting decisions or whether the Pentagon readily succumbs to congressional pressure on prime contract location and timing. It strains credulity to argue that political considerations play no part in defense contracting decisions, even as it is just as hard to accept the proposition that defense contracts represent essentially a $150 billion annual congressional bribe. The rest of this book examines these questions in some detail.

CHAPTER 2. THE POLITICAL ECONOMY OF
DEFENSE CONTRACTING

1. See Samuel P. Huntington, *The Common Defense: Strategic Programs in National Politics* (New York: Columbia University Press, 1961), part 3; and Edward Kolodziej, *The Uncommon Defense and Congress, 1945–1965* (Columbus: Ohio State University Press, 1966).

2. James M. Lindsay, "Congress and Defense Policy: 1961 to 1986," *Armed Forces and Society* 13, no. 3 (Spring 1987): 371.

3. Ibid., 374.

4. Both programs suffered huge cost overruns and serious technical problems; they became synonymous with defense waste and abuse. See A. Ernest Fitzgerald, *The High Priests of Waste* (New York: W. W. Norton, 1972); Robert J. Art, *The TFX Decision: McNamara and the Military* (Boston: Little, Brown, 1968); William Proxmire, *Report from Wasteland: America's Military-Industrial Complex* (New York: Praeger, 1970).

5. Robert J. Art, "Congress and the Defense Budget: Enhancing Policy Oversight," *Political Science Quarterly* 100, no. 2 (Summer 1985): 231.

6. Raymond Dawson, "Congressional Innovation and Intervention in Defense Policy: Legislative Authorization of Weapons Systems," *American Political Science Review* 56, no. 1 (March 1962): 42.

7. Quoted in ibid., 45.

8. David C. Morrison, "Chaos on Capitol Hill," *National Journal*, September 27, 1986, 2306.

9. Ibid.

10. Art, "Congress and the Defense Budget," 229.

11. Lindsay, "Congress and Defense Policy," 376–77.

12. Ibid., 380–81.

13. The number of amendments on most other issues increased as well during this period. See Steven S. Smith, *Call to Order: Floor Politics in the House and Senate* (Washington, D.C.: Brookings Institution, 1989), chap. 2.

14. Ibid., 374.

15. *National Defense Budget Estimates for FY 1988/1989* (May 1987), 100.

16. See U.S. Congress, Senate Committee on Armed Services, *Department of Defense Authorization for Appropriations,* part 1 (U.S. Military Posture), Fiscal Year 1985 (111) and Fiscal Year 1986 (67–68); Jack Germond and Jules

Witcover, "Reagan Hurting Himself by Bowing to Weinberger on Defense Spending Cuts," *National Journal,* December 29, 1984, 2458.

17. See Michael R. Gordon, "Data on Production Inefficiencies May Spur New Debate on Defense Contracting," *National Journal,* June 1, 1985, 1283–85; Peter J. Ongibene, "In Military Procurement, More Bucks Don't Always Produce a Bigger Bang," *National Journal,* December 12, 1981, 2192–97.

18. For a breakdown on these particular costs, see Project on Military Procurement, *Defense Procurement Information Papers: Campaign 86* (Project on Military Procurement, September 1986), 20–23.

19. Steven Roberts, "The Provocative Saga of the $400 Hammer," *New York Times,* June 13, 1984, 22.

20. Morrison, "Chaos on Capitol Hill," 2305.

21. General Accounting Office, *Legislative Oversight: DoD Appearances at Congressional Hearings during 1985* (GAO/NSIAD-86–147FS), June 1986.

22. The latter issue was the subject of a reporting requirement written into the FY 1986 Defense Authorization Act; cited in J. Ronald Fox, *The Defense Management Challenge: Weapons Acquisition* (Boston: Harvard Business School Press, 1988), 77.

23. Art, "Congress and the Defense Budget," 240.

24. David Morrison, "Warning Shot," *National Journal,* October 7, 1989, 2448.

25. Ibid., 2449.

26. Pat Towell, "Defense Panel Axes Funding for Troubled New Fighter," *Congressional Quarterly,* July 22, 1989, 1884.

27. Jon Englund, "JTIDS—Diary of a $600 Million Pentagon Fiasco," *Washington Post,* August 11, 1986, D4.

28. Aaron Wildavsky, *The Politics of the Budgetary Process,* 3d ed. (Boston: Little Brown, 1979), 63–126; Richard Fenno, *The Power of the Purse: Appropriation Politics in Congress* (Boston: Little, Brown, 1966), 23–29; and Anne Cahn, *Congress, Military Affairs, and (a bit) of Information* (Beverly Hills: Sage Publications, 1974). Although Wildavsky and Fenno are considered to be the most comprehensive works on the budget and appropriations process, both ignore the defense budget.

29. James M. Lindsay, "Congressional Oversight of the Department of Defense: Reconsidering the Conventional Wisdom," *Armed Forces & Society* 17, no. 1 (Fall 1990): 14–15.

30. General Accounting Office, *Legislative Oversight: Congressional Requests for Information on Defense Activities* (GAO/NSIAD-86–65BR), February 1986, 5.

31. Edward Luttwak, *The Pentagon and the Art of War* (New York: Simon and Schuster, 1984), 70.

32. Cahn, *Congress, Military Affairs, and (a bit) of Information,* 19.

33. J. Ronald Fox, *Arming America: How the U.S. Buys Weapons* (Boston:

Division of Research, Graduate School of Business Administration, Harvard University, 1974), 133.

34. U. S. Congress, *Department of Defense Appropriations for Fiscal Year 1986,* part 2, 86.

35. See Pat Towell, "House Members Criticize Troubled B-1 Bomber," *Congressional Quarterly,* March 7, 1987, 432; Richard Halloran, "B-1's Long-Running Battle Just Goes On and On," *New York Times,* October 17, 1988, 18.

36. "A-12 Administrative Inquiry" (Memorandum for the Secretary of the Navy, prepared by Chester Paul Beach, Jr., November 28, 1990), 29.

37. Ibid., 30.

38. John D. Morocco, "Navy Weighs Alternatives after Cheney Kills Avenger 2," *Aviation Week & Space Technology,* January 14, 1991, 18–19.

39. David C. Morrison, "Pentagon's Top Secret 'Black' Budget Has Sky-rocketed During Reagan Years," *National Journal,* March 3, 1986, 495.

40. James Kitfield, "Black Programs: Too Big to Hide?" *Military Forum* (April 1989): 22.

41. David J. Lynch, "Stealth Again Under Fire," *Defense Week,* April 26, 1986, 16; Barbara Amouyal, "Air Force May Need to Reduce B-2 Secrecy to Secure Funds, Sources Say," *Defense News,* March 13, 1989, 26.

42. Michael Gordon, "Congressmen Seek Detail on Bomber," *New York Times,* March 15, 1986, 9.

43. "Randolph Details B-2 Range, Payload, Design Rationale," *Aerospace Daily,* May 2, 1989, 175–76.

44. "B-2 Production Schedule Revealed," *Aerospace Daily,* June 27, 1989, 505.

45. Mark Thompson, "Can Stealth Fly Without Testing?" *Miami Herald,* April 23, 1989, 1.

46. Morocco, "Navy Weighs Alternatives after Cheney Kills Avenger 2," 20.

47. General Accounting Office, *Legislative Oversight: Congressional Requests for Information on Defense Activities,* 4–5.

48. General Accounting Office, *DOD Legislative Activities: Better Guidance, Accountability, and Reporting Needed* (GAO/NSIAD-86–134BR), June 1986, 5.

49. Ibid., 9.

50. George C. Wilson, "C-5A Plane Flying into More Turbulence," *Washington Post,* January 21, 1982, 16.

51. Frank Grove, "Despite Law, Air Force Lobbying for Lockheed Jet," *Philadelphia Inquirer,* June 22, 1982, 2.

52. On the B-1, see Nick Kotz, *Wild Blue Yonder: Money, Politics, and the B-1 Bomber* (New York: Pantheon Books), esp. chap. 11.

53. See Dina Rasor, "Pentagon Brass and Their Corporate Pals Team Up to Woo Congress," *Business and Society Review* (Spring 1983): 18–19.

54. Congressional Contact Tally, available from author.

55. "Lockheed, Pentagon Unite to Oppose Boeing Campaign," *Congressional Quarterly,* July 3, 1982, 1583.

56. Grove, "Despite Law, Air Force Lobbying for Lockheed Jet," 2.

57. "Lockheed, Pentagon Unite to Oppose Boeing Campaign," 1584.

58. Ibid. See also Benjamin F. Schemmer, "Budget Cutters are Only Ones Likely to Win Battle Over C-5B/747F/C-17 Airlift Alternatives," *Armed Forces Journal International* (July 1982): 44.

59. Schemmer, "Budget Cutters are Only Ones Likely to Win Battle Over C-5B/747F/C-17 Airlift Alternatives," 44. See also Project on Military Procurement, "Appendix A: Excerpts from Action/Status Computer Log," June 14, 1982, 4.

60. Grove, "Despite Law, Air Force Lobbying for Lockheed Jet," 2; and General Accounting Office, *Improper Lobbying Activities by the Department of Defense on the Proposed Procurement of the C-5B Aircraft* (GAO/AFMD-82–123), September 29, 1982, 12.

61. U.S. Congress, House Armed Services Committee, Investigations Subcommittee Report together with Separate Views, *Allegations of Improper Lobbying by Department of Defense Personnel of the C-5B and B-1B Aircraft and Sale to Saudi Arabia of the Airborne Warning and Control System* (97th Congress, 2d Session, December 30, 1984), 5, citing an article in *Defense Week* for June 6, 1982.

62. "Lockheed, Pentagon Unite," 1583.

63. Grove, "Despite Law, Air Force Lobbying for Lockheed Jet," 2.

64. General Accounting Office, *Improper Lobbying Activities by the Department of Defense on the Proposed Procurement of the C-5B Aircraft,* 22.

65. Ibid., 2.

66. House Armed Services Committee, *Allegations of Improper Lobbying.*

67. Ibid., 27.

68. Schemmer, "Budget Cutters Are Only Ones Likely to Win War Over C-5B/747F/C-17 Airlift Alternatives," 43.

69. Rasor, "Pentagon Brass and Their Corporate Pals Team Up to Woo Congress," 22.

70. Gordon Adams, *The Iron Triangle: The Politics of Military Contracting* (New York: Council on Economic Priorities, 1981), 135.

71. This is a partial summary of a report Boeing provided to the Defense Contract Audit Agency in 1975, listing the responsibilities of its Washington office; cited in Adams, *The Iron Triangle,* 132–33.

72. Adams, *The Iron Triangle,* 134.

73. Kotz, *Wild Blue Yonder,* 123–57.

74. Ibid., 135.

75. Ibid., 136.

76. Simon, *Top Guns,* 37.

77. Les Aspin, "Games the Pentagon Plays," *Foreign Policy*, no. 11 (Summer 1973): 91.

78. Fenno, *The Power of the Purse*, 85.

79. Ibid., 65.

80. Barry S. Rundquist, "Congressional Influence on the Distribution of Prime Military Contracts," (Ph.D. diss., Stanford University, 1974); R. Douglas Arnold, *Congress and the Bureaucracy* (New Haven: Yale University Press, 1979); Barry S. Rundquist and David Griffith, "An Interrupted Time Series Test of the Distributive Theory of Military Policy Making," *Western Political Quarterly* 29, no. 4 (December 1976); Bruce Ray, "Defense Department Spending and 'Hawkish' Voting in the House," *Western Political Quarterly* 34, no. 3 (September 1981); Bruce Ray, "Military Committee Membership in the House of Representatives and the Allocation of Defense Department Outlays," *Western Political Quarterly* 34, no. 2 (June 1981); Carol F. Goss, "Military Committee Membership and Defense-Related Benefits in the House of Representatives," *Western Political Quarterly* 25, no. 2 (June 1972); Leonard G. Ritt, "Committee Position, Seniority, and the Distribution of Government Expenditures," *Public Policy* 24, no. 4 (Fall 1976).

81. Ritt, "Committee Position, Seniority, and the Distribution of Government Expenditures," 487.

82. Rundquist, "Congressional Influence on the Distribution of Prime Military Contracts."

83. Murray Weidenbaum, "Measurements of the Economic Impact of Defense and Space Programs," *American Journal of Economics and Sociology* 25, no. 4 (October 1966).

84. James L. Clayton, "The Impact of the Cold War on the Economies of California and Utah, 1946–1965," *Pacific Historical Review* 36, no. 4 (November 1967): 464.

85. Even small programs can involve hundreds of subcontractors; major programs may involve many thousands. Over forty thousand subcontractors were involved in the Minuteman program (see Jacques Gansler, *The Defense Industry* [Cambridge: MIT Press, 1980], 43); over six thousand major subs worked on the B-1 bomber.

86. General Accounting Office, *Defense Department Subcontract-Level Reporting System* (GAO/ID-83–30), Report B-208826, January 21, 1983, 1–3.

The Weapons Acquisition Process

Although Congress is the most visible political actor in the defense contracting process, the military services and civilians in DOD also play important roles. One can hardly understand congressional activity without examining the broader acquisition process, that is, the organizational structures and procedures that the military services use to decide what kinds of weapons they need and how they manage programs through the process in order to reach the ultimate goal of a fielded, operationally capable weapon. This process, in fact, defines the most basic function of the peacetime military. Aside from training, the services' primary peacetime functions are developing, buying, and operating weapons.

An examination of both the formal and informal mechanisms of the process will highlight where in the process, and why, politics are most likely to intrude. Political activity occurs on two levels, internally within and among the individual services and externally between the services and the civilian leadership. The internal politics are hard to identify because they are shielded from public view. The services are generally reluctant to air their internal and intraservice disputes except when they involve organizational control over traditional missions. Each branch generally refrains from publicly criticizing the others, and nothing is gained by open discussion of the internecine squabbles that occur *within* the separate services. Behind the public facade of unanimity, however, exists a level of furious bureaucratic activity. Competing groups continually bargain, cajole, and threaten in an attempt to create and maintain coalitions powerful enough to push their pet projects up the organizational chart.

This chapter describes how the military services and DOD manage large weapons programs. Two notable observations will emerge. The first is that it is extraordinarily difficult to steer a weapon program through the maze of approvals and funding decisions that are required to make the transition from an idea to a deployed system. There are always more development ideas than money to pay for them, and competition to get initial funding included in service budgets is fierce. For the largest systems, the process takes about ten to fifteen years and can involve substantial changes in supply, personnel management, and training procedures. Once a service commits itself to developing a new weapon, it is loath to admit problems or errors that could jeopardize the program's future. Almost any outcome, even the fielding of a flawed system, is preferable to scrapping the whole project and starting over.

The second observation is that despite the formal organizational procedures involved in weapons acquisition, *informal* relationships and structures dominate. Once a weapons program begins, advocates invest heavily in building and maintaining coalitions to support it, both internally and in the broader defense community, especially in OSD and Congress. In public statements and congressional testimony, service leaders give the impression that every weapon enjoys unanimous support within the service and that everyone is working toward the common goal of fielding the system. In reality, though, there is a continual process of coalition building as different groups and branches within each service push their agendas on decision makers, promoting particular systems and trying to kill others. The chances of getting a system into production ordinarily depend more on the outcomes of these pitched bureaucratic battles than on objective effectiveness criteria. If a particular weapon fulfills a traditional service mission, the job can be easy. If not, then advocates must convince top decision makers to bring the rest of the organization along. Either way, backtracking is next to impossible once the commitment is made.

The structure of the acquisition process—and Congress's unique role in it—thus creates an environment in which traditional budget protection and promotion strategies are essential components of defense policy. The funding requests that the military presents to Congress are tarnished by the heated political battles that must be fought to propel a program to the funding stage. Politics does not enter the picture only when Congress deals with the defense money; the acquisition process is political from start to finish.

The Military Services

The individual military services dominate the acquisition process. They are responsible for evaluating their own needs, pinpointing deficiencies, and drawing up the specifications for new weapons. They manage weapons programs in both the development and production stages, negotiate contracts with contractors, and execute the resulting agreements.

Each branch of the military has its own mission: broadly speaking, the army is responsible for land warfare, the navy for control of the seas, the air force for air superiority. Strategic nuclear missions are split between the air force and the navy, although the army controls large numbers of tactical nuclear weapons. Despite increasing overlap of mission areas— the constant battle between the air force and army over the close air support mission comes to mind—each service buys its weapons separately, except for a few programs that two services manage jointly (such as the AIM-7 Sparrow air-to-air missile, which both the air force and navy use). These separate but well-guarded missions play an important role in determining what types of weapons each service prefers. How the services deal with threats posed by new systems or by the other branches reveals a number of important organizational characteristics.

The general layout of the formal acquisition process is simple, even though it involves an enormous number of individuals and overlapping steps. Every major weapon system passes through several stages as it moves from conception to deployment. Chronologically, the stages are determination of a need and concept definition, concept demonstration and validation, full-scale development, and finally production. At various points along this spectrum, normally when a program moves from one stage to the next, the secretary of defense must approve the service's activities. Also, Congress must annually authorize and appropriate money for the program. Ideally, needs are well defined at the beginning, realistic specifications are set, technical kinks are worked out in linear fashion before the project moves on to the successive stages, and programs that show obvious signs of failure are scrapped. As we will see, the services hardly ever meet this seemingly reasonable standard.

The acquisition process begins when one of the services decides that it needs a new weapon. New programs are supposed to be tied closely to a coherent military strategy, so that they improve the services' ability to carry out important missions. In the real world, however, new programs are often started in order to take advantage of a technological opportunity, perpetuate traditional service roles, or advance particularistic organizational interests.

Several factors may contribute to judgments that current systems cannot do the job. First, military intelligence might identify a threat, usually a new Soviet weapon, that renders current U.S. systems vulnerable, or they might pinpoint specific weaknesses in a currently fielded U.S. weapon. The F-15 fighter program was begun for precisely these reasons in the 1960s, when the air force concluded that two new Soviet aircraft, the MiG-23 Flogger and MiG-25 Foxbat, far outclassed the best U.S. fighter, the F-4 Phantom.[1] In response, the air force initiated the F-15 program, specifically intending to produce a plane that would best its Soviet counterparts. Similarly, the air force makes its case for the B-2 Stealth bomber by arguing that projected improvements in Soviet air defenses will prevent the B-1 from carrying out its penetration bombing mission.

Second, new military doctrines and strategies may require new tactical capabilities and new types of weapons. Defining doctrine precisely is difficult; a loose definition is that it is a military's philosophy of how best to fight. It is much easier to show its effects: "Doctrine provides a military organization with a common language, a common purpose, and a common unity of effort. Doctrine influences, to a major degree, strategic thinking as well as the development of weapons, organization, training, and tactics. Doctrine is the cement that binds a military organization into an effective fighting unit."[2] The army was in the process of revising its doctrine for fighting a conventional war in Europe when events there threw military planners into a near panic by rendering the whole effort irrelevant. According to the new plan, which is obsolete for the European theater but still used elsewhere, such as in the Persian Gulf, units were to attack second-echelon, or reinforcing, Warsaw Pact forces far behind enemy lines. Many of the weapons in the existing inventory, particularly older tactical nuclear weapons like the Lance missile, were not up to such a task. The Lance, with a range of 80 miles, cannot attack these second-echelon forces, which may be as far as 180 miles away.[3] In evaluating potential improvements to be fielded as the Lance is retired in 1995, the army decided to replace the Lance with a longer-range system. After abandoning initial efforts to use a 120-mile-range weapon called the Army Tactical Missile System (ATACMS), the army switched to the Follow-On to Lance, with a range of nearly 300 miles. Army officials described their thinking as follows: "The basic requirement is to move forward and increase the range, increase the lethality of the weapons and meet the requirements of [new Army doctrines] which say the only way to be successful is to fight battles in depth."[4] Now that the Warsaw Pact no longer exists, the army is again reevaluating its doctrine to deal with a different set of potential threats posed by Third World countries. In 1990, President George Bush canceled the Follow-On to Lance, though the army is continuing to purchase ATACMS.

Even though the military relies almost exclusively on private contractors for development and production of weapons systems, most basic research that advances the state of the art is done by a network of military laboratories. The navy's laboratory network—which does 35 percent of the service's basic research and 60 percent of exploratory development work—consists of twenty-one facilities scattered mostly around California and the northeastern United States and employs approximately forty thousand people.[5] The largest navy laboratory, the Naval Weapons Center in China Lake, California, invented the Sidewinder air-to-air missile, widely regarded as the best dogfighting weapon ever built. Still used worldwide, the Sidewinder relies on technology originally developed in the late 1940s by China Lake engineers.[6] Other in-house laboratories have made contributions as well. Night vision devices, laser-guided bomb technology, and antiradar missiles—all used with great success against Iraq in 1991—emerged from military labs.[7] Current work includes research into fiber optics, composite materials, artificial intelligence, and robotics.[8]

Defense contractors also perform some basic research, both under contract and with their own funds. Contractors are willing to use company money for defense-related research because they can market promising results to the services. Moreover, contractors who anticipate the services' needs or successfully promote their own developments are most likely to win development and production contracts. The government indirectly reimburses some of these expenditures under the Independent Research and Development (IR&D) program. Major contractors will negotiate an annual agreement with the Pentagon that specifies in general terms the types of research to be done as well as reimbursement percentages and overall spending ceilings. Unlike direct contracts, IR&D encourages contractors to manage their own research efforts efficiently, and the government benefits because the contractors also provide the funding.

Finally, the services develop new weapons to replace those already in the inventory. The need for follow-on systems stems from the fact that military hardware can last only so long before it needs replacement, either because of obsolescence or because the equipment wears out. What was once state-of-the-art rapidly becomes outmoded as new technology is developed and opponents field more capable systems. The army fields new antitank weapons to keep up with advances in Soviet armor; the air force and navy bought the High-speed Anti-Radiation Missile (HARM) to improve upon the capabilities of the older Shrike and Standard Anti-Radiation missiles.

Each service continually tries to field new versions of what can be called core weapons. In doing so, they each protect what they see as their unique missions and preserve their organizational turf and budget allocations. Air force leaders are absolutely convinced of the value of air superiority fighters and manned bombers and are always pushing to procure newer and better versions of each. In the same way, navy leaders are committed to nuclear aircraft carriers, the army to attack helicopters. These weapons fulfill distinct roles that each service sees as central to its reason for existing, and they are supported irrespective of their actual contribution to national security. Efforts to put follow-on systems into the field often last for twenty or thirty years and sometimes appear to be more closely tied to the *institutional* needs of the services rather than to objective military requirements. New generations of core systems are always on the drawing board, to the point that military leaders seem never to be satisfied with what they have in the field.

Most major new starts are initiated as follow-ons, with new systems incorporating technological advances developed since the previous ones were designed. Since new starts are extremely expensive and time-consuming, a quicker and more affordable option is to retain the basic design and incorporate improvements on the margin, which produces better performance without the cost of a completely new system. The venerable Sidewinder has been upgraded nine times since 1953, as advances in electronics and infrared guidance technology made it more potent and reliable.[9] Upgrade programs can be very useful in fixing flaws that go unnoticed until production is well under way.

The services commonly justify major new starts with a combination of the four factors cited here: a service identifies a threat to a core mission or system, which opens the door to a new requirement that stresses the importance of integrating advanced technology into the system designed in response. Typically the new system is a follow-on to one already in the inventory, with the cycle repeating every ten to twenty-five years.

The Acquisition Cycle

Once a service determines that present capabilities fall short of its needs and that it therefore needs a new weapon system, it seeks approval from either service headquarters or OSD to initiate a program start. If a program is small, that approval is likely to come from the service secretary.[10] Now the four-phase acquisition cycle begins. The service knows that it needs a weapon; it must now decide what that weapon will look like.

CONCEPT FORMULATION

Concept formulation, in which a potential weapon is conceived by members of an individual service, is the first formal stage of the acquisition process. As the term suggests, it is at this point that the military develops a concept of the weapon that will remedy identified shortcomings in the current force structure.

The service may have no detailed design specifications for the weapon system; it probably knows only in general terms what the system should do. When the army was investigating the proposed Multiple Launch Rocket System (MLRS) in the early 1970s, it defined the desired capabilities in broad terms. The army document that established a need for a new weapon system read in part, "There is an urgent need for an indirect fire weapon system to neutralize and suppress the enemy's indirect fire support and air defense capabilities [and] to perform other special purpose and general support indirect fire mission [and] . . . contribute toward the total U.S. force capability to contain and defeat the armor threat."[11] The service then translates this type of loose description into operational requirements—the missile's range and the type and number of submunitions it will disperse. Usually some small analysis contracts are awarded to contractors for work on potential weapon designs; for the MLRS, the army awarded five contracts with a total value of less than $1 million for a four-month effort to propose development strategies and designs.[12]

This early process of establishing requirements is critical because decisions about capabilities and desired performance form the core around which the entire program is wrapped. These decisions determine the overall nature of the final weapon and can be used to ensure that it will satisfy traditional service goals, missions, and biases. Once set, the requirements harden into a list of firm, unchallengeable criteria that becomes almost impossible to change, even though the key assumptions behind the requirements may be forgotten as the system moves into development.

A good example is the early decision in the F-15 program that the plane be able to fly at Mach 2.5, which was justified on the grounds that the Soviets had such a capability in the MiG-25. So great was the commitment to this goal that the air force added hundreds of millions of dollars to the program when development versions of the F-15 were able to achieve a top speed of only Mach 2.3. That huge additional investment bought the air force an increase in speed of about 150 miles an hour, a capability that had little tactical utility: "[The Mach 2.5] feature was built into the airplane in large part because the Soviet MiG-25 had it, not because of any requirement imposed by the intended operating context of the F-15. Not only that, the MiG-25 was conceived solely as a high-altitude interceptor against U.S. bombers that never materialized and reconnaissance planes now made largely obsolete by U.S. satellites. As such, the MiG-25 was an aircraft that the F-15 would most likely never even see, let alone engage, in aerial combat."[13]

The low-level dash speed requirement for the F-111 fighter bomber (its ability to fly at very low altitudes at high speeds) was increased from Mach 0.9 to Mach 1.2 for the same reason. There was no military justification for the change, but the program's advocates felt the increased speed made the F-111 look better than the existing tactical bomber, the F-105, and improved their chances of getting high-level air force approval.[14]

At the conclusion of the concept formulation stage, the service evaluates the various concepts and designs under consideration and chooses the most promising candidate. Staffers prepare detailed—if uncertain—estimates of cost, schedule, and technical risk. The selected concept design is, in the next phase, modified and adapted into what the service hopes will become a fully capable and operational system.

CONCEPT DEMONSTRATION AND VALIDATION (DEM/VAL)

During the concept demonstration and validation phase, the technologies and design assumptions behind the weapon system concept chosen in phase 1 are verified and demonstrated. Contracts are awarded to the company that will be responsible for the engineering development of the preliminary design;[15] or, increasingly, awards are made to several firms who compete for the chance to develop the system. Only a few of the many firms who submitted paper concept studies are left now; the others are eliminated from further work on the program.

Typically at this stage a program office that becomes responsible for overall management of the weapon system as it makes its way through the acquisition process is organized within one of the services' buying commands. Each of these commands oversees buying activities connected with particular missions or systems. Navy program offices for the

Sidewinder missile, the F-14 fighter, and the Harpoon antiship missile are all located in the Naval Air Systems Command, headquartered near Washington, D.C. The command is responsible for navy aircraft, missile, and associated electronics procurement.

The head of the office, the program manager, is in theory the one person with overall authority to make decisions affecting his program. As the Packard Commission noted, though, the program manager is only one of many participants who can influence the program's direction. Many of these actors will actually outrank the program manager and can insist that the program comply with a multitude of specialized requirements that are only loosely tied to performance or price. Many of these kibitzers have no "responsibility for the ultimate cost, schedule, or performance of the program."[16] The program manager's time is thus spent convincing the authorities that all the requirements are being met; he has little time left over for actually managing the program.

A major task of concept validation is assuring that the current state of the technological art will allow for cost-effective development and deployment of the final system. According to then Deputy Secretary of Defense Paul Thayer, "It is during this phase that the technical risks, which include functional performance and ability to manufacture, are both addressed."[17] Although most people would find it hard to believe, many potential weapons are weeded out because of overwhelming technical problems or prohibitively high cost.

The army, for example, abandoned an earlier version of the MLRS called the Multiple Artillery Rocket System (MARS) for just these reasons. A number of contractors had submitted design proposals in 1969 with cost estimates far higher than the army anticipated. Moreover, the army discovered that the warhead it intended to use could not destroy tanks. Less than fifteen months after it was established, the MARS program office was dismantled and the weapon canceled for reasons of "cost-effectiveness."[18] One reason the army was willing to cancel MARS was that it was not truly a core system. While the army has pressed for tank and helicopter programs with analogous problems, it was willing to put off rocket system development until a capable system could be fielded at reasonable cost.

Typically during validation one or more contractors will attempt to prove that it can do the job as promised and "fulfill the promises made in those early paper studies."[19] In the 1940s and 1950s, prototyping, or the building of a developmental version of the final product, was a common way to do this. Since development and engineering costs were relatively low then, the military could afford to build and evaluate a number of different designs: between 1945 and 1955 the air force and navy built twenty-two bomber prototypes and thirty-three fighter aircraft prototypes, only a few of which entered production.[20] Even then, however, there was a bias toward relying on paper studies and formal analyses in lieu of hardware production; prototyping was thought to slow the process and conceivably might uncover problems serious enough to jeopardize programs. Today, despite some notable successes like the F-16 and A-10 programs, prototyping is rarely used because of the prohibitively high costs involved: prototypes for the ATF will cost more than $3 billion.

The final shape of the weapon now begins to emerge. The government formalizes its final assessments of what the system will do, and contractors get a better idea of what they must ultimately design. Defense officials claim that an important check on whether an idea is feasible is whether a defense contractor will take contractual responsibility for developing the system. If no company is willing, the concept is assumed to be flawed.

Sometimes, however, a contractor will agree to—or even propose—unrealistic technical goals in order to win contracts that may be "the only game in town." As a rule, the military and contractors both tend to be overly optimistic about what potential weapons systems can do—holding such an attitude is an effective strategy for improving a company's position in competitive environments, where performance is more important than low cost. Little is done to inject any realism into these early estimates, since the services benefit as well: predictions of fantastic performance foster support within the services that propels weapons through the approval process and assists in persuading Congress to provide the necessary funding. Contractors know from experience that their designs are judged primarily on performance and that the services will be sympathetic if the weapon eventually falls short of the high initial expectations. If that happens, the most common result is that the contractor receives additional time and money to correct the deficiencies (though the A-12 cancellation indicates that the Pentagon's willingness to bail out contractors is changing). This is a major cause of the perennial cost overruns and performance shortfalls of modern weapons acquisition.

The AH-56A Cheyenne attack helicopter, ultimately canceled by Congress in the wake of enormous cost increases and intractable technical problems, is a textbook example of egregious optimism. The prime contractor, Lockheed, promised the army that the helicopter would fly twenty-five hundred nautical miles without refueling, even though the original army requirements specified a range of only fifteen hundred miles. The proposed range was far ahead of what even potential technology could achieve, but the army went along since it had too little experience to know how farfetched the estimate was. As one army official noted, "We did not know enough about the detailed technology with respect to the aircraft to know that it was not reasonable to expect that aircraft in its configuration to achieve that much ferry range."[21] The Cheyenne never came close to fulfilling those early promises. Twenty years later the newest U.S. attack helicopter, the AH-64 Apache, has less than half that range at just over one thousand miles. Building in unrealistic (and often unnecessary) requirements pushes costs higher and makes for a more difficult development effort.

By this point in the process, the cost of the proposed weapon has been estimated and reestimated several times, and budget figures have been presented by the military to Congress and to the civilian Pentagon leadership. These early cost calculations are noteworthy because they are set forth with great confidence, are backed up with reams of analysis, and are always wrong. No single statement characterizes the weapons acquisition process better than, "The final cost of a weapon will be higher than expected." It is a near certainty that weapons will in the end cost far more than originally thought. In the 1950s, cost overruns during development were huge: Merton Peck and Frederick Scherer's sample of twelve major systems noted that the *average* cost growth was 220 percent.[22] Growth in current programs is usually smaller, averaging about 10 to 35 percent from the start of full-scale development.[23]

One reason for cost growth is that cost estimating for major weapons systems is a difficult and inherently inexact science. Analysts have the daunting task of correctly guessing the cost of a system that has never been built, does things that no other system can, and embodies technology that may not even be invented yet. Students of the process have long known that predictions made in this kind of environment are "subject to gross errors."[24]

Above and beyond the uncertainties involved, though, initial estimates of cost and performance are often intentionally optimistic. Officials know that the chances of getting approval to proceed drop as costs rise and that the prospects for cancellation diminish as a direct function of how far a program has progressed. Despite the popular impression that the defense budget is bottomless, there are always more projects than money to pay for them. Promising great performance at rock-bottom prices is a good way to make your system look better than that of potential competitors, impress decision makers, and get programs started. Presenting accurate cost figures does nothing except increase a program's chances of getting killed in infancy. There is thus every incentive to low-ball initial estimates and revise them with figures that become more accurate—that is, go up—as a program moves into advanced development and finally production.

The air force estimates for the cost of the Advanced Medium Range Air-to-Air Missile (AMRAAM) followed this pattern by rising steadily from the beginning of the program. In 1977, the air force estimated AMRAAM's unit cost at $40,000 to $50,000 (in 1978 dollars). In 1980, the figure rose to $115,000, and by 1986 it was $200,000 (although one of the contractors involved in the project said the cost would be closer to $260,000).[25] There was, really, no penalty for underestimating the missile's cost to get the program under way, and by the time the missile came under severe criticism, it was too late to stop. As Thomas McNaugher notes, "In 1985 decision-makers were confronted with firmer cost and performance figures, but also with sunk costs of more than a billion dollars, two partially equipped production plants, and the political constituencies those expenditures had created."[26]

Weapons ordinarily develop a degree of bureaucratic momentum during validation. Program offices expand along with the service's institutional commitment, and the number of contractor personnel dedicated to the program, funding levels, and sunk investment grows. For the military service managing the program, the main task becomes one of moving the weapon toward production even if it means overlooking problems. Faced with a choice between accepting an imperfect system that can be improved or canceling the program and starting over, the service will naturally choose the former, especially if the program is strongly supported by service chiefs. As Fox notes, this leads to the direct suppression of potentially damaging (read *accurate*) information about its status:

> When a military Chief of Staff makes it known that he wants his service to undertake a weapons acquisition program, it is highly unlikely that unfavorable information will ever reach the Secretary of Defense through official channels. . . . Military officers are strongly motivated to achieve the objectives set by their superiors. Analysis and documentation prepared in support of a Chief of Staff's favorite programs will suppress relevant information, if necessary, rather than reveal any data likely to raise doubts in the Office of the Secretary of Defense or in Congress.[27]

Everyone involved with the program works toward overcoming or, if that is impossible, minimizing the inevitable technical problems that remain so that the system can move into full-scale development.

FULL-SCALE DEVELOPMENT

Full-scale development (FSD), the final step before production and deployment, is the stage at which "final design, engineering, and manufacturing specifications for [the] weapon system must be prepared."[28] Every aspect of a weapon—final prototypes of the weapon and all of its components, training and maintenance equipment, design of spare parts, logistic support plans—is completed. The system is tested and readied for production.[29] Ideally, the design should be pronounced finished, so that minimal changes are required during production; in practice, however, this rarely occurs.

With few exceptions, the defense contractor selected to perform FSD is guaranteed the production contract if the weapon is ultimately built. Normally the government chooses only one FSD contractor, since the costs of funding two can be prohibitive. If two or more contractors are involved, competition between them can be fierce: winning the production contract can mean tens of billions of dollars in production work over as much as a twenty-year period.

The stakes are unusually high since a commitment to FSD is tantamount to a commitment to production. Few weapons that make it to FSD are canceled; between 1955 and 1985, the services did not cancel a single weapon once FSD had begun.[30] Cancellation decisions, on the rare occasions when they do occur, have come from either the president (President Carter stopped the B-1 bomber in 1977), the secretary of defense (the B-70 bomber, DIVAD, and the A-12), or the Congress (the MBT-70 main battle tank and the Cheyenne attack helicopter).

The goal of FSD "is to develop a weapon system that will be approved for production by the Secretary of Defense."[31] Once a service is able to convince the secretary that a system is ready for production, in the next phase the weapon is produced in quantity and sent to the field.

PRODUCTION AND DEPLOYMENT

After a weapon has been defined, developed, and tested, it remains to be built and deployed. In the case of modern weapons, the production phase is often divided into two stages. The first is low-rate production, during which the contractor, using production facilities and techniques to work out any manufacturing and testing glitches, builds a small number of units. The second is full-rate production, when assembly accelerates.

Few systems make the transition from FSD to production and deployment smoothly. The modern, highly complex weapons that compose the U.S. arsenal are hardly fit for mass production; they are constructed slowly, more by craft and art than by trade skills. Moving into production before procedures and designs have been fully and carefully worked out can lead to problems. A recent example is Northrop's experience with the inertial measurement unit (IMU), a guidance system used in the MX missile. The IMU is about the size and shape of a basketball, but it contains more than nineteen thousand parts, many of which demand exacting tolerances. Northrop immediately fell behind on its manufacturing schedules, a serious problem because the MX was useless without the IMU. Of the first twenty-two missiles delivered to the air force, eight were inoperable because of IMU shortages.[32] In an attempt to speed up assembly, Northrop repeatedly tinkered with its manufacturing procedures, making an average of forty-seven hundred changes per week in early 1987![33] This led to disaster, as technical manuals and test procedures simply could not keep pace. Investigations by the air force showed that parts were improperly tested—or were used despite having failed—and that Northrop had no written instructions on how to complete basic soldering operations.[34]

Since ten to fifteen years can elapse between a weapon's conception and its deployment,[35] the services are always trying to rush the process in order to get new systems into the field as quickly as possible. One way to do this is to begin production during FSD, an overlap officially called concurrency but sometimes wryly described as the "rubber on the ramp" syndrome.

By rushing systems into the field the service can help ensure the weapon's survival. A sunk investment of several billion dollars tends to attract the marginal additional funding required to correct apparent problems. Those problems, if detected earlier in the acquisition cycle, might delay the program or give critics enough ammunition to kill it altogether.

Concurrency can save money, shorten development time, and reduce overhead. It can also motivate program managers to increase the efficiency of both contractor and government.[36] Because of its advantages, concurrency is quite common. In the 1970s it was described as the "custom,"[37] and little has changed since then.[38] The B-1B bomber, the DIVAD, the Patriot surface-to-air missile, and the M-1 Abrams tank were all concurrent programs.[39] The Harpoon antiship missile, according to one study, was 100 percent concurrent, that is, all final testing and development occurred after production had begun.[40] The army procured the MLRS on an even more ambitious and concurrent schedule. Instead of overlapping FSD and production, the army decided to skip FSD altogether and move directly from concept demonstration and validation into low-rate production, a step that shaved two years off the schedule.[41]

Yet concurrency has its risks, notably when production is begun before development problems have been ironed out and designs completed. The correcting of design problems becomes much harder once units are in the field. A technical fix applied to correct one problem may reveal a further problem that requires a fix that is incompatible with the first. Since retroactive fixes take time, the service may have completed the process on only a portion of the fielded units by the time new problems arise; on many highly concurrent programs, several versions of a weapon can be fielded at the same time, which complicates logistics by forcing maintenance networks to stock separate spare parts and technical manuals for each version.

On concurrent and nonconcurrent programs alike, the introduction of design or manufacturing changes during production forces the contractor to adjust his procedures and manuals in midstream, a task that can be complicated and sometimes even impossible. During the early stages of B-1 production, for example, Rockwell discovered that the plane's fuel tanks leaked. The B-1 was designed with integral fuel cells, meaning that there were no internal fuel tanks per se; the airframe structure itself serves as a fuel tank. Fuel leaked through the B-1's twenty-one thousand feet of metal-to-metal seams and fastener holes in the aircraft's skin, particularly in the movable wings, a problem that obviously required correction. Instead of devising one solution before the start of production, Rockwell used three different methods as wing-sets rolled off the assembly line. The first seven aircraft built used a method of silicon injections, and the next thirty-eight used silicon injections plus additional fillets. For the final fifty-five units, Rockwell designed the individual wing components with a triple redundant sealing method.[42] Since this last fix required slight alterations in the way the wing was constructed, it was impossible to retrofit the first forty-five units without completely rebuilding the wings. As of March 1988, approximately 40 percent of B-1s had fuel leaks, and 10 percent of the fleet had leaks severe enough to require grounding.[43] According to the GAO, air force officials have said that "eliminating fuel leaks is virtually impossible."[44] Although one cannot say whether such leaks, a nuisance at best, would have been designed out of the B-1 if they had been identified during development, there is no question that waiting until production had started to begin correcting the problem complicated the task enormously.

More serious issues arise when intractable development problems are detected so late in the production phase that little can be done to solve them. In the case of the much-criticized B-1 bomber, the air force discovered critical flaws in the defensive electronics suite—which was essential to the bomber's ability to penetrate Soviet radar—only after nearly all one hundred of the planes had been built. Correcting the problem was bound to be difficult and expensive, but the air force's problems worsened when it soon became clear that because of fundamental design errors the defense avionics would never be able to meet the original specifications.[45]

Other problems with the B-1B that arose after production had started were a vulnerability to bird strikes (noticed only after a plane crashed upon striking a pelican), problems with the fuel system (a factor in another crash), reliability problems with an automated on-board fault detection system, and difficulties with the terrain-following radar. Most were corrected without much trouble, but others, especially the on-board test system difficulties, persist more than six years after they were first noted.[46]

As during development, so during production costs increase, a problem that many times is attributable to inefficiently low production rates. Because modern weapons are so expensive, the services can afford to buy only small numbers of them each year. Moreover, since research and development represent only a small fraction of a program's total cost— about 3 percent through the start of FSD[47]—the services can afford to start more programs than they can realistically afford to produce. Rather than make choices about which systems to buy and which to forego, the services usually decide to buy fewer units of each system each year to stay within budget limits (Congress does the same). This pushes the annual procurement rates well below the "minimum economic rate of production, [the] lowest rate that offers an acceptable return on the investment in production facilities."[48]

Stretchouts delay the point at which weapons are fully fielded and can substantially increase unit costs. A CBO study of forty major weapons in production during 1987 concluded that half were produced at inefficiently low rates; the study found that an increase in the production rates could lower unit costs by as much as 25 percent.[49] In production, as in the earlier parts of the procurement process, the services will go to great lengths to sustain commitments to key programs. Inefficiency spread across all programs is preferred over sacrificing one or another system to achieve long-run savings.

The production process continues until the service has bought as many units as it needs or as many as Congress will allow. By the time a weapon's production run is completed, a follow-on system is normally at the beginning phases of the acquisition cycle and is being readied for production as a new and better weapon.

Although the services are the most important institutional actor in the procurement process, they cannot act alone. It is the job of the secretary of defense to impose discipline on the services and check their efforts to obtain more weapons and larger budgets.

The Secretary of Defense

The OSD has, with varying degrees of success, tried to supervise and control the services' acquisition activities. As powerless as the secretary sometimes appears to be, his authority level is far higher now than it was earlier in the postwar period. Immediately after the office was created in 1947, the first secretary of defense, James Forrestal, noted that the position had insufficient authority. Only after major reorganization of DOD in 1958 did the secretary have formal authority to "direct and control" the services rather than simply supervise them.[50]

The largest increase in the secretary's power over the services occurred during the tenure of Defense Secretary Robert S. McNamara. McNamara, through the introduction of the Planning, Programming, and Budgeting System (PPBS) and systems analysis, imposed an unprecedented level of discipline on the services.[51] McNamara upset the traditional relationship between the secretary and the services with his continual involvement in weapons programs, which the services resented as meddling. Under PPBS, the services for the first time were forced to justify their budget and acquisition requests on a mission basis, which allowed OSD to make judgments about the best way to meet, for example, strategic nuclear force requirements.

McNamara's most notable contribution to the contracting process was the concept of Total Package Procurement (TPP), in which a weapon's price, performance, and schedule were set at the beginning of FSD. A response to the enormous cost growth seen in the 1950s during development, TPP was designed to prevent contractors from taking advantage of the combination of their sole-source position and the extensive use of cost-plus-fixed-fee contracts. In that environment, contractors had absolutely no incentive to control costs, since all of their expenses were reimbursed and the government could not turn to other sources. McNamara hoped to minimize cost growth during development by settling all cost and performance terms at the very start and then using fixed-price contracts, which put maximum financial responsibility on the contractor.

In practice, though, TPP constrained both the government and contractors by locking in cost and performance requirements before important technical issues had been resolved. This led to unanticipated cost growth as well as to performance problems on major programs like the C-5A and the Maverick air-to-ground missile. The fatal flaw of TPP was that concept definition and validation efforts consisted of paper studies and analyses of technical risk, instead of actual hardware and prototype construction.[52] Total Package Procurement made it impossible for anyone to know with any certainty what the final product would look like or what it would cost.

The strained relations between OSD and the services that resulted from such innovation led Deputy Secretary of Defense David Packard in May 1969 to introduce a new acquisition management system that has survived essentially unchanged to this day. Packard hoped to minimize animosity between the OSD and the services by focusing OSD's involvement on specific, key points in the acquisition process.[53] This structure forces the services to justify their programs at these critical junctures (known as milestones) in the acquisition process to a high-level committee, then called the Defense Systems Acquisition Review Council (DSARC). As described in Packard's policy memorandum, the DSARC's purpose was to "advise . . . of the readiness of each major system to proceed to the next phase of effort in its life cycle."[54]

Initially the DSARC met at three points in the acquisition process: before concept definition, before FSD, and before production (approvals for concept definition and validation were collapsed into a single decision).[55] At DSARC meetings, the services presented data and reports on various elements of the weapons program under review. After considering the information presented, the DSARC would submit a recommendation to the secretary of defense. The council could recommend that the program proceed directly to the next stage, instruct the program office to proceed contingent upon specified changes in either program management or the weapon's technical characteristics, or advise that the program be stopped or delayed. In extreme cases, the DSARC could recommend that a program be canceled. These recommendations were then passed on to the secretary of defense, who made the final decision about the program's status.

Packard created the DSARC as part of a package of acquisition reforms, the most famous of which was the so-called fly before you buy policy. Because previous reliance on paper analysis in the definition stage had created problems in development and production, Packard placed renewed emphasis on development of hardware and prototypes. Several programs that entered production during the early 1970s, specifically the F-16 and A-10 aircraft, used prototyping.

The reporting requirements set out by the secretary of defense are designed to force the services to implement certain management objectives. By requiring documentation on reliability and maintainability, for example, the secretary hoped to force the services to think about these issues in the acquisition process—a task they might avoid if no such reports were directed.

The DSARC process has been modified many times since its inception, the most important changes involving additional review points, or milestones. Because some officials thought that the Milestone I DSARC review took place too late in the process to have much effect on programs, a Milestone 0 review was introduced in 1976 in which the services must formally receive permission to begin a major new program. This major early review gave the council some additional control over the initial acquisition stage and brought DOD into compliance with a government-wide OMB acquisition policy directive that mandated a secretarial-level decision before any major acquisition program was begun. In effect, the services required approval from the secretary of defense before engaging in any activities pertaining to a large program. Milestone 0 was dropped in 1981 by Secretary of Defense Caspar Weinberger because he felt the additional review created unnecessary delays in the acquisition process.[56] It has since been reinstated.

The memoranda that established the original DSARC process and laid out the formal structure of the defense acquisition process are periodically reissued as the policies change. Recent versions of these documents, *Department of Defense Directive, Number 5000.1* and *Department of Defense Instruction, Number 5000.2,* issued on September 1, 1987, added two more milestones (as well as creating the new

Defense Acquisition Board [DAB]). The DAB now meets at Milestone IV for a Logistics Readiness and Support Review, during which maintenance procedures, spare parts availability, and general operational readiness are discussed. At Milestone V, the DAB formally entertains discussions on whether the current system meets all of the service's needs and whether major upgrades or even entirely new programs are warranted.[57] In addition, the name of the DSARC was changed to the Defense Acquisition Board to reflect the new board's broader responsibilities and expanded membership. Unlike DSARC, which reviewed only specific programs, DAB is charged with reviewing broad acquisition policy issues and playing a larger role in the initial requirements process.[58]

Despite the best intentions of the DSARC/DAB system, the council has been only partially effective in supervising and directing the services. Board reviews are hindered by the fact that members typically receive information only after it has filtered through various staff levels in the services. Since no program office or service wants to jeopardize a major system, it ensures that little negative information makes its way to the briefing. Many critics have noted that the most important phase of the review process is the time immediately preceding the full DAB review, as various organizations within the services tug at each other to resolve or minimize problems. Program reviews are, therefore, often conducted without full and accurate information and even without full attendance by all the principals.[59]

DSARC's ability to manage is hampered by the fact that important milestones occur too late to force the services to think seriously about trade-offs or alternative ways of performing missions. By establishing the DSARC process, McNaugher writes, Packard hoped "to generate real alternatives by developing competing technologies between DSARC I and DSARC II, with the choice between or among alternatives being made at DSARC II on the basis of operational testing."[60] Yet real options are and always have been anathema to the services, who "work to exclude alternatives from the very start."[61] Unwilling and unable to explore alternatives, a program's advocates become bound by the specific option they have chosen and must reinforce the original consensus in favor of their weapons: "Successive DSARCs open the ongoing project to reexamination, during which the consensus building process that generated the original requirement may be reenacted, perhaps with new actors, or even new agencies. . . . Although Packard originally established the DSARCs as a means of reviewing progress in individual weapon projects, they often serve to generate new work with new uncertainties."[62]

Ironically, DSARC reviews are also accused of merely rubber-stamping decisions by the services, intervening only after most of the important trade-offs and decisions have been made. Despite the DAB's enlarged charter, it has little say in initial requirements, even when it meets early in the procurement process. By the time the DAB meets to discuss FSD or production decisions, it is too late to require any major program changes. As one Pentagon official put it, "On Tuesday a program comes to DSARC with a fixed price contract. The parties have made firm offers, and the offers expire on Thursday. You can't tell them they should open up and negotiate a new contract. It's a freight train, and it's impossible to stop."[63]

Despite its shortcomings, the DSARC/DAB civilian review has led to some improvements and at times has exercised strict management control. Cost growth has been reduced and occasionally, as in the army's advanced LHX combat helicopter program, a service has been denied permission to proceed. The difficulties that remain result from the uniquely powerful role the services play in the acquisition process and will resist fixes based on structural reform. As McNaugher observes, "There is no denying the need for reform, yet the kind of reforms now popular do nothing to alter the basic political incentives that shape the acquisition process."[64]

Source Selection

Over the years, the government has developed an elaborate process for selecting contractors to perform work and has established regulations that govern the contractual relationship between the government and contractors. These are designed to ensure that the government gets its money's worth and that contractors are selected fairly and on the basis of technical expertise and efficiency.

The currency of the government-contractor relationship is the defense contract, which details the work the contractor is to perform and how much the government will pay. There are two major types of contracts. Under fixed-price contracts the final price—the contractor's cost plus a profit—is agreed to in advance; the number is arrived at either through negotiations with the government or as the result of a sealed bid. Both parties understand that no price adjustments will be made. If the contract specifies, for example, that the contractor will provide a prototype aircraft for $50 million, the contractor receives that amount even if the aircraft costs $75 million to build. The extra $25 million comes out of the contractor's pocket. Conversely, if the contractor discovers a way to produce the aircraft for $30 million, it still receives $50 million and takes the extra money as additional profit. Because fixed-price contracts place full financial risk (and potential reward) on the contractor, they are normally used only when technical risks are considered manageable. In practice, fixed-price contracts enforce less discipline than might be expected. Contractors are often reimbursed for extra costs in any case, as Lockheed was on the C-5A program. Conversely, if contractors manage to reduce their costs, the government will surely reduce its payment in subsequent contracts, arguing that the contractor must reduce the amount it charges.

Under cost-based contracts, the government agrees to reimburse contractors for all costs incurred plus a specified fee. Normally a target cost—a best guess of what the final cost should be—is identified at the beginning; however, the government reimburses contractors even if the final costs exceed this total. Typically these contracts are referred to as cost-plus, giving the mistaken impression that the contractor fee is set as a percentage of the final costs. In fact, so-called cost-plus-percentage-of-cost contracts are specifically prohibited, for obvious reasons: they give the contractor every incentive to push costs as high as possible, since his fee rises accordingly. Many contracts include incentive clauses, by which the contractor's fee varies inversely with final costs—the higher the costs, the lower the fee, and vice versa. Because cost-based contracts put minimal risk on the contractor, they are often used for development work in which the technologies are new or poorly understood.

Contractors are selected to do work in a variety of ways, but the most common pattern is as follows: a service issues a Request for Proposal (RFP), which is a formal notice to industry that a contract will be let. The

RFP specifies in detail what the service wants to buy and sets out tentative quantities and delivery schedules as well as the method to be used to select the winner. If the item to be procured is relatively simple or commercially available, the service may run a sealed-bid competition. Interested contractors submit price-secret bids, which are opened simultaneously, and the contract goes to the low bidder. There are no negotiations and minimal discussion between the government and industry. Sealed bids are the purest form of competition that exists in the acquisition process.

To acquire more complex items, the service may run a competitive, negotiated procurement. Here, the RFP sets out the criteria by which the proposals will be judged. Interested contractors submit initial proposals, outlining their design and presenting cost and price data; the proposals are refined and modified in negotiations with the service. The negotiations are necessary because often the service's idea of what it wants changes on the basis of what the industry is willing to offer. Eventually, the contractors submit their so-called best and final offers (often followed by another round of negotiations and submission of best and *really* final offers), which are evaluated by a Source Selection Board set up within the procuring service. The proposals are ranked on the basis of the established criteria, the best proposal getting the contract. These competitions typically take place in the early stages of the program—in the concept definition or concept validation stages.

In the past, the contractor who won in these early stages was virtually assured of obtaining sole-source contracts for the rest of the program. This made a certain amount of sense, since choosing one company for the design phase and then handing over the blueprints to a different company for production is an expensive and often inefficient process. Moreover, companies are reluctant to produce their best designs if they know they will be given to competitors, especially when the designs include company secret or proprietary innovations.

Yet the guaranteeing of a succession of follow-on contracts leads to some obvious temptations. The most common is buying-in, which occurs when a company submits an unrealistically low bid for the development phase, knowing it will lose money. Later in the program, though, when all competition has been eliminated and contracts are sole-source, the company can recoup its losses by raising prices during production. It was this practice that motivated McNamara's ill-fated TPP policy, which locked in production prices while there was still competition.

More recently, a desire to maintain competition throughout production has changed the pattern of sole-source contracts. Increasingly, the government qualifies an additional source to compete against the original manufacturer, so that two or more companies compete for each year's annual buy of a weapon system. The high cost of establishing the second source theoretically is offset by lower unit costs and higher quality as companies are forced to compete head to head. Supporters of second-source contracting point to examples such as the Maverick air-to-ground missile, whose unit cost dropped from $122,000 to $76,000 after the air force started a competition between the original manufacturer, Hughes, and upstart Raytheon. The navy was able to lower the cost of the Tomahawk cruise missile by 35 percent after setting up McDonnell Douglas as a competitor to General Dynamics; it also convinced Texas Instruments to lower its price for the HARM by 60 percent just by threatening to set up a second source.[65]

Yet critics argue that second-sourcing does not, in fact, save enough to cover the high initial cost of qualification. Moreover, the cost savings may be overstated, since unit costs invariably drop during the course of production, even in sole-source programs. The best work to date shows that while the government may get a better, more reliable product through competition, the long-term cost benefits are at best ambiguous.[66]

Because of the value of winning contracts in an increasingly competitive environment, rivalry among the contractors is intense. The Ill Wind procurement scandal showed that some firms, and the consultants they hire, are willing to engage in criminal activity to get inside information on contract competitions. Most of the investigation focused on firms suspected of bribing government officials to either divulge information about other firms or actually rig competitions to favor their proposals over the others. Consultants hired to provide special expertise to firms preparing bids played key middlemen roles, obtaining through bribery information that would increase their own value to firms engaged in competitive proposal efforts.

Ill Wind pointed clearly to the power contract officers and program managers have during contract competitions. However, as I argue in chapter 4, the process is in general quite objective and fair. Losing contractors have a variety of protest remedies available if they perceive they lost unfairly; many of the firms who lost contracts later tainted through Ill Wind have in fact sued to reopen competitions, at great inconvenience and expense to the government.[67] Moreover, the relatively small number of individuals and contracts involved must be seen in the context of the millions of contract actions and thousands of high-level personnel involved in the acquisition process. The people and contracts under suspicion made up a minute fraction of total contracting activity.

The Defense Industry

Private companies produce nearly everything the military buys, from paper clips to aircraft carriers. Although the military deals with thousands of firms, most defense contracts are awarded to a small number of firms heavily involved in ongoing defense work; it is these companies that are generally described as defense contractors. Several hundred major prime contractors supply goods and services to the military, with about 20,000 other prime contractors and more than 150,000 smaller firms rounding out the defense industrial base.[68] These smaller firms comprise the lower tiers of the industry and supply the prime contractors with subassemblies, parts, and assorted components. Estimates of the number of people employed in the defense industry vary, depending on whether total employment (public and private) and multiplier effects are included. If all indirect and direct jobs in both the military and civilian sectors are included, the defense budget creates between 7 and 8.5 million jobs.[69] The CBO estimated that in 1981 the defense industry alone employed nearly 2.4 million people, or about 210,000 for each $10 billion in defense direct purchases.[70]

By any measure, the defense industry is highly concentrated and is made up of some enormous companies. The ten largest defense contractors received nearly $45 billion in contracts during FY 1989, or over 34 percent of the total spent on procurement (table 3–1). The top five by themselves accounted for 21.4 percent of the total. This degree of

Table 3-1
The Largest Prime Contractors in Fiscal Year 1989

Rank	Contractor	Awards in 1989 (billions)	Rank in 1958–60
1	McDonnell Douglas	$ 8.617	8
2	General Dynamics	6.899	2
3	General Electric	5.771	4
4	Raytheon	3.760	12
5	General Motors	3.691	21
6	Lockheed	3.652	3
7	United Technologies	3.556	6
8	Martin Marietta	3.337	9
9	Boeing	2.868	1
10	Grumman	2.373	17
	Total	$44.074	

Sources: Department of Defense, *100 Companies Receiving the Largest Dollar Volume of Prime Contract Awards, Fiscal Year 1989* (Washington, D.C.: Directorate for Information Operations and Reports, DIOR/PO1–89, 1990); Peck and Scherer, *The Weapons Acquisition Process: An Economic Analysis*, 613.

concentration has remained relatively stable over the past thirty years: since 1959, the top five contractors each year have collected about 20 percent of all contracts, the top twenty-five between 45 percent and 55 percent, and the top one hundred between 65 percent and 75 percent.[71] The membership of the top ten has remained steady: seven of the current ten largest were in the same position in 1958–60, and the other three followed closely: Raytheon was the twelfth largest then, Grumman seventeenth, and General Motors twenty-first.[72]

Some sectors of the industry, especially those in the lower tiers, are even more highly concentrated. Jacques Gansler combined several sources to calculate concentration ratios for a number of military markets; although the data are from 1967, there is every reason to expect that concentration is even higher now, given that many firms have left the business since then. Gansler estimates that there were twelve major

Table 3-2
Government Sales as Percentage of Total Sales

	1988	1987	1986
Northrop	92.2%	93.4%	89.7%
Lockheed	92.0	93.0	94.0
Grumman	90.4	89.4	88.4
Martin Marietta	85.4	85.9	85.1
General Dynamics	85.0	86.5	86.0
McDonnell Douglas	64.5	67.7	64.3
Raytheon	55.3	56.3	53.2
Rockwell	47.3	58.0	60.7
United Technologies	32.0	27.0	28.0
Boeing	28.3	31.5	32.7
General Electric[a]	11.4	12.4	n/a

Source: SEC Form 10K and company annual reports.
Note: Figures include civil government sales and FMS contracts through U.S.
government.
[a]Percentage of total sales made up by DOD contracts.

military markets in which the top four firms controlled over 90 percent of
the market.[73] Currently, a number of important systems—airborne radar
systems, aircraft engines, small missile and drone engines, and aluminum plating, to name a few—are produced by just two companies.[74]
Some observers, including Gansler, see this as a liability. With so few
suppliers of key components, the industry has almost no ability to surge
production in a crisis, and production lines can be held up for want of a
few long lead-time items like the IMUs for the MX.

The big contractors vary in their dependence on government. Some,
like Grumman, Lockheed, and Northrop, depend almost entirely on
government sales; others, like Boeing, United Technologies, and General Motors, are mostly commercial firms with substantial cores of
defense work (Boeing, for example, has enough orders for its commercial planes—$29 billion in orders in 1988 alone, and a total backlog of
over $50 billion—to sustain it through the next five years).[75] The per-
centage of company sales that comes from government sales for the ten

largest contractors is listed in table 3–2. Obviously, most of these companies would be in serious trouble without their defense work.

In such an environment, with literally billions of dollars in profits and company survival often at stake, contractors work hard to convince government decision makers of the virtues of their products. The contractors reinforce the services' optimism about weapons cost and performance. As I showed in chapter 2, this effort does not stop once the military gives the green light but merely moves to Congress and more explicitly political strategies designed to ensure the survival of key programs.

CHAPTER 3. THE WEAPONS ACQUISITION PROCESS

1. Robert W. Drewes, *The Air Force and the Great Engine War* (Washington, D.C.: National Defense University Press, 1987), 9–11.

2. Gen. George H. Decker, "Doctrine: The Cement that Binds," *Army* 2 (February 1961): 60, quoted in *The Defense Reform Debate,* ed. Asa A. Clark IV et al. (Baltimore: Johns Hopkins University Press, 1984), 85.

3. For a general discussion of the new army doctrine and its role in setting requirements, see John L. Romjue, *From Active Defense to AirLand Battle: The Development of Army Doctrine 1973–1982* (TRADOC Historical Monograph Series [Historical Office, U.S. Army Training and Doctrine Command, Fort Monroe, Vir., June 1984]).

4. David C. Morrison, "Another Rocket Debate," *National Journal,* March 18, 1989, 707.

5. Statement of Melvin R. Paisley, assistant secretary of the navy (research, engineering, and systems), *FY 1988/1989 Navy Research, Development, Test and Evaluation Budget,* 4.

6. Michael J. Fitzpatrick, "A Case Study in Weapons Acquisition: The Sidewinder Air-to-air Missile," *The Journal of International Affairs* 39, no. 1 (Summer 1985): 177. The Sidewinder was the brainchild of William B. McLean, a civilian physicist working for the navy.

7. Center for Strategic and International Studies, *U.S. Military R&D Management* (Washington, D.C.: Georgetown University Center for Strategic and International Studies, 1973), 37. Also, Peter deLeon, *The Laser Guided Bomb: Case History of a Development* (Santa Monica: RAND Corporation, R-1312–1-PR, June 1974).

8. *FY 1988/FY 1989 Navy Research, Development, Test and Evaluation Budget,* 8–9.

9. Fitzpatrick, "The Sidewinder Air-to-air Missile," 189. The figure is ten if the original version, the AIM-9A, is counted, even though it was never produced in quantity.

10. The acquisition approval sequence is different from the defense budgeting cycle. The secretary of defense (or another official he designates) must approve both the start of the weapons program and the service budget request that will fund it.

11. Kenneth D. McDonald, "GSRS: More than the MRL?" *Field Artillery Journal* (September/October 1974): 12–13.

12. Defense Systems Management College, *Lessons Learned: Multiple Launch Rocket System (MLRS)* (MLRS Project, Department of Research and Information, Defense Systems Management College, Fort Belvoir, Vir., July 1980), B-1.

13. Benjamin Lambeth, "Pitfalls in Force Planning: Structuring America's Tactical Air Arm," *International Security* 10, no. 2 (Fall 1985): 89–90.

14. Ibid., 97, citing Robert F. Coulam, *The Illusions of Choice: The F-111 and the Problems of Weapons Acquisition Reform* (Princeton: Princeton University Press, 1977), 41–42.

15. J. Ronald Fox, *Arming America: How the U.S. Buys Weapons* (Boston: Division of Research, Graduate School of Business Administration, Harvard University, 1974), 106.

16. President's Blue Ribbon Commission on Defense Management, Final Report to the President (The Packard Commission Report), *A Quest for Excellence* (Washington, D.C., 1983), 46.

17. U.S. Congress, Senate Committee on Governmental Affairs, *Management of the Department of Defense,* part 1, March 23, 1983, p. 69.

18. Bruce Gundmundsson, "The Multiple Launch Rocket System: On Time and Under Budget" (Case Program, John F. Kennedy School of Government, Harvard University, no. C16–87–773.0, 1987), 4. Also U.S. Department of the Army, Army Missile Command, Redstone Arsenal, *Annual Historical Summary, 1 July 1969–30 June 1970,* 3.

19. Jacob Goodwin, *Brotherhood of Arms: General Dynamics and the Business of Defending America* (New York: Times Books, 1986), 18.

20. Fox, *Arming America,* 93.

21. Ibid., 102.

22. Merton J. Peck and Frederick M. Scherer, *The Weapons Acquisition Process: An Economic Analysis* (Boston: Division of Research, Graduate School of Business Administration, Harvard University, 1962), 412.

23. Michael Rich and Edmund Dews, *Improving the Military Acquisition Process: Lessons from RAND Research* (Santa Monica: RAND Corporation, R-3373-AF/RC, February 1986), 9.

24. Frederick M. Scherer, *The Weapons Acquisition Process: Economic Incentives* (Boston: Division of Research, Graduate School of Business Administration, Harvard University, 1964), 1.

25. Thomas L. McNaugher, "Buying Weapons: Bleak Prospects for Reform," *The Brookings Review* (Summer 1986): 12.

26. Ibid., 13.

27. Fox, *Arming America*, 100.

28. Ibid.

29. U.S. Congress, House Committee on Government Operations, *Policy Changes in Weapon System Procurement*, 91st Congress, 2d Session, 1970, 51.

30. Jacques Gansler, "How to Improve the Acquisition of Weapons," in *Reorganizing America's Defense: Leadership in War and Peace*, ed. Robert J. Art et al. (Washington: Pergamon Brassey, 1985), 404.

31. Fox, *Arming America*, 107.

32. General Accounting Office, *Inertial Measurement Units for Peacekeeper Missiles* (GAO/NSIAD-87–149BR), July 1987, 2.

33. Molly Moore, "MX Reliability in Question," *Washington Post*, December 28, 1987, A12.

34. Ibid.

35. *Packard Commission*, 47, and Gansler, "How to Improve the Acquisition of Weapons," 384. The time required to move a weapon from conception to deployment (the acquisition interval) has been increasing—by approximately four to five years since the 1950s. See G. K. Smith and E. T. Friedmann, *An Analysis of Weapon System Acquisition Intervals, Past and Present* (Santa Monica: RAND Corporation, R-2605-DR&E/AF, November 1980), 36–37.

36. Congressional Budget Office, *Concurrent Weapons Development and Production*, August 1988, 4.

37. Fox, *Arming America*, 107.

38. Thomas L. McNaugher, "Weapons Procurement: The Futility of Reform," *International Security* 12, no. 2 (Fall 1987): 91.

39. Ibid., 91, citing the General Accounting Office, Report to the Secretary of the Army, *The Army Needs More Comprehensive Evaluations to Make Effective Use of its Weapon System Testing* (NSIAD-84–40), February 24, 1984. Also, Nick Kotz, *Wild Blue Yonder: Money, Politics and the B-1 Bomber,* (New York: Pantheon Books, 1988) 228–29.

40. *Concurrent Weapons Development and Production*, 15.

41. Gundmundsson, "The Multiple Launch Rocket System," 15. See also General Accounting Office, *The Army's Multiple Launch Rocket System is Progressing Well and Merits Continued Support* (MASAD-82–13), February 2, 1982, 2.

42. *Air Force Magazine*, July 1987, 29.

43. General Accounting Office, *B-1B Cost and Performance Remain Uncertain* (GAO/NSIAD-89–55), February 1989, 17.

44. Ibid., 15.

45. Ibid., 11–12.

46. General Accounting Office, *B-1 Maintenance Problems Impede its Operations* (GAO/NSIAD-89–15), October 1988, 11–16.

47. Jacques S. Gansler, *Affording Defense* (Cambridge: MIT Press, 1989), 157.

48. Congressional Budget Office, *Effects of Weapons Procurement Stretch-Outs on Costs and Schedules,* November 1987, ix.

49. Ibid., 30–31.

50. Smith and Friedmann, *Weapon System Acquisition Intervals,* 2–3.

51. See Robert J. Art, *The TFX Decision: McNamara and the Military* (Boston: Little, Brown, 1968); Richard G. Head, "Doctrinal Innovation and the A-7 Attack Aircraft Decision," in *Comparative Defense Policy,* 4th ed., ed. John E. Endicott and Roy W. Stafford (Baltimore: Johns Hopkins University Press, 1977); Douglas Kinnard, *The Secretary of Defense* (Lexington: University Press of Kentucky, 1980), chap. 3; Alain C. Enthoven and K. Wayne Smith, *How Much is Enough? Shaping the Defense Program 1961–1969* (New York: Harper and Row, 1971).

52. See Smith and Friedmann, *Weapon System Acquisition Intervals,* 3, and *Report to the President and the Secretary of Defense on the Department of Defense* (Fitzhugh Commission, 1971), 73.

53. McNaugher, "Weapons Procurement: The Futility of Reform," 89.

54. "Memorandum for Secretaries of the Military Departments, Director, Defense Research and Engineering, Assistant Secretary of Defense (Comptroller), Assistant Secretary of Defense (Installation and Logistics), Assistant Secretary of Defense (Systems Analysis)," May 30, 1969, 1.

55. *Charter, Defense Systems Acquisition Review Council,* May 30, 1969.

56. McNaugher, "Weapons Procurement: The Futility of Reform," 89. Several studies have concluded that the Milestone 0 phase is responsible, in large part, for the increased time required to field major systems. See Smith and Friedmann, *Weapon System Acquisition Intervals,* 38–39.

57. There are thus six milestones at which the DAB evaluates the progress of major programs: Milestone 0—Program Initiation/Mission Need Decision; Milestone I—Concept Demonstration/Validation Decision; Milestone II—Full-Scale Development Decision; Milestone III—Full-Rate Production Decision; Milestone IV—Logistics Readiness and Support Review; Milestone V—Major Upgrade or System Replacement Decision.

58. J. Ronald Fox, *The Defense Management Challenge* (Boston: Harvard Business School Press, 1988), 123–25.

59. *Evaluation of the Effectiveness of the Defense Systems Acquisition Review Council (DSARC),* vol. 1 (Defense Systems Management College, Fort Belvoir, Vir., April 1983), 51–60.

60. McNaugher, "Weapons Procurement: The Futility of Reform," 91.

61. Ibid.

62. Ibid., 93.

63. Fox, *The Defense Management Challenge,* 141.

64. McNaugher, "Weapons Procurement: The Futility of Reform," 102.

65. Sandra Sugarawa, "A Winning Strategy in Defense-Cost War," *Washington Post,* February 12, 1989, H1.

66. Donald Pilling, *Competition in Defense Procurement* (Washington DC: Brookings Institution, 1989).

67. See Sandra Sugarawa, "Losing Bidders Challenging U.S. Contracts," *Washington Post,* December 20, 1988, C1, and John H. Cushman, "Losing Bidder Contests Contract Involved in Pentagon Case," *New York Times,* August 25, 1988, 21.

68. Gansler, *Affording Defense,* 82.

69. Ibid., 81.

70. Congressional Budget Office, *Defense Spending and the Economy,* February 1983, 43, 64.

71. Jacques Gansler, *The Defense Industry* (Cambridge: MIT Press, 1980), 37.

72. Peck and Scherer, *The Weapons Acquisition Process,* 613.

73. Gansler, *The Defense Industry,* 42.

74. Gansler, *Affording Defense,* 259.

75. See, for example, Robert E. Dallos, "Will Success Spoil the Boeing Co.?" *Washington Post,* January 4, 1989, F1. The entire commercial aircraft industry, controlled by Boeing, McDonnell Douglas, and Aerospatiale (maker of the Airbus), is enjoying an unprecedented boom as airlines worldwide are simultaneously expanding and replacing an increasingly aged fleet.

Campaign Contributions by Defense Contractors

Defense contractors, through their PACs, are active contributors to congressional campaign coffers (at least those of incumbents). Critics of the current campaign finance system note that this raises the specter of routine conflicts of interest, as members of Congress decide the fate of contractors who may have donated thousands of dollars to their reelection efforts. In this respect, General Dynamics' donation of money in the hopes of keeping the F-16 program alive is no different from the National Association of Realtors donating money in the hopes of retaining the mortgage interest tax deduction. In another sense, though, contributions made by contractors are different, since most of the large firms depend almost entirely on defense contracts (see table 2–2). People will always need houses, with or without the tax advantages; kill the F-14, and the Grumman Corporation all but vanishes.

Given the stakes involved and the disturbing potential for quid pro quos, the scope and character of the activity of the defense contractor PACs must be investigated. Do contractors contribute money in the expectation that members will support key programs? or do donations serve only to keep lines of communication open? Do contractors target fence-sitters, hoping to sway them with a large contribution? or does money flow mostly to those already predisposed to support weapons programs? Establishing the direction of the causal arrow between contributions and votes (the classic political science version of the chicken/egg question) is almost impossible yet central to the whole issue. Does the appearance of impropriety—a contractor who each year depends on Congress to pass his program and who showers thousands of dollars in contributions on key members—justify restrictions? Where does the burden of proof lie?

This chapter attempts to answer these questions by reviewing important examples of scholarly efforts to fix the direction of the causal arrow and by examining patterns of contributions for a selection of fifty defense contractors. The analysis focuses not only on where PAC money goes, but *when* it arrives. Defense contractors are unique in that their interests are potentially imperiled every time the defense budget winds its way through Congress. These regular budget cycles, if they are reflected in the timing of contributions, may reveal clues about contractors' motivation.

Sorting Out Cause and Effect

What effect does PAC money have on votes? Although there is not enough room for a complete treatment here, I can outline the basic themes of the debate.[1] Critics claim that PAC money distorts the political process by allowing (or forcing) legislators to tailor their voting behavior to attract much-needed campaign money. Defenders of PACs claim that they support those members of Congress who are already disposed to support their interests and use contributions to purchase, if anything, access. Money is the foot in the door; it enables an interest group to make its case to a member who may (or may not) be sympathetic.

The debate is often rancorous, and both sides resort to misleading tactics. Many corporate PACs give themselves innocuous names that obfuscate the fact that they seek to promote highly specific interests. We can be fairly certain that defense contractors' views of good government and active citizenship do not include cutting the defense budget so that governments can build more parks and community colleges. And presumably they do not encourage their employees to push for those goals.

On the other side, critics consistently make the basic error of equating coincidence with cause when examining contribution patterns. Common Cause, for example, routinely publicizes the contribution records of members of Congress, showing that those who supported a bill affecting a particular interest group received large donations from that group. The implication is that the money determined how the members voted, even though the conclusion cannot be supported (or refuted) merely by establishing that money and votes tend to go together. The alternative—often equally unverifiable—explanation is that PACS merely contribute to those members with a history of supportive behavior.

When Congress began reviewing the Clean Air Act in the early 1980s, Common Cause revealed that members who were expected to favor relaxing environmental regulations received much larger contributions from the affected industries (steel, autos, chemicals, and so forth) than those who wanted to keep the law intact.[2] Simply noting the coincidence between votes and contributions, however, reveals nothing about whether the votes were caused by those contributions.

In nearly every case, members who received large contributions had histories of voting in favor of (or against) the industry interests affected. Indices of environmental and probusiness voting behavior prepared by the League of Conservation Voters (LCV) and the National Association of Businessmen (NAB) show how members of the relevant committees voted in 1979 and 1980 on issues like those raised by the Clean Air Act revisions.[3] With few exceptions, members with high NAB and low LCV scores (representing a probusiness, nonenvironmental voting record) received the most from industry groups, while those with low NAB and high LCV scores received the least.

Questions of causality can be resolved only by analyzing the independent effect of campaign contributions while holding constant other vote influences like party, ideology, and constituency interest. Sophisticated analyses of various issues have shown that PAC money sometimes has an independent effect, but that it is almost always small in comparison to that of other factors.[4] Moreover, PAC influence tends to be heaviest when Congress is considering narrow technical issues—milk price supports, the amount of oil that can be imported on non–U.S. built and operated ships, truck weight limits—about which the broad public has little knowledge and weak or nonexistent preferences. This invisibility, in fact, is often necessary in order for PACs to have much impact. As Larry Sabato notes, "PAC contributions are [more] likely to influence the legislature when the matter at hand is specialized and narrow, or unopposed by other organized interests."[5]

Such a requirement rarely applies to defense issues in Congress, which are almost always controversial and of interest to a wide variety of publics, especially if the survival of a major weapons program is at stake. Because any study of the effects must be part of a comprehensive model of voting on defense issues, the reader should refer to the following chapter, which examines among other things the effect of PAC contributions on a congressional decision to cut funding for two nuclear aircraft carriers. That analysis shows that PAC money had absolutely no effect on how the members voted.

The issue, though, need not be limited to whether PAC money buys votes; an examination of overall contribution patterns is still instructive. By looking into the timing of PAC activity and whether it responds to critical periods in the budget process, one can also shed light on the relationship between contractors and members of the House and Senate.

PAC Activity among Defense Contractors

The largest PACs among companies that are heavily involved in defense contracting (table 4–1) include most of the top fifty companies, all of the top ten, and twenty-seven of the top thirty. The list is not meant to be exhaustive, but rather a data base that should provide an idea of how defense issues affect contribution patterns. The selection thus excludes many large PACs whose parent corporations are only peripherally involved in defense contracting or whose defense work comprises a tiny share of their total business. In 1987, for example, IBM was awarded $1.79 billion in contracts, a large absolute amount but less than 5 percent of its total sales of more than $50 billion. GTE received $1.5 billion in contracts against total sales in 1987 of $16.5 billion (9.1 percent); AT&T $638 million against $35.2 billion in sales. These companies and others like Philip Morris and the major oil companies are probably less concerned with defense than with other policy issues, and these concerns will be reflected in their PAC activity.

The level of PAC activity by defense contractors has increased markedly since 1978, rising 784 percent through 1988 (table 4–1). This is roughly comparable to the increase among all corporate PACs, which gave $5.6 million to incumbents in 1977–78 and $45.1 million in 1987–

Table 4-1

Defense Contractor PAC Activity

Total Contributions (Incumbents)

1978	1980	1982	1984	1986	1988
$870,167	$1,755,146	$3,840,471	$5,666,420	$6,462,537	$6,820,519

Activity, 1985–88

| Political Action Committee Name | PAC Donations (Incumbents) | | Contracts |
	87–88	85–86	in 1989 (mill)
1. Lockheed Employees PAC	$ 383,070	$ 349,208	$3,651.5
2. Textron Inc. PAC[a]	357,681	364,850	908.5
3. Northrop Employees PAC	330,790	268,984	631.1
4. Rockwell International Corporation Good Government Committee	313,908	337,050	2,132.8
5. Boeing Company PAC	303,885	235,875	2,868.4
6. FMC Corporation Good Government Program	303,845	213,730	795.8
7. United Technologies Corporation PAC	287,017	192,425	3,356.3
8. Non-Partisan Political Support Committee for General Electric Company Employees	285,860	215,650	5,771.0
9. General Dynamics Corp. Voluntary Political Contribution Plan	269,299	334,783	6,899.2
10. Hughes Aircraft Company Active Citizenship Fund	262,650	205,625	3,014.9
11. Allied-Signal PAC	254,575	215,100	905.6
12. McDonnell Douglas Good Government Fund	234,800	207,325	8,151.3

Table 4-1
(continued)

Activity, 1985–88

Political Action Committee Name	PAC Donations (Incumbents)		Contracts
	87–88	**85–86**	**in 1989 (mill)**
13. Grumman PAC	232,325	231,389	2,373.1
14. Martin Marietta Corporation PAC	221,774	137,925	3,336.6
15. Tenneco Employees Good Government Fund	196,600	331,750	915.9
16. Litton Industries Inc. Employees Political Assistance Committee	196,375	178,984	1,436.6
17. Harris Corporation-Federal PAC	189,550	170,300	286.2
18. TRW Good Government Fund	181,273	164,448	1,293.6
19. Westinghouse Electric Corp. Employees Political Participation Program	165,220	134,460	1,649.6
20. LTV Aerospace and Defense Company Active Citizenship Campaign	156,900	124,250	533.2
21. Raytheon Company PAC	150,250	162,243	3,760.7
22. Motorola Employees Good Government Committee	103,675	106,879	378.3
23. Colt Industries Inc. Voluntary Political Committee	99,875	126,425	130.6[b]
24. BDM International, Inc., PAC	99,150	113,850	187.3
25. Corporate Citizenship Committee of ITT	92,900	103,500	1,163.3
26. Singer Company PAC	92,900	99,126	758.0
27. Bechtel Group, Inc. PAC	77,400	85,402	135.9

Table 4-1
(continued)

Activity, 1985–88

Political Action Committee Name	PAC Donations (Incumbents) 87–88	85–86	Contracts in 1989 (mill)
28. Ciba-Geigy Employee Good Government Fund	75,580	80,200	na
29. Gencorp Inc. PAC[c]	68,965	72,580	788.7
30. Eaton Corporation Public Policy Association	68,300	80,350	304.5
31. Bath Iron Works Corporation PAC	67,850	115,459	217.8
32. E-systems PAC (includes several)	63,361	22,458	284.2
33. McDonnell Douglas Helicopter Company PAC	62,800	53,400	775.9
34. Morton Thiokol PAC	59,750	42,400	514.0
35. Constructive Citizenship Program of Texas Instruments	59,450	55,800	946.3
36. Honeywell Employees PAC (including subsidiary PACs)	57,500	44,500	1,555.4
37. Gould Inc. Responsible Government Association	56,550	68,900	171.0[d]
38. Electronic Data Systems Employees' PAC	52,346	46,550	175.5
39. Goodyear Aerospace Corp. PAC	45,150	10,000	na
40. Air Products and Chemicals Inc. PAC	43,925	36,400	na
41. Beech Aircraft PAC	37,540	45,450	104.3
42. Kaman Corporation Good Government Fund	37,150	29,483	168.0

Table 4-1
(continued)

Activity, 1985–88

Political Action Committee Name	PAC Donations (Incumbents) 87–88	85–86	Contracts in 1989 (mill)
43. NAVISTAR International Corporation Good Government Committee	36,860	26,648	na
44. Fairchild PAC	26,600	98,975	na
45. Sundstrand Good Government Support Fund	21,845	10,688	131.7
46. Cubic Employees' PAC	20,400	37,150	na
47. LTV Corporation Active Citizenship Campaign	16,950	9,800	757.0
48. Lear Siegler Inc. PAC	$0	7,750	99.3
49. Sperry Corporation PAC	$0[e]	56,110	1,158.2
Total	$6,820,519	$6,462,537	

Source: Federal Election Commission.
[a]Includes Avco Corporation.
[b]1987 total.
[c]Includes Aerojet General Corporation.
[d]1987 total. Acquired by Nippon Mining in 1987.
[e]Merged with Burroughs to form Unisys in 1986, and contract data no longer broken out separately starting in 1989. Contract total is for Unisys Corporation.

88 (an 805 percent increase).[6] Lately the rate of increase has slowed considerably, however, with contributions up only 20 percent since 1984 and only 5.5 percent since 1986. The small increase in 1986–88 took place as the defense budget started to drop after 1985. None of the defense PACs are among the largest donors to congressional campaigns, and all are dwarfed by the biggest PACs: in 1987–88, the Realtors Political Action Committee contributed more than $3 million to federal candidates, and the ten largest PACs gave a total of $21 million.[7] However, the defense PACs have some wealthy allies in ideological PACs that support a strong national defense: the Council for National Defense and the National Security Political Action Committee (which spent more than $10 million in 1987–88).

Some summary statistics for the defense PACs are shown in tables 4–2 and 4–3. As expected, defense PACS contribute most heavily to members of the military committees, in terms of both average levels and the percentage of members who receive money. Members of the House who sit on the military committees receive from four to six times as much money as their less fortunate colleagues. The difference in the Senate is smaller, but committee members still received about 50–200 percent more money from defense PACs than nonmembers until 1988. Virtually everyone on the House committees receives money, although a high percentage of nonmembers receive some money. This pattern at least suggests that contractors target those members who have the most influence over the shape of the defense budget.

Defense PAC money also has a strong ideological streak and is concentrated among those who are generally supportive of the defense industry. Republicans do much better than Democrats at attracting contributions and receive a disproportionate share. Even though Republicans in the House are in a perpetual minority position, they still collected about half of the PAC money. In the Senate, being in the majority tends to offset the ideological bias of PAC money. The Democratic share of Senate defense PAC money nearly doubled between 1986 (when they were still in the minority) and 1988 (when they had recaptured the chamber). The Republicans, though, still received over 50 percent of the 1988 defense PAC money. As a whole, the Republican share of the ever-increasing PAC pie is actually shrinking, dropping nearly 11 percentage points between 1986 and 1988.

Table 4-2

Average Level of PAC Contribution per Election Cycle

House

	1978	1980	1982	1984	1986	1988
HASC Member	$ 3,908	$ 6,111	$12,896	$18,624	$25,211	$27,141
HADS Member	4,178	9,933	34,959	50,414	47,910	63,872
Nonmember	1,424	2,792	5,111	6,273	7,556	8,120

Senate

	1978	1980	1982	1984	1986	1988
SASC Member	$26,796	$16,443	$26,539	$54,000	$44,531	$24,620
SADS Member	4,793	22,066	23,274	35,059	46,169	24,994
Nonmember	6,118	7,012	16,123	16,587	28,396	27,440

Percentage of Members Receiving PAC Money

House

	1978	1980	1982	1984	1986	1988
HASC Member	92.1%	93.0%	84.4%	97.8%	97.8%	100.0%
HADS Member	75.0%	90.0%	90.9%	91.7%	100.0%	100.0%
Nonmember	76.7%	79.9%	88.9%	92.3%	88.6%	90.7%

Senate

	1978	1980	1982	1984	1986	1988
SASC Member	16.7%	52.9%	76.5%	78.9%	60.0%	75.0%
SADS Member	53.8%	31.3%	70.6%	82.4%	64.7%	77.8%
Nonmember	37.1%	64.7%	67.2%	73.8%	70.3%	79.0%

Table 4-3
Partisan and Ideological Distribution of Defense PAC Money (Incumbents)

	1978	1980	1982	1984	1986	1988
Total						
Total Contributions	$870,167	$1,755,146	$3,840,471	$5,666,420	$6,462,537	$6,820,519
Democrats	$414,294	$ 974,279	$1,626,937	$2,423,490	$2,643,036	$3,426,218
Republicans	$455,873	$ 780,867	$2,213,534	$3,242,930	$3,819,501	$3,394,301
Percent to Democrats	47.6%	55.5%	42.4%	42.8%	40.9%	50.2%
Percent to Republicans	52.4%	44.5%	57.6%	57.2%	59.1%	49.8%
House						
Total Contributions	$595,899	$1,188,293	$2,567,081	$3,569,432	$4,142,467	$4,756,699
Democrats	$340,428	$ 624,018	$1,139,897	$1,904,003	$2,141,360	$2,543,014
Republicans	$255,471	$ 564,275	$1,427,184	$1,665,429	$2,001,107	$2,213,685
Percent to Democrats	57.1%	52.5%	44.4%	53.3%	51.7%	53.5%
Percent to Republicans	42.9%	47.5%	55.6%	46.7%	48.3%	46.5%

Table 4-3
(continued)

	Senate					
	1978	1980	1982	1984	1986	1988
Total Contributions	$274,268	$ 566,853	$1,273,390	$2,096,988	$2,320,070	$2,063,820
Democrats	$ 73,866	$ 350,261	$ 487,040	$ 519,487	$ 501,676	$ 883,204
Republicans	$200,402	$ 216,592	$ 786,350	$1,577,501	$1,818,394	$1,180,616
Percent to Democrats	26.9%	61.8%	38.2%	24.8%	21.6%	42.8%
Percent to Republicans	73.1%	38.2%	61.8%	75.2%	78.4%	57.2%

Contributions by Defense Ideology (Percentage of Total Contributions)

	1983–84	1985–86	1987–88
Most Hawkish (NSI = 100)	34.5%	44.6%	47.2%
Most Dovish (NSI = 0)	5.9%	9.5%	9.4%
Hawkish (NSI >50)	73.3%	73.0%	66.1%
Dovish (NSI <50)	27.7%	27.0%	33.9%

More important, PAC money overwhelmingly flows toward members who favor high defense spending. The distribution of money according to how members rate on the National Security Index (NSI), a voting index prepared by the hawkish Committee on National Security (see chapter 5), is shown in table 4–3. Nearly one-half of defense PAC money flows toward members with a perfect prodefense voting record (NSI = 100), and less than one dollar in ten is contributed to the most dovish members (and nearly all of it to members of the military committees). Overall, defense PAC money is split two to one in favor of hawks.

CAMPAIGN CONTRIBUTIONS AND THE
BUDGET CYCLE

One way of analyzing the effect of PAC money is to examine whether contractors accelerate their campaign activity when their pet programs are in jeopardy. The nefarious image many people have of PACs is that they race to the Hill whenever their interests are threatened and sprinkle thousands of dollars on wavering members to procure their short-term support. Again, although the coincidence of timing is not proof of vote-buying, the lack of coincidence would make such a conclusion less compelling. The PACs do have memories, and their recollection of a member's support at a critical time would probably not fade with the passage of a few months. The additional time, though, allows other issues to become important, and it gives both sides a chance to reconsider their support.

Every year as Congress works through the budget cycle, defense contractors, at least in theory, are at risk of having their programs eliminated or cut back, especially if they are in development. First during committee hearings and markup, then on the floor of the House and Senate, and finally during the House-Senate conference, contractors face political risks. Defense PACs can be expected to increase their activity during these times with the intention of securing at a minimum access to important legislators.

Weekly PAC contribution patterns were plotted against the timing of congressional activity on the defense budget during the 1985–86 budget cycle to see if such surges in fact occur (fig. 4–1). The figure is a representation of weekly contributions by the forty-nine PACs listed in

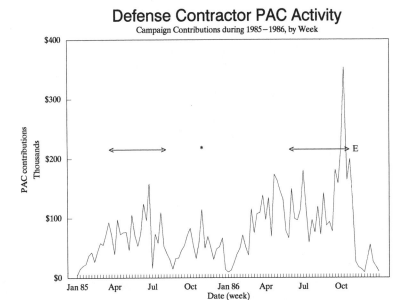

Defense Contractor PAC Activity
Campaign Contributions during 1985–1986, by Week

4-1

Timing of PAC Contributions, All Defense PACS, 1985–1986

table 4–1; each point reflects the dollar amount contributed in each week. The horizontal lines indicate the periods during which Congress considered the defense budget in each year, from the date of the first authorization committee markup to the date when both chambers voted on the final conference version of the defense budget. In 1985, the House vote on the conference report was delayed by several months and is indicated by the asterisk. The *E* designates the election of 1986.

The PACs sharply accelerate their campaign activity during the latter part of the election cycle (table 4–4). Of the $8.1 million given,[8] nearly two-thirds was given during 1986 ($5.1 million, or 63 percent), the remainder in 1985 ($3 million, or 37 percent). The average daily contribution in 1986 was $19,478, compared to only $11,624 in 1985. Over one-third of contributions were made in the last four months of the campaign ($3 million, or 37 percent). Activity virtually ceases after the election, the defense PACs giving less than $200,000 between November 5, 1986 (the day after election day), and December 31, 1986.

Table 4-4

Timing of PAC Expenditures

All Contributions (Challengers and Incumbents)

	Cycle	1985	1986
	$8,117,552[a]	$3,033,790	$5,083,762
		37.4%	62.6%

	Coincidence with Budget Cycle	
	1985	1986
Average Daily Contribution	$11,624	$19,478
Average during Budget Cycle	$16,940	$20,465
Average 10 Days before Conference	$ 9,525	$29,537
Average during Conference	$17,573	$47,287
Average 10 Days after Conference	$ 7,901	$29,625

[a]This figure is higher than the total given in table 4-1 because it includes contributions to challengers as well as corrections, amendments, and other changes made to the data prior to final release of "D" index, which was used to calculate figures in table 4-1.

Contribution patterns tend also to mirror the defense budget process in Congress; the pace picks up as Congress begins considering the defense budget and slows after the final conference vote. If we consider the season as beginning with the first markup session and ending after the vote on the conference bill, the amount of money contributed during this period will reveal the degree of acceleration. A second indicator calculates donations made while the House and Senate are in conference (which can be the most critical period in the cycle).[9]

In 1985, subcommittees of the Senate Armed Services Committee (SASC) began marking up the FY 1986 defense budget on March 27; the full committee ended markup on April 4. The HASC began its markup on April 30 and ended on May 8. Both chambers voted on versions of the bill in June: the Senate on the fifth, the House on the twenty-seventh. From there, House-Senate conferees worked out a compromise package during July 11–25. The Senate approved the agreement on July 30, but the House vote was held up by disputes over strategic programs, including the MX missile and Star Wars. After repeated delays, the House finally approved the authorization bill on October 29. Because of the time between the Senate and House conference bill votes, PAC activity between the start of the Senate markup and the Senate conference vote makes up the first indicator, with the second incorporating the two weeks before the October House vote.

The dating of the 1986 cycle was straightforward: initial markups took place on June 10; the final floor votes were August 9 for the House, August 15 for the Senate; the two chambers met in conference from September 23 to October 14; and both approved the conference version on October 15, 1986.

For both years, contributions during the budget cycles were higher than average (table 4–4). In 1985, the average daily level during the cycle was $16,940, compared to only $11,624 during the rest of the session. The much smaller jump in 1986 may reflect increases in overall activity because of the upcoming election: the daily average during the cycle was $20,465, compared to $19,478 during other days.

More striking is the jump that occurs during the conference, a phenomenon that is less likely due to some extraneous factors. During the 1985 conference session, daily contributions jumped to $17,573. This is an increase not only over the average for the year, but also over the daily levels immediately before and after the conference. Contributions averaged only $9,525 per day during the two weeks immediately before the conference session, and $7,901 in the two weeks after (note also the sharp dip in activity in July of 1985, which occurred immediately after the House voted on its version of the Authorization Act, and the peak in October, during the week when the House voted on the final conference bill). The pattern holds in 1986. The average daily level of PAC activity was $47,287 during the conference, compared to $29,537 in the two weeks before and $29,625 in the two weeks after. Obviously, during this important period defense contractors are working to protect their programs and ensure that funding is included in the final conference version of the defense budget.

It does appear, then, that defense contractors act strategically by using PAC resources when their money might be expected to do the most good. Few other PACs behave this way; most of the time their contributions are based on the electoral cycle.[10] When PACs do time their activity to coincide with the legislative cycle, it is usually seen as pernicious, an indication of an explicit vote-for-money trade. Sabato notes the example of the National Automobile Dealers Association (NADA), which was trying to fend off a Federal Trade Commission ruling requiring used car dealers to list defects in their cars. NADA contributed to sixteen members of the House soon after they became cosponsors of legislation to defeat the commission's ruling.[11]

CAMPAIGN CONTRIBUTIONS AND
PROGRAM CRISES

To see if defense PACs resort to the same behavior on a smaller scale, I will investigate two controversial episodes in the House, both of which were critically important to the contractors involved. The first is a congressional vote on a measure that prevented the army from establishing a second source for a tank engine (this incident is discussed in detail in chapter 6). The second is the vote in 1982 to replace Lockheed C-5Bs with Boeing 747s (see chapter 2). In both cases one can track the daily activity of the relevant PACs to see if they responded to the crises by increasing their contributions. One can also look at campaign contributions before and after the vote to see how supporters and opponents were treated in subsequent election cycles.

AVCO and the M-1 Tank Engine Second Source

Journalistic accounts of the congressional debate of July 1983 over whether the army should set up a second source to produce the M-1 tank turbine engine made much of the political contributions made by the existing engine builder, AVCO Corporation, at the time of the vote. AVCO, claimed the *Wall Street Journal,* had engaged in a number of scurrilous practices to ensure that Congress would protect the company's sole-source position. In the four months prior to the vote, the company's PAC had given $5,000 to HADS chairman Joseph P. Addabbo, after having given him only $500 during the 1982 cycle. It had given $10,000 to members of the HASC Subcommittee on Military Procurement during the 1982 cycle, and further, had given money to four subcommittee members the day after the vote. The *Journal* also stated that AVCO's contributions had risen in 1983–84, the PAC having given twice as much from January to June of 1983 as it had during the same months in 1981.[12] "AVCO places its money well," the article judged, "and it had no shortage of influential allies in Congress when its engine monopoly was threatened."[13]

AVCO's sole-source contract was preserved by a vote of 241–187.

Did PAC contributions determine the vote? AVCO of course denied the charge and said that its competitors (Garrett, Pratt & Whitney, and Detroit Diesel Allison), who stood to benefit from the second-sourcing provision, all had given money as well.[14] The parent companies of these firms contributed a total of $655,747 to Congress during the 1983–84 cycle, over three times as much as AVCO's $194,650.[15] Moreover, even after AVCO's sole-source position was assured, it continued to contribute heavily, giving nearly $70,000 in 1984 to the House alone. Contributions dropped markedly in 1985–86, however, falling to only $40,150, because AVCO was purchased by another defense contractor, Textron, in January 1985. After absorbing AVCO and its PAC, Textron's contributions rose to $376,050 in 1985–86, making it one of the largest contractor PACs (including both incumbent and challenger contributions).

AVCO's contributions were not sharply tilted in favor of those who supported it on the M-1 engine vote. During 1983–84, the PAC contributed $128,880 to 147 House members, all but one of whom voted on the provision. Of the 187 members voting against AVCO, 40 (21 percent) received money, the average contribution being $740. Of the 241 who supported AVCO, a higher percentage received money (106, or 44 percent), but the average contribution was only slightly higher ($904) than that given to opponents; 135 members supported the company even though they received no money. It is hard to conclude, judging from these numbers, that AVCO succeeded in buying the vote.

Yet AVCO clearly accelerated its PAC activity when its program was in trouble. The timing of the corporation's PAC expenditures for each week of 1983–84 is shown in figure 4–2; important events are identified with letters: V signifies the actual vote on the amendment, R the date of the Armed Services Committee report, E the election; the horizontal line indicates the period from the Procurement Subcommittee markup to the final vote on the conference bill, which was reported September 12. The company's PAC gave $7,800 to the House in the midst of the Procure-

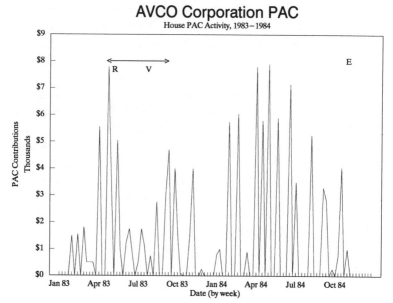

4-2

Timing of AVCO Corporation PAC Contributions, 1983–1984

ment Subcommittee deliberations, including $4,800 to members of the military committees and $1,500 to the Speaker of the House, Thomas P. ("Tip") O'Neill (D-Mass.). Contributions made by AVCO averaged $1,733 per week during the period between HASC markup and the conference vote; during the remainder of the cycle, the average was $1,114 per week.

Lockheed and C-5B

Lockheed's contribution patterns during 1981 and 1982 are shown in figure 4–3. The horizontal line in the figure indicates the time that elapsed between the Senate vote to buy 747s and the final votes on the conference report that restored full C-5B funding (the Senate approved the report on August 17, the House the following day). Lockheed contributed $184,880 in 1981–82 but faced an array of opponents ranging from Boeing (which contributed $125,000) to McDonnell Douglas

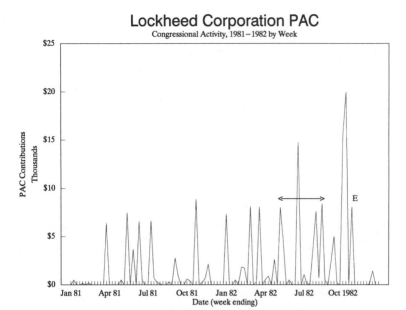

Lockheed Corporation PAC
Congressional Activity, 1981–1982 by Week

4-3

Timing of Lockheed Corporation PAC Contributions, 1981–1982

($136,675) to airlines, banks, and other firms that stood to benefit from the government's absorbing the surplus 747s. More important, the timing of Lockheed's contributions during 1982 showed only marginal response to the Senate vote (which was unforeseen). Between the Senate vote on May 13, 1982, and the final conference report which rejected the Senate's position (issued August 16), Lockheed contributed $32,830 to members of the House and Senate, with $27,830 going to House members alone. The PAC did contribute $11,330 to House members within two weeks after the House initially voted to reject the Senate provision and $8,400 within two days of the final conference report approvals.

Lockheed's contributions heavily favored those who supported it on the C-5B vote, but its PAC did not exact retribution against everybody who voted against the company. Twenty-seven of the 117 House members who voted to buy 747s (that is, those who voted against Lockheed's interest) received money from Lockheed in 1981–82. Of these, 14 received money again in 1983–84; in twelve of those cases, contribution levels *rose,* and in only one instance did they drop. Some of the increases were sharp: Vic Fazio (D-Cal.) received $500 in 1981–82, voted against the C-5B, and was punished with a $3,000 contribution in the next election cycle; Lawrence Coughlin (R-Penn.) received $200 in 1981–82, $2,000 in 83–84; Bernard Dwyer (D-N.J.), $400 in 1981–82, $2,250 in 1983–84. More surprising, though, is that in the 1983–84 cycle Lockheed contributed to 16 members that it had bypassed in 1981–82, even though they voted the *wrong way* on the 747/C-5B issue. Most of the contributions were small, but a few were noticeable: Thomas Foley (D-Wash.), Frank Wolf (R-Va.), and Donald Young (R-Alaska) each received $1,500. Norman Dicks (D-Wash.), point man for the pro-Boeing forces, did himself little long-term damage by attacking Lockheed's prize program. He received $1,600 from Lockheed in 1981–82 and a total of $4,450 in the next two election cycles (1983–86), although that did not match the $11,000 he received from Boeing during the same period.

The same held for the Senate. Of the 60 senators who voted on May 13, 1982, to buy 747s, 21 received money in 1981–82 and 15 in 1983–84. Many of those senators saw their Lockheed contributions increase by thousands. Pete Domenici (R-N.M.) and William Armstrong (R-Colo.) both went from nothing in 1981–82 to $5,000 each in 1983–84. Ted Stevens (R-Alaska) received $500 in 1981–82 but $4,500 in 1983–84. Slade Gorton, a Republican from Boeing's home state, Washington, saw his Lockheed donations rise from $500 to $3,000. The average contribution to those *opposing* Lockheed more than doubled during these years, from $1,143 to $2,543.

Senators who supported Lockheed, not surprisingly, did even better. Although the 39 members who voted with Lockheed in 1982 did not receive a disproportionately large share of the PAC's campaign dollars (only 11 received money, and their average was $1,364), they reaped the rewards the following election cycle. Twenty senators received contributions in 1983–84 averaging $3,993. William Cohen (R-Maine) went from nothing to $9,000; Thad Cochran (R-Miss.), $0 to $8,000; Roger Jepsen (R-Iowa), $500 to $7,000.

At the same time, though, Boeing's contributions exacted few penalties for defection on the Lockheed vote. Both Cochran and Cohen received $2,000 in 1983–84; Jepsen received $4,000, and J. Bennett Johnston (D-La.) $5,000. In 1983–84, Ted Stevens, who voted to buy

747s in 1982, received less from Boeing ($4,000) than he did from Lockheed ($4,500).

This muddied picture can be explained in two ways. First, PACs may not be willing to abandon incumbents on the basis of one vote—no matter how crucial—because they never know when they might need their support in the future. Second, the same company may need a member's support on several issues arising simultaneously. At the same time as the 747/C-5B controversy, Lockheed was fighting attempts to curtail C-5B production in favor of the C-17 advanced cargo aircraft and working to maintain support for the Trident submarine-launched ballistic missile program. The company was working on the F-117 Stealth fighter, a highly classified program, as well. All of the large contractors work on many projects and must build coalitions for each; it thus becomes more difficult to make connections between contributions and a single vote.

Both of these explanations run counter to the traditional money-for-votes theory of PAC activity. It may also be that defense PACs are not very smart, in that they often make decisions that appear to run counter to their self-interest. Sabato has noted that "like any decision making process, PAC candidate selection is less rational in practice than it appears on paper."[16] He goes on to quote at length an industry lobbyist describing the problems large corporations have in making these decisions: "In every major corporation you have a headquarters with a certain set of attitudes, and then facilities scattered all over the country with other attitudes. One facility's relationship with a member of Congress may be ideal, the headquarter's relationship with him may be nonexistent, and the Washington office might have mixed feelings. The more players you have the more complicated it becomes."[17] Moreover, contribution patterns that overwhelmingly favor prodefense legislators are not entirely rational, if the purpose is to ensure a majority. Why should contractors give money to members who are already likely to support key programs? Member of Congress who are prodefense will not, presumably, abandon the B-2 bomber or the MX for the lack of a $5,000 check. If PAC money truly bought votes, it would make far more sense to give to defense moderates or to members who are undecided. Yet that is not what PACs do.

The M-1 and C-5B incidents highlight some of the difficulties analysts have in sorting out the effects of PAC donations and cast doubt on the argument that money can persuade otherwise recalcitrant members to support a company's position. On any one issue, several companies, often more, are usually competing head to head, and all resort to campaign activity. Furthermore, members not infrequently have reason to support a contractor on one project, even as they oppose it on another. Especially for the major contractors, the network of programs, subcontractors, and PAC contributions is so intricate that at least some members will face conflicts irrespective of how they vote: no matter how they decide, they will help some supporters and hurt others. PAC money may provide members with some clues as to where their support lies, but it will not as a general rule guarantee their vote.

CHAPTER 4. CAMPAIGN CONTRIBUTIONS BY
DEFENSE CONTRACTORS

1. The most complete, and best, treatment is Larry J. Sabato, *PAC Power: Inside the World of Political Action Committees* (New York: W. W. Norton, 1985).

2. *Dirty Money . . . Dirty Air: A Common Cause Study of Political Action Committee Contributions to House and Senate Committees Reviewing the Clean Air Act,* May 1981.

3. See Michael Barone and Grant Ujifusa, *Almanac of American Politics 1982* (Washington, D.C.: Barone, 1981), lxv, and member profiles.

4. See W. P. Welch, "Campaign Contributions and Legislative Voting: Milk Money and Dairy Price Supports," *Western Political Quarterly* 35, no. 4 (December 1982); Henry Chappel, Jr., "Campaign Contributions and Voting on the Cargo Preference Bill: A Comparison of Simultaneous Models," *Public Choice* 36 (1981); Henry Chappel, Jr., "Campaign Contributions and Congressional Voting: A Simultaneous Probit-Tobit Model," *Review of Economics and Statistics* 64, no. 1 (February 1982); Gregory M. Saltzman, "Congressional Voting on Labor Issues: The Role of PACs," *Industrial and Labor Relations Review* 40, no. 2 (January 1987).

5. Sabato, *PAC Power,* 135.

6. Harold W. Stanley and Richard G. Niemi, *Vital Statistics on American Politics,* 2d edition (Washington DC: Congressional Quarterly Press, 1990), 167–68.

7. Ibid., 165–66.

8. This figure is higher than the total given in table 4–4 because it includes contributions to nonincumbents.

9. Data on markup sessions, committee votes, floor action, and conferences

were taken from the House and Senate versions of *Legislative Calendar, 99th Congress: Armed Services Committee,* 1985–86.

10. Sabato, *PAC Power,* 90–92.

11. Ibid., 92. Kirk Brown analyzed the congressional vote on the FTC rule and found NADA contributions to have influenced members' voting behavior. See "Campaign Contributions and Congressional Voting," paper prepared for the annual meeting of the American Political Science Association, September 1–4, 1983.

12. Brooks Jackson, "AVCO Makes Judicious Use of Gifts to U.S. Congressmen," *Wall Street Journal,* October 13, 1983, 1, 24.

13. Ibid., 1.

14. Ibid., 24.

15. Data are from the Federal Election Commission "D" index. The figures are Garrett (Allied Signal, $143,350), Pratt & Whitney (United Technologies, $285,280), and Detroit Diesel Allison (General Motors, $227,117).

16. Sabato, *PAC Power,* 80.

17. Ibid.

Defense Contracts and Voting in Congress

If you cry jobs on the floor of the House, you'll get laughed out of the joint.
—Representative Norman Lent (D-N.Y.)

How accurate is the popular wisdom that says members of the House and Senate—even committed doves—approve of defense programs because their constituents benefit? According to this view, members will abandon their opposition to a weapon system when substantial defense contracts or subcontracts are allocated to their congressional districts or states; the deciding factor is not military effectiveness, cost, or quality, but whether their constituents need jobs. There are innumerable examples of such behavior: Senator Alan Cranston's (D-Cal.) and Senator Howard Metzenbaum's (D-Ohio) fight for the B-1 bomber, described in chapter 1, is cited as evidence for this position. Liberal Senator Ted Kennedy (D-Mass.) is a vocal opponent of most large defense programs, except those that use jet aircraft engines built by General Electric, a large employer outside of Boston. Congressman Tom Downey (D-N.Y.) similarly opposes many weapons systems but has been a key player in the successful fight to keep Long Island–based Grumman Aircraft's F-14 fighter production line open, even after the navy tried to close it. Clearly, something is going on here. If local interests in fact determine congressional attitudes on weapons systems, the defense budget protects the United States from foreign threats less than it satisfies a multitude of competing local economic interests.

The dominance of this view is all the more surprising and important because it contradicts scholarly work on the question. With rare exceptions, comprehensive studies of congressional voting behavior on defense issues have concluded that local economic benefits have no bearing on members' support of either particular weapons programs or defense spending as a whole. Resolving this conflict is important. As I will show in chapter 6, contractors routinely spread subcontracts over a wide geographic area in order to maximize the number of legislators with a stake in defense programs. Contractors are political sophisticates and presumably would not invest the time and effort required to spread the wealth if doing so did nothing to gain them allies on the Hill.

Here I examine the question of parochial voting on a specific weapons system: whether to fund two nuclear aircraft carriers, each worth nearly $3.5 billion. The analysis shows that some members did indeed vote on the carrier issue in accordance with the district level spending the contracts would produce. However, the influence of local spending is small compared to that of other factors—such as whether members are hawks or doves on defense—and played no role in determining which side won. Local spending appears to have the same type of effect on congressional votes as PAC money: it buys access and in a few cases may sway members to vote against their preferences but does not govern vote decisions.

Parochial vs. Policy Voting

Accurately specifying the reasons members of Congress vote the way they do is a fundamental problem of political science. Of special interest is the degree to which members vote on the basis of localized, district level economic benefits. Legislators, the thinking goes, are likely to support policies and programs that promote the well-being of their constituents, and the intensity of their support should increase along with the local stakes. Members from agricultural states are more supportive of farm price supports than representatives of industrial areas, and the latter are more likely to favor legislation that protects manufacturing jobs. It follows, then, that members will vote for defense projects that result in contracts for local businesses, even if the project is hard to justify on its merits. As former senator Philip Hart (D-Mich.) put it, "It is not politically hard for me to vote against, say, a new aircraft carrier. But if the shipyard were in my state and five thousand people were waiting for the work, I would be examining very closely, and perhaps less critically, all those reasons why the carrier might be essential to national security."[1]

A broader version of the received wisdom is that members from defense-oriented areas will vote for programs that benefit their districts, support the defense budget as a whole, and embrace belligerent or aggressive foreign policies.[2] An aggressive foreign policy will, according to this argument, produce higher defense budgets and more public support for defense programs, which would indirectly result in more programs and economic benefits for local contractors. Continued exposure to prodefense arguments from constituents might also shape a member's voting preference. Self-interest (that is, direct pork barrel voting) might be less important than a "generalized identification of interests with the well being of the Department of Defense and its 'complex' of allies."[3]

Despite the prevalence of the popular view of pork barrel voting, careful studies of local benefits and voting have shown little connection between the two.[4] The main analytical method involves comparing district or state level defense spending to voting behavior on defense issues. The expectation is that higher spending will be reflected in more supportive voting patterns. Only a few researchers have been able to show any link at all, and the positive relationships are tenuous. Bruce Russett, for example, found a tiny correlation ($r = 0.14$) between the location of defense bases and prodefense voting in the Senate. But the connection nearly vanished once he controlled for region: southern senators were, in general, more hawkish than their colleagues, and they also benefited disproportionately from defense bases.[5] Most of the studies conclude that parochial interests do not explain congressional votes on defense issues. Researchers explain that legislators vote in accordance with their ideological predispositions rather than with district economic interests. Prodefense hawks will support most defense programs irrespective of their local economic consequences, and doves will oppose them.

Yet there are enough examples of district-interest behavior that one cannot accept these research findings as conclusive. Constituents expect their representatives to promote and protect their districts' economic interests, and members can hardly be considered rash if they vote to keep local defense contractors (or any other firms in their districts) in business. It may be very difficult to separate the effects of economic interests from other factors that enter into a particular vote decision, and this may account for the disappointing research findings on this question.

In chapter 2 I noted some of the difficulties involved in this type of research, notably the problems entailed in measuring the location of defense subcontracts. Determining the link between spending and voting is hard if this key independent variable is unknown.

On the other side of the vote/spending equation, measuring a legislator's preference for defense spending is often just as hard. Normally, roll call votes in favor of the annual defense authorization act are used to identify a prodefense preference, but they actually reveal little of interest. Because most members consistently vote for most types of defense spending, voting patterns are fairly stable. Between 1980 and 1987, both the House and Senate approved the annual defense authorization bills by huge margins: the average vote was 303–95 in the House and 86–7 in the Senate. Furthermore, the standard interpretation that a vote for the defense bill reflects a preference for defense spending is often wrong. During the last years of the Reagan administration, most nay votes on final defense authorizations were cast by Republicans who thought the budget was *too low*. In 1986, the authorization bill passed 255–152. Yet 143 Republicans opposed the measure because they wanted a larger budget without restrictive SDI provisions. The same thing occurred in 1988, when only 41 of 168 Republicans voted for the FY 1989 defense budget, dissenters again citing SDI and other arms control provisions as their reason for opposing it.[6] President Reagan, hardly one to support lower defense spending, vetoed the 1989 defense budget for the same reason, although critics claimed that he simply wanted to make the Democrats, most of whom voted for passage, look weak on defense in an election year.[7]

One might be tempted to simply reverse the conventional interpretation in these cases and conclude that opposition to the bill constituted a hawkish vote, but this too is unsatisfactory. Many strong prodefense Democrats voted for the measure, which thus put hawks on both sides of the issue. Support for the budget came from an unlikely alignment of prodefense Democratic conservatives and their more liberal colleagues. The latter voted for the budget—even though they felt it was far too high—precisely because of the provisions that offended Republicans.

One way of surmounting this measurement problem is to construct proxy measures of defense voting, inferring legislators' true preferences from roll call votes on a range of specific defense policies. Although these votes do provide some clues as to how members feel about the defense budget, they are often totally divorced from any type of local district benefits. One such index included, in addition to votes on the defense authorizations and appropriations bills, votes on cotton quotas, appropriations for the Peace Corps, and support for a conference of the Organization of American States.[8] Another included votes on Senate confirmation of Richard Burt to the State Department and of Kenneth Adelman to the Arms Control and Disarmament Agency.[9] Why congressional voting on these issues should be related to local defense spending is, to be sure, less than clear.

If one expects members to consider defense questions on the basis of how much local spending is involved, then the members must believe that voters will be able to form an opinion on whether the districts' interests are adequately represented. This means constituents must pay attention to their elected representatives' votes and listen to potential challengers who may be able to exploit them. Constituents must also be able to connect the votes to their own economic self-interest or believe a challenger who draws the link for them. This is surely a difficult task on most of these votes, given that a substantial portion of the public cannot recall even their representatives' names, much less their voting records.

The best way to test the pork barrel hypothesis would be to examine votes on a specific weapon system—preferably one that is large and expensive—to see if members' votes depend on the local economic benefits produced by that weapon. Only a few scholars have attempted to do this, and the results are generally in line with the policy-voting perspective. Robert Bernstein and William Anthony determined that ideology (along the hawk-dove continuum) was the dominant factor in the widely publicized Senate vote in 1970 on the Anti-Ballistic Missile system. James Lindsay examined Senate voting on the ABM system, MX missile, B-1 bomber, and SDI and concluded that local spending and constituent pressure played an insignificant role in shaping the outcomes. Richard Fleisher determined that voting for the B-1 did depend on local spending but only to a very small extent.

All three of these studies looked at voting in the Senate, where the impact of a given level of defense spending is smaller than at the congressional district level. Congressional districts (except in those states which encompass only one at-large district) are much smaller and less populous than states and will therefore be more affected by a given amount of defense spending. In general terms, "House members, who lack statewide constituencies, represent fewer interests and any given interest is likely to loom more imposingly in a House member's calculations than a single interest in a large complex state. House members may be said to reflect more directly the interests of their constituencies, and they provide an important link between citizens and their government that senators cannot provide."[10] Representatives also tend to focus more attention on their districts and are generally less concerned with national issues than senators. Congressional districts are usually more homogeneous than states and less frequently involve trading off the interests of different groups. We would thus expect the economic and political forces that may compel a member of the House to vote to protect district interests to be diluted at the state level.[11]

Another reason to discount these findings for the Senate is that they involved highly controversial strategic issues that are probably less likely to elicit strong pork barrel responses than, for example, conventional (non-nuclear) weapons programs. Members might be unwilling to sweep aside serious substantive objections to the MX missile, SDI funding, or any strategic nuclear system in order to secure work for their district. They would be more likely to do so for less contentious systems, such as tactical aircraft, ships, or conventional weapons. The best way to find evidence of district-interest voting on defense would be to examine voting and spending in the House, using accurate spending data at the congressional district level for weapons not closely tied to strategic nuclear issues.

Voting and Spending on Nuclear Aircraft Carriers

Because of a unique confluence of congressional voting actions and availability of data, it is now possible to solve many of the measurement problems that plagued past work and subject the pork barrel hypothesis to a rigorous test. On May 7, 1987, the House of Representatives considered two amendments to the FY 1988 Defense Authorization Act, one introduced by Lynn Martin (R-Ill.), the other by Dave McCurdy (D-Okla.). The McCurdy amendment sought to delete funding for one of the two new Nimitz-class nuclear aircraft carriers (designated CVN 74 and CVN 75 by the navy) that the Reagan administration requested in the 1988 budget; Martin's amendment, which sought to transfer some of the carrier money to operations and maintenance accounts, would have killed both carriers.[12] The amendments lost by wide margins, Martin's by 124–294, McCurdy's by 145–267.

The debate over the amendments revolved around both substantive issues and the effect the contracts would have on local economies. Martin claimed not only that the navy had violated an agreement with Congress not to seek money for any carriers until FY 1992, but also that funding of the carriers would soak up funds needed for other programs. She also stated that Secretary of the Navy John F. Lehman had testified before HASC in 1986 that no new carrier construction would be needed until the early 1990s, when the navy would make its initial requests for the new carriers needed to replace the *Midway* and the *Forrestal,* World War II vintage carriers.

The navy responded that it had decided to ask for early funding only after it learned that by accelerating construction it would save nearly $1 billion. Newport News Shipbuilding, the prime contractor, was then in a position to begin building the new ships as soon as it finished two nuclear carriers currently under construction. Without the early money, the company would have to shut down operations for several years while it waited for the new construction to start. With back to back funding, the production line would remain "warm," and workers would retain their jobs skills instead of having to relearn them after not working for four or five years. An important side benefit was that the work force would enjoy continuous employment, with no layoffs during the time between the completion of the current ships and the start of work on the new ones.

The economic value of the aircraft carriers could be expected to be important to Congress for several reasons. First, the contracts were huge and vitally important to the domestic shipbuilding industry, which in 1987 was in the midst of a serious and prolonged downturn. Even in an era of increasing navy budgets, shipbuilders were reeling from the Reagan administration's decision to end construction subsidies in 1981, an act that rendered U.S. firms unable to compete with foreign companies for commercial orders.[13] Between 1982 and 1986, the number of shipyards in the United States dropped from 110 to 74, and employment in the industry was down 25 percent in the same period.[14] The collapse of the commercial market left the remaining companies almost entirely dependent on navy contracts: only 11 percent of U.S. shipbuilding capacity was engaged in private work in 1987, compared to 44 percent in 1978.[15] Unlike businesses in some other industries, shipbuilding firms and suppliers had nowhere else to go for work. The aircraft carriers would account for a significant portion of the industry's business and would produce thousands of much-needed jobs. According to the navy's estimates, each $1 billion in shipbuilding contracts produced 27,000 direct and 15,000 indirect jobs.[16] The subcontracts alone would therefore produce approximately 133,000 jobs over the life of the construction effort.

Second, both supporters and opponents of the aircraft carriers were acutely aware of how the economic benefits were distributed. As part of the intensive lobbying campaign that preceded the vote on May 7, the navy and Newport News Shipbuilding, through its parent company, Tenneco, prepared and distributed a report detailing the dollar amount of subcontract work that would be performed in each congressional district if carrier funding were approved. Although the report provided information only on supplied products (subcontracts), it noted that the total of $3.16 billion in subcontracts represented approximately 45 percent of the total value of the system. The other 55 percent ($3.86 billion) would pay for prime contract work performed by Newport News Shipbuilding.[17] According to the report, 310 congressional districts in 44 states benefited, with dollar amounts ranging from $1,000 to $372 million. The navy calculated district level spending by means of a model derived from the distribution of work on the previous two carriers Newport News Shipbuilding had built.

For some contiguous districts in urban areas (such as Los Angeles, Philadelphia, and Chicago), the navy could not pinpoint the location of subcontract work; in these cases the navy allocated the total amount of spending to each of several districts. Despite these minor measurement problems, one can treat the data as representing the true value of the work done in each district because the navy reported it as such to Congress.

Much of the floor debate on the carrier amendments did focus on parochial and economic arguments. Congressman Herbert Bateman (R-Va.), who represents the Norfolk district where Newport News Shipbuilding is located, argued that a delay in funding would hurt many segments of the industrial base: "It is not just shipbuilding jobs for my district. It is a question of jobs in the domestic steel, coal, and electronics industries and other jobs that would be lost."[18] Congressman Robert J. Lagomarsino (R-Cal.) stated that the economic benefits extended far beyond the shipbuilding industry: "While the carriers are built in Newport News, it is important to remember that everyone benefits. Obviously, the national defense benefits. So does the depressed American shipbuilding industry. The new ships require massive amounts of American steel, American coal, American electronics, and American aircraft and fittings. Today, 44 states share in the industrial effort supporting the carrier program."[19] Congresswoman Martin, who had little patience with the pork barrel arguments, expressed displeasure with the navy's tendency to stress them:

> One of the least delightful things about this debate has been part of the level on which I believe the Navy has been acting. I do not fault the Virginia delegation for trying to protect for its state some of the most incredible jobs, and, frankly, pork of the century. Were it my district, I would do the same. But our obligation is a different one. It is to make sure that this Nation is ready, and that the Nation's security will not be impaired even to the benefit of one, two, or three states. Some members, if they are back in their office, may have received a copy of what their districts will get.[20]

At the conclusion of the House debate, Congresswoman Martin asked her colleagues to consider the budgetary and military implications of the carriers rather than the parochial issues. Holding the subcontract report—which she termed a "goody list"—aloft, she said, "I respect the people with whom I serve more than that. I don't think ultimately that [district benefit] is the way most of them are going to make a decision on this."[21]

If pork barrel voting is to be found anywhere, it is here. The economic benefits were huge and critical to the welfare of an entire industry. The weapon system itself was noncontroversial in that carrier opponents argued not that the ships were unacceptable on strategic or moral grounds, but that they were unaffordable. Members hinted at the consequences opponents would face in their districts by turning their back on much-needed jobs.

Even after the question was settled and the contracts awarded, the jobs issue continued to arise. During the Virginia gubernatorial Republican primary of 1988, both contestants scored Democrats, including presidential candidate Michael Dukakis, for failing to support the aircraft carriers. Former senator Paul S. Trible asked, "How can Dukakis justify eliminating two carriers that are essential to our security and provide 7,000 jobs for Virginia?"[22] The local newspaper chided both Trible and his opponent, Virginia Attorney General J. Marshall Coleman (who had made similar statements), for arguing in economic, rather than military, terms. "Someone," the *Norfolk Virginian-Pilot* announced in an editorial, "should explain to Mr. Trible and Mr. Coleman the difference between military procurement and welfare."[23]

Testing for a Relationship between Jobs and Votes

Any model of how members voted on the carrier amendment must take into account factors that the researcher believes went into each decision. The initial hypothesis is that members voted on the basis of a combination of policy, parochial, and personal factors. A functional representation of such a model looks like this:

$$\text{Vote}_i = f(\text{spending}_i, \text{ideology}_i, \text{personal}_i, \text{other}_i)$$

That is, we postulate that the vote of the ith member of the House is a function of the local spending in that member's district, his or her attitudes on defense issues, personal and idiosyncratic factors, and additional factors that are excluded from the analysis. What remains is to devise a way of measuring each of these factors.

Spending, the easiest variable to specify, is represented simply by the amount of carrier work done in each district, as calculated by the navy report. The other factors pose more challenging specification problems. A member's attitude on defense spending represents his or her predisposition to support or oppose weapons systems in general; it fixes a member's a priori opinion on the carrier question and represents the policy aspects of the vote decision. Other things being equal, members who tend to support most weapons (hawks) will presumably be likely to support the aircraft carriers, and those who oppose most weapons (doves) to oppose them. Because attitudes on defense in general, and the carriers in particular, are unlikely to be simply one-dimensional, measuring them accurately requires a mix of different indicators, not just one. The present model uses four such indicators: score on the National Security Index (NSI) (a measure of past defense voting), political party, membership in the Military Reform Caucus, and whether a member's district contains a major naval installation.

The first indicator, NSI, is a member's score on a congressional voting index prepared by the American Security Council, a prodefense, nonprofit organization. At the end of each Congress, the council's NSI scores each member on ten congressional votes in the previous two sessions that the council considered important to maintaining a "peace through strength" military posture. Members receive scores of 0–100, with 100 being a perfect prodefense orientation (correct votes on all ten issues, based on the council's opinion) and 0 representing the most dovish position (incorrect votes on all ten issues).[24] Since I want to identify members' attitudes prior to the carrier vote, the 1985–86 NSI index is used for those members in both the Ninety-ninth (1985–86) and One-hundredth (1987–88) congresses. For freshman members elected in November 1986, the model incorporates scores from 1987–88.

The second indicator of defense attitudes is a member's party affiliation, either Democrat or Republican. In general, Republicans are more hawkish than Democrats. In the mid-1980s, Democrats had come to oppose many elements of the Reagan defense buildup, and we can expect that they would be less supportive of large, expensive weapons such as aircraft carriers.

The third indicator is membership in the Military Reform Caucus, which has been active in military reform and favors smaller, cheaper, and less complex weapons systems. The caucus has explicitly challenged the navy's preference for large aircraft carriers.[25] Other things being equal, even hawkish caucus members should be more likely to support the Martin amendment to stop carrier funds than nonmembers.

The final indicator of a member's defense attitude is whether he or she represents a district with a major navy installation. Large facilities employ thousands of workers, both civilian and military. Navy personnel presumably support navy programs and expect their representatives to do the same. Naval bases might even be indicative of a more parochial interest in the aircraft carriers, particularly those facilities that will become home port for the new ships. Members from naval districts should reflect these concerns.[26]

Personal factors that affect the vote decision are those which represent elements of a member's personal experience that may be relevant to the carrier issue. This is, admittedly, only crudely approximated by whether a member is a retired naval officer. Navy experience should have imbued the member with a sense of the importance of the navy's mission to national defense; it provides a filter through which members view defense issues.[27]

A second personal factor is the level of campaign contributions to members by the PAC of Newport News Shipbuilding's parent company, Tenneco. Although in the previous chapter I cast doubt on the hypothesis that PAC donations buy votes, I include them in the analysis because the vote model provides the best way of determining how much of an independent influence PAC expenditures had on this issue. According to Federal Election Committee data, the Tenneco Inc. Employees Good Government Fund gave $199,000 to House members during the 1985–86 election cycle and in 1987 before the May 7 votes on the two amendments (FEC campaign finance data do not list separately the activity of company subsidiaries).

Obviously, even a comprehensive model of voting cannot take every possible independent variable or causal factor into account. Members may vote on the basis of cues and follow the lead of certain prominent

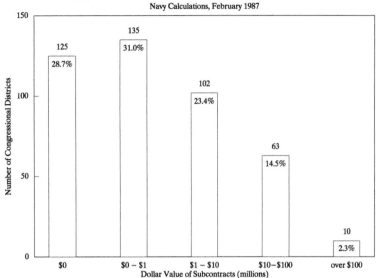

5-1

Distribution of Aircraft Carrier Subcontracts, by Size

members of the House or particular delegations. Logrolling may come into play as well, with members voting against their personal preferences because they are promised a future reward (or reminded of a past debt) by party leaders, committee chairs, or rank-and-file members trying to build coalitions for their own pet issues. Since most of these deals will be private, they cannot be introduced as an additional control; they must be lumped together and considered part of the unexplained portion of the vote decision.

The size and distribution of the carrier subcontracts are shown in figure 5–1. Three hundred ten congressional districts in forty-four states received some piece of the carrier work; the median district subcontract value was $1.2 million, the mean $10.2 million. Ten districts had more than $100 million in subcontracts, and seventy-three districts $10 million or more.

Some of the simple bivariate relationships between the independent variables and the votes on the Martin amendment are shown in tables 5–1a through 5–1e. According to these tables, the strongest determinant is

Table 5-1

Cross-tabulations of Martin Amendment Vote with Independent Variables[a]

(a) Vote by political party membership

	Democrat	**Republican**
Keep Carriers	157	139
	(63%)	(80%)
Delete Carriers	91	35
	(37%)	(20%)

Chi^2 (2 df) = 13.4

(b) Vote by NSI Score

	NSI = 0 (most dovish)	**NSI = 100 (most hawkish)**
Keep Carriers	36	128
	(35%)	(89%)
Delete Carriers	66	16
	(65%)	(11%)

Chi^2 (2 df) = 77.2

(c) Vote by membership in the Military Reform Caucus

	MRC Member	**Nonmember**
Keep Carriers	65	231
	(63%)	(72%)
Delete Carriers	38	88
	(37%)	(28%)

Chi^2 (2 df) = 3.2

(d) Vote by Navy Career

	Navy Career	**No Navy Career**
Keep Carriers	33	263
	(80%)	(69%)
Delete Carriers	8	118
	(20%)	(31%)

Chi^2 (2 df) = 2.3

Table 5-1

(continued)

(e) Vote by existence of naval facilities in district

	Naval Facility in District	**No Naval Facility in District**
Keep Carriers	31	265
	(84%)	(69%)
Delete Carriers	6	120
	(16%)	(31%)
Chi^2 (2 df) = 2.3		

[a]Includes members paired for and against.

a member's position on the hawk-dove continuum as reflected in the NSI score. Only 11 percent of the most hawkish members of the House voted to delete the carriers, compared to nearly two-thirds of the most dovish members. Strong relationships also exist between the vote and political party; the connection between the vote and the other variables is all in the expected direction, but it is possible that the patterns shown are simply a coincidence. At least we can be confident that the model encompasses some of the important variables of interest.

At the bivariate level, the connection between voting and spending is less clear. Although nearly all of the members whose districts received more than $100 million in subcontracts voted to keep the carriers (9 out of 10), that result could be due to the fact that, independent of spending, those members were much more conservative on defense issues than the rest of the House. Representatives from the $100 million and up districts had an average NSI score of 75, while their 425 colleagues had an average score of just over 53. So, we would expect that these 10 members would probably have voted to keep the carriers even if their districts were to receive no subcontracts. It can hardly be said, based on this correlation alone, that spending determined their vote.

At lower levels of spending, the relationships weaken further. The voting behavior of members from three different types of districts is shown in table 5–2: those with at least $1,000 in subcontracts (the minimum nonzero value), those with more than $1 million, and those with more than $10 million. In each case, these groups are compared to

Table 5-2

Bivariate Relationship between Spending and Votes

District Subcontract Value

	$0	Above $1,000	Above $1 million	Above $10 million
Keep Carriers	88	208	118	50
	(73%)	(69%)	(70%)	(73%)
Delete Carriers	33	93	51	19
	(27%)	(31%)	(30%)	(27%)
Average NSI score	60	51.4	51.1	47.5

the set of legislators representing districts with no subcontracts. Also given is the average NSI score for each category, in order that we may distinguish between changes due to spending and changes due to different attitudes on defense issues. The patterns show that the percentage vote to keep the carriers stays relatively constant as the amount of spending goes up; this would appear to challenge the notion that members are voting on the basis of parochial interests. At the same time, though, the hawkishness of each group declines slightly, which could cancel out the effects of spending increases. Clearly more is going on here than can be accounted for by any simple calculation; one must turn to more sophisticated techniques to isolate the causative influence of spending, while holding the effects of the other variables constant.

The Probit Model

The formal statement of the voting model is as follows:

$$Vote = b_0 + b_1 Spending + b_2 NSI + b_3 MRC + b_4 Navydist + b_5 Retnavy + b_6 Party + b_7 PAC + e$$

The variables are

Vote   = 1   if member voted against the Martin amendment to delete funding for CVN 74 and CVN 75 in the FY 1988 defense budget. This indicates support for the carriers

       = 0   if member voted for the Martin amendment

Spending   =   the square root of the dollar value of carrier subcontracts
                 awarded in member's congressional district

NSI   =   member's National Security Index score, 100th Congress
                 for members first elected in 1986, 99th Congress for
                 others

MRC   = 1 if member belonged to the Military Reform Caucus
                 during the 100th Congress
            = 0 otherwise

Navydist   = 1 if member's district contained a major navy installation
                 or facility
            = 0 otherwise

Retnavy   = 1 if member is a retired naval officer
            = 0 otherwise

Party   = 1 if member is a Republican
            = 0 if member is a Democrat

PAC   = 2 if member received more than $2,500 in campaign
                 contributions from the Tenneco Inc. Employees Good
                 Government Fund between January 1, 1986, and May 7,
                 1987
            = 1 if member received between $1 and $2,499
            = 0 if member received no campaign contributions

The vector composed of the b's is the set of parameters that we want to estimate. The model will be run for the entire House as well as for important subgroups, such as Democrats and Republicans, and regional blocs. Since members of these different groups will tend to vote together, controlling for these differences allows us to better determine if the model accurately predicts voting behavior, and if so, whether different types of members will respond differently to district level economic stakes.[28]

The model incorporates the square root of local spending for two reasons. First, district spending varies over a wide range (between $0 and $372,000, since spending is measured in thousands of dollars). This introduces the risk that the effect of spending will be seriously overestimated; the high-spending districts, because they are so far from the average, may have a disproportionate influence on the results. Second, the marginal effect of one dollar in spending will probably drop as the overall spending level increases. A change from $0 to $25 million in local spending will likely have more impact on a member's decision to support the carriers than an equivalent $25 million increase from $200 million to $225 million. Both of these problems are solved by taking the square root of spending: the transformed variable takes values between 0 and 610 and incorporates the diminishing returns from higher spending. A square root transformation is more appropriate than other candidates, such as logarithmic transforms. The square root curve rises more gently and flattens out much later than the logarithmic function and is also easier to interpret.

Accounting for these diminishing returns is important even in the context of the probit model, which already assumes that the effect of any one independent variable shrinks as the cumulative probability density moves closer to either 0 or 1. This provides some check on diminishing returns, yet the degree of control depends on the value of the density function itself. The square root transformation introduces an additional check that is independent of the shape of the density function. Furthermore, if one is to properly specify the model, the shapes of the underlying relationships between dependent and independent variables should be identified. If spending affects voting in a nonlinear fashion, then the variables should reflect it.

Probit techniques are the appropriate method for estimating parameters when the dependent variable (here, Vote) takes on only two values (here, the values are 0 and 1). The technical details are important, but it is possible to understand the model even if one is not familiar with the technique. Put simply, this probit model estimates the effect of the different independent variables on the probability (between 0 and 1) that a member supported or opposed the aircraft carriers. Readers who are unfamiliar with probability density functions and interpretation of probit coefficients can skip the tables showing the parameter estimates and rely on the figures, in which the relationship between voting and the various independent variables is shown more clearly.

The coefficient estimates for voting on the Martin amendment are shown in tables 5–3 and 5–4. Equation (1) shows the result for the entire House. Although the overall size of the effect of each variable cannot be directly deduced from the table, it is possible to assess the statistical

Table 5-3

Probit Results on Martin Amendment

Equation	(1)	(2)	(3)
Variable	**Entire House**	**Republicans**	**Democrats**
Constant	−.066	−.98	−.046
Subcontract spending	.00085	.0071*	−.00038
	(1.11)	(2.37)	(0.43)
Member of Military	−.19	−.53*	.11
Reform Caucus	(1.11)	(2.37)	(0.43)
National Security Index	.015***	.019**	.013***
	(5.62)	(3.37)	(4.22)
Political party	−.56*		
	(2.43)		
Navy base in district	.42		.14
	(1.48)		(0.43)
Retired naval officer	.0095	−.26	.65
	(0.39)	(0.78)	(1.55)
Campaign	.17	.12	.28
contributions	(1.06)	(0.62)	(0.69)
N	422	175	247
% correctly predicted	76.5	82.3	74.9
% null	70.1	79.4	63.6
−2(log likelihood)	224.5	73.6	143.9

t-ratios in parentheses

*p < 0.05

**p < 0.01

***p < 0.001

significance of the coefficients—the precision of the estimate and the corresponding relative certainty that it is not in fact zero—through normal t-statistics. From this, we can be most certain that ideology, as measured by the NSI, is an important determinant of votes on the Martin amendment. While few of the other variables show evidence of signifi-

Table 5-4

Probit Results on Martin Amendment (High-Spending Districts [over $100 million] Removed)

Equation	(4)	(5)	(6)
Variable	**Entire House**	**Republicans**	**Democrats**
Constant	−.078	−.98	−.057
Subcontract spending	.00062	.0071*	−.00098
	(0.630)	(2.37)	(0.86)
Member of Military Reform Caucus	−.13	−.53*	.20
	(0.82)	(2.12)	(0.96)
National Security Index	.016***	.019**	.015***
	(5.72)	(3.36)	(4.31)
Political party	−.64**		
	(2.69)		
Navy base in district	.40		.12
	(1.42)		(0.37)
Retired naval officer	.073	−.26	.61
	(0.29)	(0.78)	(1.43)
Campaign contributions	.15	.12	.23
	(0.94)	(0.66)	(0.56)
N	412	170	242
% correctly predicted	76.5	81.8	74.0
% null	69.7	78.8	63.2
−2(log likelihood)	220.6	73.6	139.9

t-ratios in parentheses

*p < 0.05

**p < 0.01

***p < 0.001

cant effect, all but one (Party, which will be discussed shortly) are at least in the expected direction.

Spending, it appears, has almost no effect on members' voting behavior. The coefficient is minuscule and fails to meet even lenient standards of statistical significance. Even if we could assume that the coefficient was significant, the small size counsels against concluding that local spending matters. In figure 5–2 can be seen the effect of district subcontracts on the probability that a hypothetical House member voted to keep the carriers (probit models require that all variables except the one of interest be set in advance, since the effect of any one variable will change when the other variables change). The value on the vertical axis indicates the predicted probability that a member will vote to preserve funding for the aircraft carriers, with levels of 0.5 or above indicating a preference to keep it. This does not mean that everyone with probability above 0.5 will support the carriers, but rather that they are more likely to do so than not.

Since a member can choose only one of two positions—voting for or against the amendment—the probabilities of that member choosing one or the other can best be visualized in terms of an experiment with a certain probability of success. For members with 0.5 probability of voting to support the carriers, on average, half of them will vote to support and half to oppose. In this case, it is as if each member flipped a fair coin and voted Yes if the coin came up heads, No if tails. Since on average half the flips will be heads and the other half tails, the most likely outcome is that half the members vote yes, half no. Similarly, for members with 0.90 probability of support, it is as if they used the same process but used a weighted coin that came up heads 90 percent of the time. For each probability level, our best guess is that the fraction of all members with that level will vote to support the carrier. The actual number of members voting to support will have a binomial distribution centered on $p \times x$ (the number of members in the sample with probability p).

The hypothetical member in figure 5–2 is a Democrat from a non-navy district, a member of the Military Reform Caucus, and a person who has no navy experience and has received no campaign contributions from Tenneco.[29] The three separate curves allow us to see how variance in a second characteristic—defense ideology—will affect voting; NSI takes three values, 100 (most hawkish), 0 (most dovish), and 53.6 (the average value for the entire House). For doves, $100 million in local stakes—a colossal value representing about 2,500 jobs—increases the probability that a member will vote for the carriers from only about 0.43

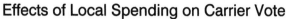

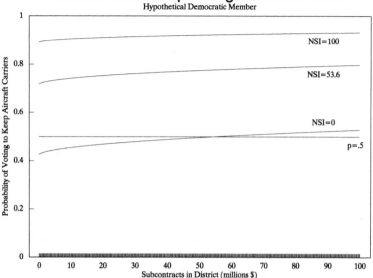

5-2

Effects of Local Spending on Carrier Vote

to 0.53. One billion dollars in district spending increases the probability only to 0.59. For hawks, who are more likely to support the carriers irrespective of local stakes, the effect of $100 million is smaller still, raising the probability of a procarrier vote from 0.89 to about 0.93. Most significant, almost no votes are changed from opposition to support by district spending. Only doves from districts with less than approximately $55 million in subcontracting are presumed to vote against the carriers (that is, below the 0.5 threshold). If one assumes that the prime contractor could sway votes by strategically allocating subcontracts, he could afford to buy only an insignificant number; by the navy's count, only thirty-two districts actually had more than $55 million in subcontracts, including the multiple counts resulting from the navy's inability to break out single values for some districts. The cost of acquiring each additional supporter is extremely high.

There would be little point in trying to buy votes, moreover, since a winning coalition already existed among those members inclined to support the carriers regardless of their local stakes. In a House vote 218 votes are needed to guarantee a victory. Regardless of how subcontracts were distributed, the navy and Tenneco could be reasonably confident of at least 40 percent support, the probability that those most opposed to the aircraft carriers—doves with no local spending—would vote to retain funding. This simple method alone predicts 185 votes, 32 votes shy of a majority. But that figure is understated, since the House's mean NSI score is 53.6, and the median score is 60. Both the navy and prime contractor Tenneco could be confident of a safe majority to retain the warships irrespective of how the economic benefits were distributed. Judging from the House vote as a whole, strategically distributed spending would have made little difference and would have been unnecessary even if it could have attracted votes. The wide distribution of subcontracts to two-thirds of the congressional districts may have been a way of cementing support rather than an attempt to buy it.

How, then, did members make up their minds? Ideology, as measured by the NSI, exerts the strongest effect. The single best predictor of how a member voted on this issue is his or her expressed preference on defense issues in general. Through the use of separate equations for Democrats and Republicans (equations 2 and 3 in table 5–3), one can show how support depends on NSI score (figure 5–3). For both parties, as expected, doves are far less likely (between 40 and 50 percent) to have voted for the carriers than hawks. A surprising feature of the graph is that dovish Republicans are, it seems, less likely to support the carriers than dovish Democrats for all values of NSI below 28. How can this be, if Republicans are more conservative on defense issues than Democrats? This is partly the result of the fact that very few Republicans have low NSI scores; in the One-hundredth Congress, only 9 out of 175 Republicans had a score of 50 or below, and only 2 scored 0. Moreover, though the sample size is small, these dovish Republicans did oppose the carriers, voting 5–4 (56 percent) in favor of the Martin amendment, as opposed to their dovish Democratic colleagues with similar scores, who rejected it 79–90 (47 percent). This pattern reverses at the hawk end of the NSI scale. Among members who scored 100, Democrats voted down the amendment 17–5 (77 percent), Republicans by 111–11 (91 percent). So, although the tiny Republican sample prevents generalizing, the surprising result does reflect the actual data.

Tenneco PAC contributions had no effect on the vote. In every case

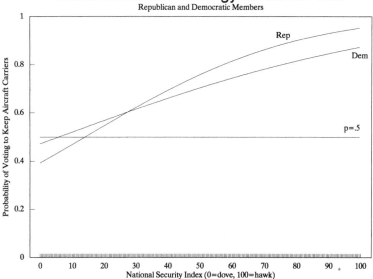

Effect of Defense Ideology on Carrier Vote

Republican and Democratic Members

5-3

Effect of Defense Ideology on Carrier Vote

that was estimated, the coefficient was small and indistinguishable from zero. Although Tenneco's contributions were large and extensive, they did not influence a single vote. Tenneco's campaign money flowed overwhelmingly to those members who were already inclined to support large defense programs such as aircraft carriers as well as to members of the defense committees. Although member support does appear to rise along with contributions, the effect is entirely due to prior defense attitudes. Once these are taken into account, the independent influence of PAC money vanishes. Once again, the mere fact that money and votes tended to go together proves nothing about which came first.

One quick way of dispelling the notion that Tenneco used PAC money to effectively buy votes is to examine table 5–5, which shows the distribution of votes and PAC money for Republican hawks (those with NSI scores of 100). Legislators who received over $2,500 from Tenneco are, curiously, less likely to support the ships than both those who received moderate contributions—between $0 and $2,499—and those

Table 5-5

Effects of PAC Contributions

Republicans with NSI = 100

		Voted to Keep Carriers	Voted to Delete Carriers	Total
PAC Contribution	$0	50 (86%)	8 (14%)	58
	$0–2,499	47 (98%)	1 (2%)	48
	$2,500 +	14 (82%)	3 (18%)	17
	Total	111 (90%)	12 (10%)	123

who received nothing. Obviously, PAC money alone could not guarantee that a member would vote the way Tenneco wished.

The separate equations for Democrats and Republicans show that Republican votes are affected by district level economic interests, a relationship missed by the model for the entire House. The coefficient for spending in equation 2 in table 5–3 is relatively large, an order of magnitude greater than the coefficient in the Democratic model (equation 3), and it is statistically significant—the chances of producing this estimate if there is in fact no such relationship (i.e., that the true coefficient value is 0) is 1 in 50. Apparently Republicans and Democrats responded differently to district economic stakes.

The effect local spending has on the vote decision of two hypothetical Republican members, one a member of the Military Reform Caucus, the other a nonmember, is shown in figures 5–4 and 5–5. The steep slope of the different curves shows that the vote decision changes dramatically as the amount of district subcontracting rises. For dovish Republican non-MRC members (those whose NSI = 0), the probability of supporting rises from 0.18 for those with no local spending to nearly 0.9 for those with $100 million in subcontracts (figure 5–5). More moderate spending can change the vote as well; $20 million raises the probability of supporting the carriers to the threshold level of 0.5.

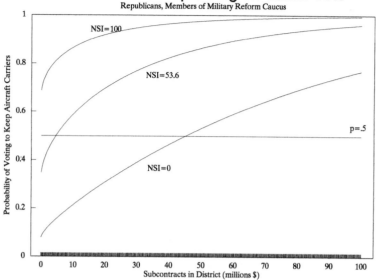

5-4

Effects of Local Spending on Carrier Vote, Republican Members of Military
Reform Caucus

The influence of spending decreases as hawkishness rises, although
the effect remains substantial. For Republican MRC members with NSI
of 100 (fig. 5–4, top), $50 million in subcontracts raises the probability
of support from 0.68 to nearly 0.97. A more surprising result is that
moderate and dovish Republicans—those whose NSI is 53 or less—are
predicted to oppose funding (probability of support = 0.38) if their
districts do little or no work, although it took less than $5 million to push
them over the 0.5 threshold. Spending has the greatest effects for the
most dovish Republicans and transformed strong opposition into strong
support. Tenneco could have, if it had wished, had some influence on all
but the most hawkish Republicans by judiciously distributing subcontract work. Because so few Republicans are doves, however, and so
many districts had at least some spending, the subcontract allocation was
irrelevant to the outcome.

A few tests emphasize that the connection between spending and
votes is real, not an artifact of the methods used here. Excluding the

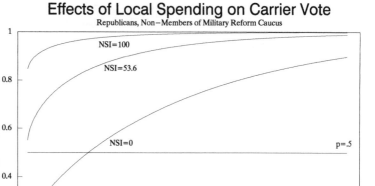

5-5
Effects of Local Spending on Carrier Vote, Republican Nonmembers of
Military Reform Caucus

highest value districts, those over $100 million, had no effect on the
coefficients or on the overall relationship (table 5–4). Discounting the
navy's calculations for the groups of districts that did not have separate
values (by dividing the total for each set among all districts included)
actually strengthened the spending/vote relationship. Finally, the data in
simplified form show the average amount of subcontracting performed in
the districts of carrier supporters and opponents (table 5–6). The difference between the districts of Republican procarrier and anticarrier members is striking. Among more hawkish Republicans—those with NSI
scores over 50—carrier supporters received, on average, over ten times
as much work for their districts as did opponents. This does not prove
that these Republicans voted as they did because of the level of subcontracts that their districts did, or did not, receive. It does, however,
weaken the argument that the probit model inferred too much from the
data.

Why did some Republican members pay attention to district eco-

Table 5-6

Average District Subcontracts by Vote, Party, and Defense Attitudes

Republicans

	Keep Carriers	Delete Carriers
Hawkish	$15,118,900	$ 1,222,230
n	135	31
Dovish	$ 8,164,250	$ 3,914,000
n	4	5

Democrats

	Keep Carriers	Delete Carriers
Hawkish	$11,848,400	$17,814,000
n	44	9
Dovish	$12,717,200	$11,764,400
n	113	81

nomic interests when most of their colleagues did not? The answer may lie in the character of the aircraft carrier issue—as well as its timing—and in the members' response to the two (see table 5–7). Of the thirty-six Republicans who split on the vote, twenty came from the Midwest, and another nine represented northeastern states, including two from Ohio and three from New York. Three of four Iowa Republicans, all four Republicans from Wisconsin, and the entire Nebraska delegation voted to delete funding. Most of these geographic areas are either agricultural or industrial and in 1987 were still suffering from the severe farm and industrial slumps of the mid-1980s. Members had to have been sensitive to the hardships and surely noticed the disparity between the economic benefits produced by the huge defense buildup, which graced some parts of the country with literally hundreds of billions of dollars in defense contracts, and the prolonged economic difficulties their own regions endured. The lack of substantial subcontract opportunities must have been especially apparent in states like Nebraska, which received only $56,000 worth of work.

The votes these members cast against the aircraft carriers were atypi-

Table 5-7
Republican Members Opposing the Carriers

Name	State	1988 NSI Score	Subcontracts
Kolbe	Arizona	100	$ 4,133,000
Brown	Colorado	80	649,000
Hefley	Colorado	100	75,000
Gingrich	Georgia	100	2,203,000
Fawell	Illinois	90	661,000
Martin	Illinois	90	59,000
Coats	Indiana	80	1,400,000
Leach	Iowa	0	738,000
Lightfoot	Iowa	78	4,507,000
Tauke	Iowa	50	0
Myers	Kansas	80	0
Morella	Maryland	22	10,511,000
Pursell	Michigan	100	132,000
Schuette	Michigan	100	0
Upton	Michigan	100	141,000
Frenzel	Minnesota	100	0
Buechner	Missouri	100	0
Bereuter	Nebraska	80	0
Daub	Nebraska	90	56,000
Smith	Nebraska	80	0
Gregg	New Hampshire	90	37,000
Roukema	New Jersey	80	911,000
Fish	New York	60	1,462,000
Green	New York	20	3,082,000
Houghton	New York	90	14,717,000
Gradison	Ohio	100	1,499,000
Regula	Ohio	90	15,000
Smith, D.	Oregon	100	0
Smith, R.	Oregon	80	0
Walker	Pennsylvania	100	557,900
Schneider	Rhode Island	10	732,000*
Sundquist	Tennessee	100	0

Table 5-7

(continued)

Name	State	1988 NSI Score	Subcontracts
Gunderson	Wisconsin	90	0
Petri	Wisconsin	90	6,000
Roth	Wisconsin	90	1,054,000
Sensenbrenner	Wisconsin	70	0

*paired for

cal of their generally conservative stances on defense issues. Even though Iowa, Wisconsin, and Michigan are known to be more dovish on defense issues than other states, their representatives usually voted with the hawks in Congress. They cannot be described as soft on defense. The Nebraska delegation, consisting of Douglas Bereuter, Hal Daub, and Virginia Smith, had NSI scores of 80, 90, and 80, respectively. The same was true for others: Wisconsin congressmen Steven Gunderson, Thomas Petri, Toby Roth, and James Sensenbrenner had, respectively, scores of 90, 90, 90, and 70. One-third of the carriers' Republican opponents had the maximum NSI score of 100. On the controversial and often ideologically polarized issues selected for the NSI, such as aid to the Nicaraguan Contras and strategic nuclear policy issues, most of these members could be counted on to vote with their party. Aircraft carriers are less closely coupled to superpower relations and raise a different set of questions, including affordability and the possibility that money might be taken from other programs to pay for them. Hawkish Republicans with large district stakes in the ships might be inclined to overlook such problems; those with little direct economic interest would be less so. A possibility, then, is that Republican opponents would have in fact preferred to vote for the aircraft carriers but chose to vote against them because support might have alienated too many constituents. The lack of a heavy local stake induced them to vote against their own policy preference.

Midwestern Republicans in particular took a viable position in voting against the aircraft carriers. Their prodefense stances would go unquestioned because of their hawkish votes on other defense issues, yet they could demonstrate their concern about local unemployment and farm problems by voting down an extremely expensive piece of military hardware. Members from the same areas who represented districts with large subcontracts would have fewer problems justifying their support for the ships because of the jobs and other benefits that resulted. The average level of subcontracting performed in the districts of Republican supporters, $15 million, would produce about eight hundred direct and indirect jobs; $1 million, the average level in opponents' districts, about fifty-five. It therefore appears as though subcontracts could have persuaded these recalcitrant Republicans to vote in line with their ideological orientation.

Democrats behaved differently. Even some Democrats whose districts performed large amounts of work voted against the carriers: ten of the Democrats with local stakes above $50 million voted to delete funding. Of these, seven came from districts that had to share an amount of subcontracts because they represented contiguous districts that were not broken out separately. Four of these districts were in southern California, the area with one of the heaviest concentrations of defense industry in the country; the other three were from the Chicago area. Nine of the ten had NSI scores of 0, which means that even large subcontracting totals could not overcome their opposition; their votes were not for sale. In an extreme case, Congresswoman Marilyn Lloyd (D-Tenn.), though generally conservative on defense issues, was unmoved by $145 million in subcontracts (or about six thousand jobs) only three years after her district finally lost the Clinch River Breeder Reactor. Unlike Republicans, whose opposition could be weakened by a local stake, dovish Democrats refused to sell their support.

The inferences to be drawn from these results can be stretched only so far. On a procurement decision that as much as any other weapon system should have generated vote preferences based on economic benefits, only a small number of members were induced to abandon their policy preferences for parochial reasons; and even then the discrepancies resulted from the lack of benefits rather than an abundance. This cannot be considered a generalized finding applicable to the entire House; as James Lindsay points out, "The fact that *some* members of Congress vote against their private policy beliefs by no means warrants the conclusion that *most* legislators do."[30]

At the same time, the results cannot be dismissed. The lack of doves who voted for the carriers on the basis of local benefit may reflect the relatively small value of work performed in many districts. Members who could safely ignore the economic effects of $10 million or even $50 million in local subcontracts and vote in accord with their dovish policy preferences might behave differently when much larger amounts are involved. After all, even the defense budget's severest critics become vocal and persistent advocates of local prime contractors or military bases when the money flow is threatened. The location of economic benefits might have been crucial in determining the outcome of the carrier debate if the vote had been close; in that case the support of the recalcitrant Republicans could have been pivotal. Furthermore, the fact that some members are moved by district level benefits does establish a useful general principle, one that has eluded systematic research for some time. If defense contractors possessed enough sophistication to be able to predict which members would be most easily swayed by district interests—and by inference which members would be unlikely to respond—they could more easily overcome the inherent zero-sum character of strategic subcontract allocation: namely, that short of simply adding work to the program the only way to give one district more money is to take it away from another. Although such delicate and complicated political calculations could not plausibly determine the specific distribution of subcontracts, a broad geographic distribution of suppliers is a reasonable way of increasing the chances of hitting susceptible members.

If subcontracts cannot guarantee that members will protect the programs that produce them, they can serve many of the same political-strategic purposes as PAC contributions. As I indicated in chapter 3, most observers of PAC activity conclude that campaign contributions have little impact on votes per se but instead purchase access, or the ability to lay claim to a member's time. Awarding subcontracts to a particular congressional district might be another way of doing the same thing; contractor personnel and lobbyists undoubtedly have more success in getting a member's attention when they can show that he or she has a direct political and economic interest in the issue at hand. Moreover, we can almost always expect the member from the district in which the prime contractor is located to be a vocal and persistent advocate of crucial programs. The allocation of subcontracts seems to be a way of opening doors and gaining access.

CHAPTER 5. DEFENSE CONTRACTS AND VOTING
IN CONGRESS

1. Quoted in Adam Yarmolinsky, *The Military Establishment* (New York: Harper Colophon Books, 1971), 39.

2. Stephen A. Cobb, "Defense Spending and Foreign Policy in the House of Representatives," *Journal of Conflict Resolution* 13, no. 3 (Fall 1969): 358–59.

3. James Clotfelter, "Senate Voting and Constituency Stake in Defense Spending," *Journal of Politics* 32, no. 4 (November 1970): 983.

4. Robert A. Bernstein and William W. Anthony, "The ABM Issue in the Senate, 1968–1970: The Importance of Ideology," *American Political Science Review* 68, no. 3 (September 1974); Barry Bozeman and Thomas E. James, "Toward a Comprehensive Model of Foreign Policy Voting in the U.S. Senate," *Western Political Quarterly* 28, no. 3 (September 1975); Cobb, "Defense Spending and Foreign Policy in the House of Representatives"; Stephen A. Cobb, "The Impact of Defense Spending on Senatorial Voting Behavior," in *Sage International Yearbook of Foreign Policy Studies,* vol. 1, ed. Patrick J. McGowan (Beverly Hills: Sage Publications, 1973); Stephen A. Cobb, "Defense Spending and Defense Voting in the House: An Empirical Study of an Aspect of the Military-Industrial Complex Thesis," *American Journal of Sociology* 82, no. 1 (July 1977); Clotfelter, "Senate Voting and Constituency Stake in Defense Spending"; Richard Fleisher, "Economic Benefit, Ideology, and Senate Voting on the B-1 Bomber," *American Politics Quarterly* 13, no. 2 (April 1985); Charles Gray and Glenn W. Gregory, "Military Spending and Senate Voting," *Journal of Peace Research* 5, no. 1 (1968); James M. Lindsay, "Parochialism, Policy, and Constituency Constraints: Congressional Voting on Strategic Weapons Systems," *American Journal of Political Science* 34, no. 4 (November 1990); Wayne Moyer, "House Voting on Defense: An Ideological Explanation," in *Military Force and American Society,* ed. Bruce Russett and Alfred Stepan (New York: Harper and Row, 1973); Bruce Ray, "Defense Department Spending and 'Hawkish' Voting in the House of Representatives," *Western Political Quarterly* 34, no. 3 (September 1981); Bruce M. Russett, *What Price Vigilance? The Burdens of National Defense* (New Haven: Yale University Press, 1970).

5. Russett, *What Price Vigilance?,* 75.

6. Pat Towell, "Over GOP Protest, Hill Clears Defense Bill," *Congressional Quarterly Weekly Report,* July 23, 1988, 2046.

7. Pat Towell, "Veto of Defense Bill Ups the Political Ante," *Congressional Quarterly Weekly Report,* August 6, 1988, 2143–45.

8. Cobb, "The Impact of Defense Spending on Senatorial Voting Behavior," 168–69.

9. Frank Whelon Wayman, "Arms Control and Strategic Arms Voting in the U.S. Senate: Patterns of Change, 1967–1983," *Journal of Conflict Resolution* 29, no. 2 (June 1985): 247.

10. Ross K. Baker, *House and Senate* (New York: W. W. Norton, 1989), 46.

11. Lindsay, "Parochialism, Policy, and Constituency Constraints," 14.

12. Press release from Representative Martin's Washington office, released May 6, 1987.

13. John Stocker, "Shipbuilding Agenda for Bush," *Journal of Commerce*, January 31, 1989, 10.

14. Shipbuilders Council of America, "Production Worker Employment in Major U.S. Shipbuilding & Repair Facilities," October 1986.

15. Robert F. Morrison, "Study Finds Shipyards Dependent on Navy," *Journal of Commerce*, September 15, 1988, 3B.

16. U.S. Congress, Senate Committee on Armed Services, *Department of Defense Authorization for Appropriations for Fiscal Year 1986*, part 2, February 1985, 809.

17. "Supplied Products (Estimated) for Aircraft Carriers CVN 74 & 75," February 1987. See George C. Wilson, "Navy Lobbies to Add 2 Carriers," *Washington Post*, March 29, 1987, A5.

18. *Congressional Record*, May 7, 1987, H3281 (daily edition).

19. Ibid., H3285.

20. Ibid., H3280.

21. Ibid., H3288.

22. Quoted in "The Military and Politics: Building Carriers," *Norfolk Virginian-Pilot*, August 15, 1988, 6.

23. Ibid.

24. In the 1985–86 congressional sessions, the American Security Council selected the following ten votes:

HJ Res 181	MX Missile Appropriations	March 28, 1985
HR 2577	Contra Aid	June 12, 1985
HR 1872	Binary Chemical Weapons Production	June 19, 1985
HR 1872	SDI Authorization	June 20, 1985
HR 1872	ASAT Testing	June 26, 1985
HR 1555	Assistance to Angolan Rebels	July 10, 1985
HJ Res 3	Nuclear Test Ban Negotiations	February 26, 1986
HR 4800	Easing of Export Controls	May 21, 1986
H Con Res 350	Compliance with SALT II Limits	June 19, 1986
HR 5052	Contra Aid	June 25, 1986

25. See Stephen Canby, "Military Reform and the Art of War," in *The*

Defense Reform Debate: Issues and Analysis, ed. Asa A. Clark IV et al. (Baltimore: Johns Hopkins University Press, 1984), 141–42.

26. Navy districts are defined here as those that contain one of the following types of navy installations: shipyards, air stations, ship stations, navy bases, weapons stations, submarine bases. Districts containing only marine corps installations, reserve facilities, hospitals, construction battalions, or technical facilities are not coded as navy districts. Data on base location are from United States Navy, Office of Legislative Affairs, *Major Naval (Navy and Marine Corps) Installations and Activities in the United States* (NAVSO P-3626, June 1985).

27. This information is taken from the biographical information contained in the *Almanac of American Politics 1988* (Washington, D.C.: National Journal, 1987).

28. On the nature of these group influences, see Barbara Hinckley, *Stability and Change in Congress,* 4th ed. (New York: Harper & Row), 210–32.

29. In the model, this means that the variables Navydist, RetNavy, and PAC are set to 0, and that MRC is set to 1. Unless otherwise noted, all of the stylized members analyzed here are constructed with these characteristics.

30. James M. Lindsay, "Parochialism, Policy, and Constituency Constraints: Congressional Voting on Strategic Weapons Systems," 951.

Congressional Influence in Defense Contracting

Political considerations are normally more important in choosing contractors for individual weapons systems. . . . Basic decisions are made and contractors are chosen with an eye to their potential reception on Capitol Hill.

—Lawrence J. Korb

A key assumption underlying the political model of the defense contracting process is that the Pentagon awards contracts specifically to gain support in Congress and that members of the House and Senate can tell the Pentagon which firms to choose. Defense contracts, critics argue, are funneled to wavering legislators to secure their votes on defense budgets, and large contracts are parceled out to districts of the department's friends. Yet all careful studies of the subject have found rumors of rampant political infestation to be exaggerated. This apparent discrepancy arises largely because much of the political activity that pretends to influence DOD source selection is, ultimately, for show: congressmen and senators take credit for securing contract awards when, in all likelihood, they had no influence whatsoever in the final decision; they seek to mitigate the consequences of losing large contracts by criticizing DOD source selection decisions and suggesting that the winning firm benefited from unsavory political advantages.

The fact is that there is little an individual legislator can do to determine where prime contracts go. The prime contract award process is structured to preclude routine political meddling by legislators who want to channel contracts to their constituents. The scope of the source selection process immunizes it against the kinds of political pressures that legislators can bring to bear: contractor proposals are evaluated and winners are selected in a highly formalized setting; DOD contracting activities are governed by a large body of law and departmental regulation; and losers have a variety of administrative and judicial remedies available to them if they suspect unfair treatment.

Congressional politics, then, normally does not affect prime contractor source selection—but it intrudes in other ways. Although members cannot, in general, create constituencies by demanding that a particular contractor receive a major contract, they can protect existing constituencies by making it very difficult for the Pentagon to cancel or scale back ongoing programs; there are large differences between award advocacy and funding advocacy. Successful funding advocacy involves either writing restrictive language into the authorizations bill that prohibits DOD from taking specified actions (such as opening up a program to competition) or simply gaining enough support in Congress to put money in the budget where none was requested.

Political considerations are most evident in subcontracting decisions made by the prime contractor. In selecting subcontractors, prime contractors become political targeteers, allocating subcontracts to maximize regional economic and political effects. The effect is to spread subcontracts over as many states and congressional districts as possible, so that a large number of members have at least some economic stake in the program.

Yet these two examples of political infiltration are not the same phenomena as those identified by more general pork barrel explanations. In nearly all cases where the pork barrel theory is applied, the full story is more complex than critics will admit. Although some members of Congress are concerned only about the effects of defense contract decisions on their local economies, the institution will generally vote to kill large weapons systems if their sole effect is to produce jobs. Such judgments, to be sure, rely on fine distinctions between legitimate national security concerns and disingenuous rationalizations. But as the aircraft carrier analysis in the last chapter demonstrated, local stakes do not guarantee support and neither does the lack of vested interest rule it out.

The Politics of Source Selection

A major problem in studying the politics of defense contracting is that it is extremely difficult, even impossible, to prove that a contract award was made on political grounds. The Tactical Fighter Experimental (TFX) contract—the development program that led to the F-111 fighter/bomber—illustrates the problem.

In late 1962, DOD announced that General Dynamics had won the competition to develop a new generation of combat aircraft. The aircraft, called TFX, would function as both a fighter and a bomber and was likely to be the only large aircraft program of the 1960s. The entire program was estimated to be worth $5.8 billion in 1962 dollars; in real dollars, roughly two-thirds the size of the B-1 program. Secretary of Defense Robert McNamara awarded the contract to General Dynamics even though the Air Force Source Selection Board had unanimously recommended, through four separate rounds of evaluation, that the contract go to Boeing, the other company competing for the award.

The announcement unleashed furious criticism. Boeing's supporters claimed that General Dynamics had won the contract on the basis of political considerations. McNamara, they argued, gave the award to General Dynamics because it would build the TFX in Texas, home of Vice President Lyndon Johnson and a state vitally important in the election of 1964. In this respect, Boeing was at a disadvantage because it would have built the plane in solidly Republican Kansas. Moreover, critics pointed out, several high-ranking DOD officials, most notably Deputy Secretary of Defense Roswell Gilpatric, had professional ties to General Dynamics prior to taking their current jobs. The contention that General Dynamics did not win the contract on merit was reinforced when the aircraft ran into serious cost and technical problems.

Two weeks after the announcement, Senator Henry Jackson (D-Wash.), who represented the state in which Boeing's headquarters were located, called for a congressional investigation into the contract award. The resulting McClellan Hearings, held in two sessions in 1963 and 1970, examined every conceivable aspect of the contract award. Yet despite what Chairman John L. McClellan (D-Ark.) called "one of the longest and most extensive congressional investigations ever undertaken,"[1] the committee was unable to show that the award was politically motivated; the main conclusion was that McNamara's decision was a bad one. There was simply no hard evidence that politics had played a role in the final decision.

Several years after the hearings, one study concluded that McNamara had chosen General Dynamics because he wanted to compel the air force and navy to purchase one aircraft and felt he was more likely to succeed in that effort with the General Dynamics plane.[2] Yet there are many government officials who felt at the time—and who remain convinced today—that McNamara was looking after the political interests of the president.[3]

In the 1970s, the awarding of the M-1 tank contract to Chrysler raised a different set of issues. Once again, a service decision (in this case, the army's) was reversed by the service secretary. The army wanted to award the contract to General Motors, Chrysler's competitor, but was overruled by Secretary of the Army Donald Rumsfeld. Rumsfeld argued that Chrysler's design was better able to meet NATO standardization requirements, an explanation one former OMB official considered a smokescreen for a hidden agenda. Chrysler won the award, according to this official, because President Ford was worried about the automobile industry, especially since the presidential election of 1976 was approaching. Chrysler was in serious financial trouble and needed some form of assistance; a defense contract was a better way to provide it than other forms of government aid, such as a bailout guaranteed loan.[4] However plausible this theory may sound, it is less than compelling: Chrysler got a government loan anyway, and the contract award was announced a week after the election, on November 12, 1976.

Perhaps as a result of cases like these, many people involved in weapons acquisition believe that congressmen and other politicians can effectively lobby on behalf of specific companies and that political considerations determine which company will win contracts: "[One] congressman stated that many of his colleagues had an attitude of 'the next big contract will not go to the state which won the last big one.' An executive of a major contractor reported that 'many of us believe that the Pentagon and the politicians merely say, "whose turn is it this time?" ' "[5]

Again, research by academics reached the opposite conclusion. One set of studies, done at the Harvard University Graduate School of Business Administration, examined a number of large-scale programs through the 1950s and early 1960s.[6] It concluded that "the direct effects of politics in the weapon acquisition processes tend to be exaggerated."[7] The authors, recognizing that their conclusion was at odds with prevailing opinion, left open the possibility that they did not dig deeply enough into the decision-making processes to uncover political effects. But, they add, "we can only report what we have seen: that politics counts for less in selecting weapons contractors than many people think."[8] Later work covering the 1960s and 1970s, also done at Harvard, reached the same conclusion.[9] The author of that study found only one program out of several hundred of which it could be said that congressional influence determined the outcome.[10]

The source selection process is structured so that congressional influence (award advocacy) cannot play a major role. Because of the statutory authority involved in the contracting process and the tremendous attention given to the awarding of defense contracts, the system is set up to maximize objectivity and minimize political influences at the source selection stage.

All contracts that DOD awards must adhere to the Federal Acquisition Regulation (FAR) (48 CFR Chap.1, Parts 1 to 51), implemented in September 1983. The activities of the department are under the additional authority of the Department of Defense FAR Supplement (48 CFR Chap. 2) and the regulations promulgated by the individual services. These laws spell out precisely the manner in which defense contracting is to be conducted and specifically cover source selection in competitive negotiated contracts (the kind involved in many large programs, including the TFX).

Contractors who think the law has been broken can protest any award decisions. They may either appeal decisions to the contracting officer or higher levels within DOD, GAO, or the General Services Board of Contract Appeals or seek remedy through the courts.[11] Although protest procedures by themselves will not prevent DOD from allowing political considerations to prejudice contract awards—since it can easily concoct nonpolitical justifications—blatant favoritism or bias in source selection, to the point where department regulations or federal law has clearly been broken, will likely be reversed under the scrutiny of protest procedures.[12]

The Ill Wind procurement fraud investigation shows what can happen when those in the procurement process violate laws and regulations. As I indicated in chapter 3, the contractors who lost awards to competitors found guilty of unlawful activities immediately began protesting, and several major awards were overturned.[13] Although suspected political influence is hardly thought to involve such blatant violations of normal practice as that uncovered in Ill Wind, the lack of any evidence confirming suspicions of *political* influence may well indicate that they are unfounded.

The way in which DOD evaluates competing contractors' proposals makes political manipulation unlikely. Proposals and technical evaluations can entail many months of work and involve hundreds of people. One survey of six programs found that proposal evaluation for large programs required an average of 267 analysts and 35,000 hours of work.[14] The analysis of proposals alone is a monumental task, as the amount of data contractors submit in their proposals can be staggering. A single proposal for a modern combat aircraft may run close to 100,000 pages. The five companies competing for the C-5A contract submitted a total of 240,000 pages in their proposals; with multiple copies, the entire set weighed some thirty-five tons![15]

The groups charged with evaluating the specific aspects of a contractor proposal (cost, technical risk, maintainability) normally ignore the political ramifications of their decisions. The engineers responsible for assuring that a plane's wings stay attached in flight do not care which legislators their conclusions may annoy. According to one study, "Department of Defense respondents were not concerned about which city won a major contract, or the economic consequences to a given area if it won or lost a specific contract. Instead, they projected an image of professionals administering the contract award process, and being above the political battles and lobbying that existed in many major weapons system contract awards."[16] Although the secretary of defense can overturn the recommendations produced by the source selection process, as happened with the F-111 and XM-1, he is likely to arouse considerable suspicion if he does so. Such rejections are very rare.[17]

Nearly all participants in the procurement process, from legislators to defense officials to contractors, agree that once the acquisition cycle reaches the source selection phase, congressmen and senators cannot influence decisions. Too much bureaucratic machinery is in motion, and entrenched advocates have already taken position around certain proposals or contractors for reasons that have little to do with politics. Craig Liske and Barry Rundquist report that "virtually never, at this stage, can any congressmen or group influence a decision on which firm will get the contract. . . . Even for someone with 'clout,' like a committee chairman, it is difficult to determine where a procurement contract will finally go."[18]

At the early stages in the acquisition cycle, then, responsibility is too fragmented and dispersed to permit political contamination. At the later stages, most decisions have been cast in stone. Neither phase is amenable to congressional meddling.

The Politics of Contracts and the Politics of Bases

The political neutrality of the source selection process stands in stark contrast to the ways in which DOD and Congress handle military bases. Historically the military has had far more discretion in deciding where to locate its facilities and always steers clear of members of the Armed Services and Defense Appropriations committee in deciding which bases to close. Between 1952 and 1974, the army and air force closed 125 major military installations, only 9 of which were in districts represented by members of the House military committees. R. Douglas Arnold estimates that bases in committee members' districts were about half as likely to be closed as were other installations.[19]

The Pentagon is more likely to make explicit political decisions on base matters than it is on source selection, a phenomenon entrenched in the political lore of Congress. The politicized nature of the process was highlighted by the navy's strategic homeporting plan, which was designed to disperse the fleet to fourteen new ports and budgeted nearly $1 billion for the construction of major new facilities. Many in Congress criticized the plan as nothing but a way of doling out navy pork to more congressional districts. The strategic rationale was that an increase in the number of ports would complicate Soviet strategic targeting, reduce the navy's vulnerability to sabotage and conventional attack, and make the fleet more efficient by porting battle groups together and putting them closer to areas of possible action.

The program's critics regarded the navy's reasoning as an attempt to coat a blatant political move with thin national security arguments. A retired vice admiral, John Shanahan, said, "All of this is politically motivated. I just cannot find any tactical or strategic justification for spreading the fleet up and down the East and West coasts and in the Gulf of Mexico. It's a game."[20] Navy officials admitted that the homeporting plan would increase congressional support for a six-hundred-ship fleet: "What better way is there to build a constituency than to spread around ships? It's a buy-in for the Navy," said one.[21]

Few failed to notice that most of the new homeports were to be built in the districts or states of powerful congressional allies of the DOD, including many who sat on the military committees.[22]

Any discretion the military sees fit to exercise in choosing which facilities should be built and which should be shut down is cause for concern in Congress, which fears politically motivated decisions. The military might punish its congressional enemies by closing facilities in their districts (the often unstated converse is that members can prevent closures by threatening to withdraw support on other issues).[23] Representative Patricia Schroeder (D-Colo.) claimed in 1976 that "the [base closing] lists which come out of the Pentagon seem to be more based on politics than on military utility,"[24] an analysis vindicated by the way DOD handled the base closing question ten years later.

In February 1986, in response to a congressional request, Secretary of Defense Weinberger named three installations that DOD wanted to close. Each was in the district of a Democratic critic of President Reagan's defense budgets—House Speaker Tip O'Neill (D-Mass.), William H. Gray III (D-Penn.), and Schroeder.[25] No one was astonished when all three objected. Senator Gary Hart (D-Colo.), who was affected by the Colorado closure, argued that Weinberger was "trying to put his critics on the defensive."[26] The bases were unlikely to be closed on the secretary's recommendation; such was not even the intent. On the contrary,

Weinberger was trying to make critics of large defense budgets look bad when they protect spending in their own districts, and he recommended the bases be closed for that reason. Similar maneuvers are rarely attempted with major weapons systems.

Schroeder made the same point again in 1990, when Secretary of Defense Cheney released a list of candidates for closure as part of the FY 1991 defense budget; she noted that nineteen of the twenty-one bases targeted for closure were in Democratic districts, as were over 90 percent of the personnel reductions.[27] Along with the proposed base closings, Cheney indicated that he would expand several other domestic installations; figures released by the Democratic Study Group showed that 98 percent (2,265 out of 2,304) of these additional jobs were in Republican districts (though the increases were small).[28] Moreover, the study group argued, three-quarters of the personnel reductions involved Democratic members of either HASC or House Ways and Means; both were sure to become involved in defense and tax issues of "keen interest to the Administration."[29] The implied message was that President Bush and Cheney would horse-trade for votes on these key issues. HASC Chairman Aspin concurred, saying the way Cheney handled the proposed list "creates hostages for the Administration. Vote against a veto override, your base is safe. Vote to override, your base is threatened. This puts a political gun to the head of a member with a base in his or her district."[30]

To defend itself against DOD's caprice—or so Congress says, even though the obvious intent is to protect local benefits—Congress has constructed a series of impenetrable barriers that effectively strip the Pentagon of its ability to close bases. By requiring advance notice of proposed closures, mandating long waiting periods, and forcing the military to slog through the morass of environmental impact reports, Congress prevented DOD from closing any major installations between 1977 and 1988; DOD gave up even trying between 1979 and 1985.[31]

The impasse over base closings was temporarily resolved in 1988, when Congress established a bipartisan commission to select bases to be closed. Congress instructed the commission to compile a list of proposed closures, which was to be accepted or rejected as a whole; members were prohibited from protecting individual bases on the "hit list." The genius of this plan was that it was impossible to oppose in principle, since no member could support the idea of keeping outdated installations open.

When the commission reported its list in December 1988 (recommending that eighty-six bases be closed and fifty-nine others be partially closed or "realigned,") members whose districts suffered predictably screamed foul. They began a loud public campaign to protect their bases, criticized the commission's work, and tried to overturn the decisions.[32] They failed: the House rejected an attempt to reverse the base closings, voting 381–43 to accept the recommendations.[33] This exercise, however, provided political cover for affected members, since they were not the ones who made the final decisions; that blame fell to a group of faceless bureaucrats whose work was, in the words of an affected member, "fatally flawed."[34]

Both DOD and Congress treat contracts and bases differently because the rules governing the two are different. Congress can easily stall base closures and realignments, but there is no FAR counterpart or other rules to prohibit DOD discretion—at least in proposing bases for closure, as opposed to actually following through. The Pentagon uses bases for political purposes because it can; such activities are much rarer in the procurement process.

Congressional Politics and Defense Contracts

The reason people believe politics drives defense contracting is that most players in the process, especially those in Congress, pretend that it does; fostering the impression is a useful electoral tool. Although congressmen and senators have little influence over DOD source selection, they often behave as though they do. If members convince their constituents that they can determine the outcome of contract competitions, they can then claim credit for the resulting awards. Some are blunt in claiming to wield influence. One member, complaining about the number of retired officers who return to the Pentagon as lobbyists, noted that he ran into them "every time I go to the Pentagon to obtain a contract for one of my constituents."[35] Another, a senator from Pennsylvania, advertised his influence in a letter to firms in his state: "Let me know if you are bidding on government contracts. I have been influential in gaining award of these contracts, but you must let me know if you want me to help."[36] This credit claiming is important, as it gives constituents the impression that their representative is actively fighting for their interests. Constituents who believe this message are likely to return the favor through campaign contributions and votes.

Before 1970, this type of credit claiming was a routine part of the political landscape. The Pentagon allowed selected legislators—often those most sympathetic to DOD—to publicly announce contract awards to firms in their district or state before the general public was notified by news release. This practice certainly fostered the impression that the member's efforts had had a hand in the award, particularly since the information was selectively provided to the military's congressional allies. Congress stopped the practice in 1971, in part because of criticism like that voiced by Senator John Williams (R-Del.), who argued, somewhat disingenuously, that "political influence in the awarding of Government contracts should not be encouraged, nor should either the Congress or the Administration condone a policy which gives the appearance of influence peddling."[37] Many members supported change, no doubt, because they rarely were on the receiving end of this benefit, not because of any philosophical objections to the practice.

Credit-claiming activities have led constituents to expect help from their representatives on contract matters; members are often contacted by local defense contractors who are unhappy about DOD decisions. Usually these contacts occur after a firm has lost a contract competition. These matters are treated with the utmost seriousness by both members and Pentagon officials, who solemnly vow to investigate and report back on how the award decision was reached.

Usually, however, the member's function is simply to find out why a constituent lost a contract. One Armed Services Committee member explained, "We owe it to any constituent to investigate their complaint. I'd call upon the Pentagon and ask, 'what happened?' And they would respond. Usually, since the process is open to public scrutiny, they follow the rules—it's the contractor [who is at fault]. We'd get back to the contractor and say 'The Pentagon abided by the rules, and here's what you didn't do right.' We give them information they might otherwise not have, since the contractor usually hears nothing other than 'you didn't win.' "[38] Constituents who expect their representative to overturn a contract award invariably leave disappointed. Individual members of Congress just do not have that kind of power.

Vocal activity in support of local defense contractors is designed more for domestic consumption, to convince voters that the member is looking after their interests.[39] In the words of one congressman, "To be very candid about it, the effort has to be made because the public expects it."[40] Award advocacy is a ritual that stresses appearance over substance: "A congressman will inquire about a selection at the request of an influential constituent, even when he doubts that it will make any difference. The service responds to the congressional inquiry with cordiality, but such inquiries have little impact at the operating levels where the source selection decision is usually made. The constituent, however, leaves Washington convinced that dealing with the government is all a matter of politics."[41] HASC Chairman Aspin works hard at this credit-claiming function; since 1987 he has funneled over $200,000 to the Aspin Institute, a nonprofit organization designed to help Wisconsin businesses obtain defense contracts. During the election campaign of 1988, Aspin said the institute helped bring $500 million in contracts to the state, a claim discounted by a Milwaukee paper, which noted that "many of those Wisconsin firms probably would have received the contracts without the help of Aspin and the Institute."[42]

When members fail to engage in these symbolic activities they may find themselves with serious political problems. In the California Senate race in 1970, for example, successful challenger John Tunney charged that incumbent George Murphy had not worked hard enough to bring contracts to the state. Tunney claimed that the $8 billion F-15 contract had not gone to North American Rockwell, which is based in southern California, because "Murphy did practically nothing in California's behalf."[43] Even though there is no substance to claims of influence, appearances do matter, and legislators work hard to maintain the illusion.

Authorization Language and Programmatic Direction

One way that members can exercise some indirect influence over the placing of defense contracts is through their control of the language that authorizes the Pentagon to spend money. By inserting the appropriate language into the annual authorization bill, members can prohibit or compel specific action. Such efforts are effective if the language finds its way in and are highly visible to constituents.

Many times this activity involves programs for which the primary motivation is pork barrel politics, and no conceivable national security justification exists for restrictive language. The provisions may reach absurd levels. For years, Congress forced the Pentagon to buy high-sulphur U.S. coal to heat bases in Germany and prohibited the conversion of those bases to more economical oil heat.[44] The result is that while the U.S. Army has stockpiled only enough ammunition to last a few weeks in a sustained conventional conflict, it has enough coal to last for four years. Robert Higgs, who chronicled the story of this coal boondoggle, characterized it as "inexcusable from the standpoint of genuine concern for national security."[45] Similar provisions prevent the military from recycling aluminum, force it to buy small transport planes it neither wants nor needs, and mandate milk as part of the standard military ration.[46] Congress has used provisions to impede competition, as when it prohibited the navy from giving photocopies of the blueprints of the Trident submarine to a potential second source.[47] HASC Chairman Aspin plays as well, having added millions of dollars for trucks that the army says it does not (or does, depending on the source) want; that the contractor is in Wisconsin, Aspin's home state, is no accident.[48]

Congress, to its credit, occasionally rejects some of the more ludicrous efforts to aid local interests. In 1982, Senator Charles Percy (R-Ill.) failed—barely—in an attempt to force the navy to reopen a contract competition to buy reconnaissance cameras. His reason? As one newspaper account put it, "An Illinois company that *hadn't even bid on the original project* [said it could] make a better one."[49]

Such provisions have no purpose other than to force the military to channel money to specific firms or districts. The economic rationale is simple, as the diffused costs and concentrated benefits give the recipients every reason to support the provisions and opponents little reason to fight them. The costs are hardly noticeable to the millions of people who pay but vital to the small number who reap the reward. This is classic pork barrel.

At times, however, these provisions involve substantive disputes between Congress and DOD over which weapons systems and how many of each the military should buy. Although it is easy to characterize such disputes as parochial politics, the pork barrel aspects of congressional action in these cases are less clear. Congress funded both the A-7 and A-10 attack aircraft after the air force no longer wanted them.[50] By forcing the air force to buy more A-10s, Congress was probably concerned less about pork than about overcoming the service's lukewarm commitment to the close air support mission (see chapter 8). The air force was never enthusiastic about the A-10 and wanted to buy as few as it could.

There is also a budgetary component to rewriting the authorization language. Congress adds money to the budget almost every year, in an annual game in which the air force requests no money for C-130 cargo aircraft, secure in the knowledge that Congress will put the planes in for them (it did in 1987 and 1988, buying twenty-six aircraft). In playing along, the air force gets the planes it wants, but at Congress's direction; the service need not siphon money from other programs to pay for them.

Authorization Language on Major Programs

Charges of pork barrel politics are often made about much larger programs, especially when Congress refuses to cancel a major weapons system. Two examples are Congress's refusal in 1983 to allow the army to establish a second source for the M-1 tank engine and the decision in 1989 to restore funds for the F-14 fighter aircraft, which the secretary of defense had attempted to cancel. In both cases, many observers attributed Congress's actions to nothing more than the flagrant pursuit of pork. But as the following case studies show, the full stories are richer than this simple explanation allows. Readers should not take these descriptions to be the definitive interpretation of events; they are rather intended to show that more was involved than pork barrel politics. Parochial concerns cannot offer a complete explanation for the actions, and strategic and military calculations played a larger role than critics will admit. Obviously, local jobs were of major concern to the affected legislators, who can hardly be blamed for fighting to protect their constituents. Those members, however, would not have been able to protect their pet programs if the only argument they could have mustered was that jobs were at stake.

THE M-I TANK ENGINE

Section 107 of the Department of Defense Authorization Act of 1984 directed that "the Secretary of the Army may not make a contract for the purpose of establishing a second source for production of the engine for the M-1 tank." The clause gave AVCO Corporation a legally binding lock on M-1 turbine engine production, despite serious reliability problems and large cost increases.

The provision was Congress's response to the army's attempt to establish a second source for the M-1 engine. The army justified its decision by arguing that a second source would improve quality, reduce costs, and improve surge capacity (the ability to increase production in a crisis). Three companies had submitted bids for the second-source proposal, and the lowest bid beat AVCO's current price by over 20 percent.

Defense officials bitterly criticized the prohibition, citing it as being nothing but a pork barrel grab:

> Too often, Members of Congress emphasize the public works aspects of the defense budget. A second production source of the M-1 tank engine is a recent example. The Army, after much congressional criticism over its failure to use competitive procurement, proposed a second source for the M-1's engine when the AVCO Corporation proved an unreliable supplier.
>
> Instead of rewarding the Army for this endeavor, Congress explicitly prohibited a second supplier. The message sent to the Pentagon was clear: Congress is not serious about reforming DOD spending practices.[51]

Members of the Connecticut delegation, who represented the area in which AVCO is located, encouraged this interpretation by appealing on behalf of the twelve thousand residents who worked on the program. Congressman William Ratchford (D-Conn.) put it in terms of a challenge: "So I say to the Members, 'Don't think it couldn't be you, and don't think it couldn't be your state.' "[52] An aide to Congressman Nicholas Mavroules (D-Mass.), whose district borders AVCO's plant, was even bolder, saying flatly, "It's a pork barrel issue."[53]

Most members, though, saw it differently. The pork barrel implications quickly faded as defense officials and members argued over Congress's proper role in managing procurement programs. Defense officials blasted Congress for micromanaging and obstructing efforts to increase competition; one cited the M-1 provision as "the most egregious example" of Congress trampling on the Pentagon's management efforts.[54]

Congress's response was equally testy. Members responded that the establishment of a second source so late in a program made no sense and that the army had "cooked" its analysis to produce misleading data which showed that competition would save money. Two members of HASC, Dan Daniel (D-Vir.) and William L. Dickinson (R-Ala.), took the unusual step of publicly responding to DOD's attacks. They wrote a lengthy missive that was published in *Armed Forces Journal International,* whose editors noted that the two congressmen have "no parochial interest whatever in who builds the M-1 tank engine or where it is built."[55]

Daniel and Dickinson challenged every element of the army's decision and of the analysis that justified it. They noted, for example, that the army wanted sufficient production capacity to build 568 engines per month (or 6,816 per year), even though the maximum production rate for other components was 150 per month. At the time the army planned to reduce the annual M-1 buy to 720 tanks per year, or 60 per month. Furthermore, second-sourcing the engine made little sense because the army would continue to purchase other tank subsystems—target sights, engine parts, transmissions, and hulls—from single suppliers.[56] They pointed out that the army artificially inflated the number of engines needed over the entire M-1 program in order to make second-sourcing appear more economical. Later, it was revealed that the army had arrived at the number by estimating spares requirements twenty-three years into the future, a task an Armed Services Committee staffer termed, in hearings, as "just plain dumb."[57]

Daniel and Dickinson concluded that Congress rightfully stepped into the M-1 program, not because of parochial issues of concern only to the Connecticut delegation, but to prevent the army from making a poor program management decision. The action reflected a "judgement that the Army failed to make a case that second sourcing of the tank engine was in the national interest. What we found is that the Army never really did know why it wanted to second-source the engine—only that it wanted to do it. What began as an analytical exercise evolved gradually into a matter of pride as the Army struggled to prove all along that it knew what it was doing."[58]

Obviously, the Connecticut congressional delegation was concerned about protecting hometown jobs. But 235 other members (many of whom had no stake in the project) voted down an amendment to delete the restrictive position. Even accounting for logrolling, personal favors, and the like, one is left to conclude that there was more involved here than just pork.

THE F-14 FIGHTER

Executives at the Grumman Corporation knew early in 1989 that the company's premier aircraft, the F-14, might be in trouble. Although Reagan's final defense budget request included money for eighteen F-14 fighters, Bush's secretary of defense, Cheney, was rumored to be considering canceling new F-14 construction as an economy measure.[59] Cheney ended speculation in April 1989 when he announced that he would cut F-14 funding in the FY 1990 budget, continuing only with an upgrade program that converted older F-14A models to the more advanced D configuration.[60] The cancellation would all but end Grumman's forty-year position as the navy's major aircraft manufacturer: in addition to losing the F-14, Grumman faced the end of its A-6 attack, E-2C airborne early warning, and EA-6B electronic jamming aircraft programs.

The day after Cheney's announcement, the Long Island congressional delegation met with him in an attempt to persuade him to reverse his decision. Having failed, members of the delegation, including Democrats Tom Downey, George Hochbrueckner, and Robert Mrazek and Republicans Norman Lent and Raymond McGrath, decided that they would fight the decision in Congress. After suffering several setbacks, they convinced HASC to restore funding for eighteen new F-14s in 1990 and 1991 and defeated a floor amendment that attempted to restore the cut. Grumman had to agree to end the program following the FY 1992 buy but gained three more years of production work, which allowed for a "softer landing."

As with the M-1 story, it is easy to characterize the fight over the F-14 as nothing more than the pursuit of pork.[61] Grumman employed more than five thousand people on the program, all of whom stood to lose their jobs if the cancellation stuck. Clearly job preservation was the primary consideration for the central congressional players, but it cannot explain the behavior of several hundred other members who also voted to restore funding.

Cheney canceled the plane for fiscal reasons, as part of an effort to shave $10 billion from his FY 1990 budget request. The F-14 is the most expensive fighter in the military inventory. Stopping F-14 production in 1990 would have saved, by the secretary's calculations, $2.4 billion by 1994.[62] Furthermore, a new naval fighter is scheduled to enter the inventory in the late 1990s, about the time that the navy will start retiring F-14s; this made further production an unnecessary luxury.

The Long Island delegation's case for restoring the F-14 was based on four arguments. They claimed that Cheney's cost savings were overstated, that the F-14 follow-on might not be ready on time, that the navy would face a shortfall in F-14 inventories in the late 1990s, and that allowing Grumman to leave the fighter aircraft business would leave McDonnell Douglas as the sole manufacturer of naval aircraft. In retrospect, some of the arguments about future F-14 needs appear weak, particularly given the military's likely response to events in Eastern Europe and the Soviet Union. The navy now plans to reduce the number of carrier battle groups from fifteen to twelve, which means that existing F-14 inventories may well be sufficient to meet future needs. But at the time of Cheney's decision, no such plans were contemplated, and the Soviet military threat still loomed large.

Downey, Hochbrueckner, and the other representatives from Long Island claimed that Cheney's cost analysis was flawed and that the true price of the F-14 was $50 million per copy, instead of $75 million as the secretary had said. Canceling the contract in 1990 also meant that the government would pay substantial termination costs to Grumman. Cheney had proposed spending $771 million in 1990 to upgrade six F-14s; this was only $365 million less than Reagan's last budget, which requested $1.136 billion for twelve new F-14Ds and six upgrades.[63] HASC voted to fund twelve new F-14Ds, along with twelve upgrades and advance procurement for $1.01 billion, or only $230 million more than Cheney's original request.[64] The marginal cost of each additional F-14 was thus far less than the $75 million Cheney claimed.

Second, Cheney was betting heavily that the F-14 follow-on, the Naval Advanced Tactical Fighter (NATF), would be ready on time and that Congress would provide stable funding levels. Both assumptions appeared questionable at the time, given the history of the NATF program as well as the Pentagon's experience with joint navy-air force aircraft programs. The NATF is a naval variant of the air force ATF, which has already fallen behind schedule by four years, with first production deliveries now slated for 1999 instead of 1995 as originally planned.[65] The air force is also having trouble mastering the advanced technology involved and may fall short of the initial cost or performance estimates.[66] These problems will affect the NATF program, which is reported to lag behind the air force ATF by about three years.[67]

Moreover, many doubt the navy's dedication to the NATF, given the fact that since World War II the service has never adapted an air force aircraft for use at sea.[68] Congress was sufficiently edgy about the navy's level of commitment that it mandated navy-air force cooperation on the ATF as a condition for continued funding. The navy may interpret the restriction loosely or even ignore it altogether, something it has done before. In the 1970s, Congress ordered the navy and air force to purchase a single lightweight fighter. Rather than buy the F-16, which the air force selected in a competitive fly-off, the navy developed the aircraft which lost that competition into the F-18.[69] Comments from navy personnel did little to calm such fears; one naval officer said of the program, "We will still buy the same plane. For the Navy version, we will have to change the wings, change the fuselage, change the control surfaces and maybe the avionics. However it will still be the same aircraft."[70] Navy officials have also said the NATF needs larger wings, more fuel-carrying capacity, and heavier weapons than the ATF as well as the ability to attack ground targets.[71]

A looming problem is that the air force ATF may be too large to operate from carriers. The prototypes are each slightly longer and heavier than the F-14 and have a longer wingspan; if past experience with prototypes holds, the production models will be even heavier.[72] Adding room for a second crew member in the navy version will make the plane even longer, and reinforcing the aircraft to withstand the stress of carrier takeoffs and landings will add between four thousand and ten thousand pounds.[73] The total weight may be too heavy for existing aircraft carrier catapult systems, and the navy has said it will not "redesign its catapults and carrier decks to accommodate an NATF heavier or larger than the F-14."[74]

Cheney may have canceled the F-14 in part to force the navy into accepting the NATF. In the absence of the F-14, the navy would have no alternative to the NATF. Faced with making a choice between a system it dislikes for institutional reasons and no system at all, the navy would have to relent. Other secretaries, McNamara especially, have used this strategy to force commonality. Preserving the F-14 gave Grumman a chance to promote its own version of an advanced fighter, an updated F-14 called the Tomcat 21.[75]

The Long Island delegation argued next that the navy would have too few fighters in its inventory if the NATF failed to enter production as scheduled. On this point, Tomcat supporters had to counter an internal classified navy study that predicted a surplus of F-14s.[76] Congressman Hochbrueckner called the report hogwash; his position was strengthened when both the chief of naval operations and the navy secretary agreed that the navy would indeed face a shortfall without new F-14D production.[77] If Grumman lost the F-14 in 1990, there would be no way to ramp up production in the late 1990s if the shortfall became a reality. "If [the ATF is delayed]," said Lent, "and someone called up Grumman in 1999 saying 'start building,' there wouldn't be anyone there at Grumman to answer the phone."[78]

Those delays quickly developed. In May 1990, Cheney announced that ATF production would start in 1996 (two years later than planned), with the NATF delayed yet again: production was slated to begin in 2000, rather than 1998, and first deliveries were to be made no earlier than 2001. Grumman may have indeed found some breathing room, especially if the ATF shows the same sorts of problems that doomed the A-12. In the wake of the A-12 cancellation, the navy has taken another look at the A-6 attack aircraft and is even considering a ground attack version of the F-14 as an interim solution.[79] Even before the A-12 was canceled, the navy had proposed buying additional F-14s through 1997, giving Grumman four more years of production.[80]

The fourth and weakest argument in favor of restoring Tomcat production was that the cancellation of the program would hurt the defense industrial base by leaving the United States with only one manufacturer of naval aircraft, namely, McDonnell Douglas. Apart from the fact that this would happen anyway when Grumman stops building F-14s in 1993, the argument fails to consider that eventually at least one additional manufacturer, and perhaps three, would come on line depending on who wins the ATF competition (for which Lockheed, Boeing, and General Dynamics are teamed against Northrop and McDonnell Douglas). Moreover, Grumman may have a new opportunity to compete for the eventual replacement for the A-12, a competition it originally lost to McDonnell Douglas and General Dynamics.

There is no doubt that the key motivation behind the Long Island delegation's efforts to save the F-14 was to protect local jobs. However, they knew that their case for restoring funds had to be based on more substantive arguments. Both Grumman and congressional staff members said that the saving of jobs, by itself, would not have convinced other members to support the plane; one staffer involved claimed that the jobs issue was not even explicitly mentioned to many members.[81] In the Senate, where key support came from Senator Jim Sasser (D-Tenn.), chairman of the Budget Committee, who had no parochial stake in the program, the jobs issue was peripheral.

That the F-14 action was not a pork barrel issue, at least for Congress as a whole, becomes more evident when the rescue of the F-14 program is contrasted with earlier efforts to protect contracts on Long Island. The most visible and controversial was the attempt in 1986 to restore funding for the T-46 trainer aircraft, which the air force canceled after stubborn development problems proved impossible to correct. Like the F-14, the T-46 was manufactured on Long Island, but by Fairchild Republic, whose headquarters are near Grumman's.

In 1985, the air force became dissatisfied with the way Fairchild was managing the program. When it became clear that the T-46 program was in trouble, a large congressional battle developed between the New York delegation and the air force. Senator Robert Dole (R-Kan.) complicated matters by publicly urging the air force to drop the T-46 from the FY 1987 defense budget. Dole was acting as advocate for Wichita-based Cessna Aircraft Company, which had proposed an upgrade program for its T-37 trainer aircraft as an alternative to the T-46. The New York delegation, in September 1985, asked the air force to grant Fairchild additional time to solve the aircraft's shortcomings.[82] When the problems proved intractable, the air force decided in March 1986 to scrap the program. Fairchild said it would close its doors unless the decision was reversed.[83]

After congressional wrangling that rivaled the effort on the F-14 program, the Senate voted 79–14 to accept the air force's recommendation and cut funds for the T-46 in the FY 1987 defense budget.[84] The House, though, approved the HASC provision to restore funding.[85] William Dickinson (R-Ala.), ranking Republican on HASC, had no patience for what he saw as a pure pork barrel issue: "Many of the very people who voted to cut the defense budget Friday led the fight to stuff the T-46 into the budget Monday. The T-46 is a $3 billion program of airborne pork . . . a program that wasn't even included in the $320 billion budget request that some people called bloated."[86] Senator Alfonse D'Amato (R-N.Y.) considered the T-46 important enough to filibuster for forty-eight hours, preventing the Senate from approving a final budget package as the fiscal year ended. The entire federal government shut down for two days until D'Amato relented, having failed to save the program.

Although the New York delegation was able to gain a small concession by successfully inserting language into the 1987 defense budget that mandated a T-46 vs. T-37 fly-off competition, the program was effectively killed. Fairchild indeed shut down its Long Island operations, and thirty-five hundred jobs were eliminated.

The New York delegation was unable to save the T-46 largely because the program had little to recommend it besides the fact that jobs were at stake. Although the program involved fewer people than the F-14, it was still considered vital by representatives from the area. The T-46 competed with other congressional interests, most notably the Kansas delegation's support of Cessna, but the same was true of the F-14, the funds for which were taken from other programs in navy accounts. Moreover, the Long Island delegation also failed to save the A-6 upgrade program, which was canceled in 1989. One is left to conclude that a key difference between these programs and the F-14 was that pork barrel considerations, by themselves, cannot convince a majority of members to support a program of this size.

Congressmen and senators put special language into the authorization bill and direct the Pentagon to spend money because these activities are highly visible and get lots of hometown coverage. Even if they are unsuccessful, members still get credit for trying. Senator Phil Gramm made this point on the base-closing issue: "I come up here and say, 'God

have mercy. Don't close this base in Texas. We can get attacked from the
South. The Russians are going to attack Texas. We need this base.' Then
I can go out and lie down in the street and the bulldozers are coming and I
have a trusty aide there just as it gets there to drag me out of the way. All
the people . . . will say, 'You know, Phil Gramm got whipped, but it was
like the Alamo. He was with us until the last second.' "[87]

Adding program-specific language to the authorization bills is a simple strategy, and it bypasses all of the complicated procurement rules and
regulations. It plays to the credit-claiming and position-taking functions
so vital to members of Congress.[88] Together with subcontract targeting
(see below), it is a form of influence that is allowable, effective, and
often used.

Subcontract Targeting and
Geographic Spreading

Subcontracting is the most political aspect of the actual contract
award process. Scholars and procurement analysts have long suspected
that prime contractors distribute subcontracts—orders for raw materials,
equipment, and parts not manufactured by the prime contractor—
throughout the country with an eye toward maximizing the geographic
spread of acquisition programs, which gives many members an economic stake in the program. The strategy requires primes occasionally to
select suppliers on the basis of geographic considerations: "It happens.
But you'll never get anyone to admit it. . . . There'll be a situation where
someone will say we're getting 'X' from New York and 'Y' from
Connecticut. We'd better get 'Z' in California or Seattle."[89] One high-
ranking DOD procurement executive indicated flatly that this sort of
targeting occurs routinely.[90]

By giving more congressmen and senators an economic stake in a
weapons program, the prime contractor stands a better chance of avoid-
ing budget cuts or cancellation. According to Aspin, "If it comes down
to cutting a weapons system, one whose economic benefits are localized
in a single state, or in one or two congressional districts, is more likely to
be cut than one that, through contracting and subcontracting, has managed to spread its economic largess throughout the country."[91] The

services, too, have a clear interest in encouraging subcontract spreading, since it "[provides] ready and calculated answers to the questions of uncommitted congressmen."[92] The discussion in chapter 5 demonstrated that in some very limited instances local stakes can sway a member's vote, even if district subcontracts do not invariably lead to blind support.

Subcontracts are better suited for political targeting than prime contracts. There are only so many choice prime contracts to go around, but one prime contract can be divided into thousands of subcontracts, each of which can be used as an incentive or reward for an individual member. The selection of subcontractors, unlike prime contract source selections, is often affected by congressional pressure because primes have more discretion to respond favorably: "Congressmen will often argue that it is in the interest of national security to keep a particular supplier in business, even when he may not have been the low bidder. Such arguments, passed down to a prime contractor through the DOD from Congress, have considerable weight."[93] There is little doubt that DOD encourages this type of activity by its primes.

Subcontract spreading strategies are easy for prime contractors to implement. Apart from perhaps some production control or quality assurance problems—the kind that might require periodic visits from the prime—it makes little difference to a prime contractor in Connecticut whether a standard part is produced in New York, Texas, or California. Managing a distant sub is no more difficult than managing a local one. And since many smaller parts involved in military programs are standard, costs will not vary considerably. Subcontract targeting is an effective, low cost, and low risk strategy for ensuring a weapon system's political health.

Congressmen have more influence over subcontracts than they do over prime contracts because the rules, both formal and informal, that govern the two processes are different. Subcontracting activities are not subject to the same FAR constraints as prime contracting, and companies passed over for subcontracts generally cannot protest. Primes typically have a free hand in selecting subcontractors because they, not the Pentagon, make most subcontracting decisions. Subcontracts are, finally, much less visible, so they generate less national attention and controversy.

Despite the apparent ease and prevalence of subcontract targeting, it has been difficult to show that it occurs. The problem can be traced to the lack of information on subcontract location, as noted in chapter 2.

Subcontract data are likely to appear only when a program is in trouble in Congress. Then, the Pentagon and the prime contractor often assemble a list of subcontracts that details work done at the state or congressional district level. These data are circulated on the Hill, to impress upon members their economic interest in the program.

The analysis in this chapter uses such data to analyze four systems in detail: the B-1 bomber, the AH-64A Apache attack helicopter, the F-15A fighter, and the nuclear aircraft carriers described in chapter 5. Aggregated state-level subcontracting data on the B-2 bomber, the F-14 fighter, DIVAD, and the V-22 Osprey are subjected to less rigorous analysis. Using these data, we can answer the simple question of whether such targeting in fact occurs, and, if so, to what extent prime contractors use the strategy to help their programs survive the budget process.

COMMITTEE-CENTERED TARGETING

Consider first the possibility that prime contractors use their subcontracting discretion to strategically pick suppliers in districts represented on the military committees—a subcontracting version of the distributive hypothesis outlined in chapter 2. Just as prime contracts would presumably gain the attention of committee members and give them a motive as well as the ability to protect the program responsible, so too could subcontracts. By examining subcontracts in this way one can determine the seriousness of the measurement problems of prime contracts because it becomes possible to determine precisely where work is done. An indication that strategic subcontract targeting is occurring would be, as in the distributive hypothesis, the presence of higher levels of it in the districts of committee members than in those of nonmembers. Alternatively, members on the committees may be more likely to get any amount of subcontracts than are nonmembers.

District level data are available for nuclear aircraft carriers, the AH-64A helicopter, the F-15 fighter, and the Target Acquisition and Designation Sight/Pilot Night Vision Sensor (TADS/PNVS), the fire control system for the Apache. The two-way distribution for both committee members and nonmembers as well as the average amount of subcontracts in the districts of nonmembers, HASC members, and HADS members is given in table 6–1.

Evidence that the prime contractors targeted subcontracts to committee districts is strong only for the aircraft carrier program. Committee members were more likely to receive subcontracts than nonmembers and—at least those on the Armed Services Committee—more likely to receive higher dollar amounts. For the Apache program, the evidence is weaker: although members of the Defense Appropriations Subcommittee received more subcontracts than nonmembers, overall, committee members were less likely to have work for their districts than nonmembers.

The evidence is weaker still for the F-15 program, for which committee members not only were less likely than nonmembers to receive work, but also received smaller amounts of work for their districts. The average subcontract level in nonmember districts, $21 million, is high largely because one district in southern California received a $1.1 billion subcontract for Hughes Aircraft, manufacturer of the F-15's radar. If that award is eliminated as an outlier, nonmember districts average $15.5 million, still higher than award levels in committee members' districts.

These relationships between committee membership and subcontracting are interesting but inconclusive. The targeting of committee members is not, by any standard, a major factor influencing the location of subcontracts. Even for the aircraft carriers, the correlation between committee membership and subcontract levels may result from factors having little to do with politics.

MAXIMIZING THE GEOGRAPHIC SPREAD OF SUBCONTRACTS

One of the best programs to examine for evidence of strategic subcontract distribution is the B-1 bomber. The B-1 has had a long and labored history, surviving one cancellation, cost overruns, and technical snags. Critics have alleged from the program's inception that subcontracts have been spread over as wide an area as possible.[94] An air force officer involved with the B-1 admitted this, stating that "one major goal of the program was to distribute subcontracts throughout the country in a manner designed to produce the most votes in Congress."[95] Rockwell is alleged to have purposely subcontracted out major portions of the aircraft

Table 6-1
Committee-Centered Subcontract Targeting

CVN-74/75

	Subcontracts in District	No Subcontracts
Committee member	49	12
	(80%)	(20%)
Nonmember	261	113
	(70%)	(30%)
Total	310	125

	Average Subcontracting Level
Member of HASC	$16,027
Member of HADS	$ 6,494
Nonmember	$ 9,482

AH-64A Apache Helicopter

	Subcontracts in District	No Subcontracts
Committee member	36	25
	(59%)	(41%)
Nonmember	238	136
	(64%)	(36%)
Total	274	161

	Average Subcontracting Level
Member of HASC	$12,766
Member of HADS	$21,571
Nonmember	$13,657

F-15

	Subcontracts in District	No Subcontracts
Committee member	23	30
	(43%)	(57%)

Table 6-1
(continued)

Nonmember	214	168
	(56%)	(44%)
Total	237	198

	Average Subcontracting Level
Member of HASC	$ 9,063
Member of HADS	$ 2,074
Nonmember	$21,039

TADS/PNVS

	Subcontracts in District	No Subcontracts
Committee member	24	37
	(39%)	(61%)
Nonmember	151	223
	(40%)	(60%)
Total	175	260

	Average Subcontracting Level
Member of HASC	$1,169
Member of HADS	$1,144
Nonmember	$2,039

that it could have just as easily built itself; the idea, of course, was to increase the value of work done in other areas of the country.[96] The charge is heard often that the B-1 is spread out over three hundred congressional districts and forty-eight states.

Subcontract data, although dated, are available for the B-1A. In the mid-1970s, the Council on Economic Priorities prepared a report on the economic impact of the B-1 that included development and total program expenditures listed by state.[97]

Yet the mere existence of a broad distribution of subcontracts says nothing by itself; Rockwell may have had no choice but to subcontract in forty-eight states if necessary suppliers were located throughout the country. One must find some sort of control that will separate technologically required from politically motivated distributions. One way of doing this is to examine subcontracts for comparable commercial and military programs. Commercial programs will be unaffected by political calculations.[98] Civilian aerospace manufacturers will select their suppliers on the basis of price, quality, and delivery schedule; there is no reason to expect subcontract distributions to reflect anything but economic efficiency. Commercial programs, then, form a control group against which military programs can be measured. Substantially different distributions would support the hypothesis that political considerations affect the placing of military subcontracts. In table 6–2 are listed the percentage of subcontracts in each state for the B-1, together with supplier distribution data for two large commercial aircraft programs.[99] The B-1 data are adjusted to reflect only production expenditures, since the commercial data are for mature production programs. Using B-1 development expenditures, I estimated B-1 subcontracting levels in states with less than $1 million in subcontracts.[100]

By any measure, B-1 subcontracts are far more spread out than subcontracts for either of the commercial programs: 43.5 and 56.6 percent of the commercial subcontractors are in the same state as the final manufacturer. Only 28.5 percent of the B-1 work is done in Rockwell's home state, California. Commercial suppliers are located in fewer than half as many states (twenty-two and twenty-three) as B-1 suppliers.

Several measures of industrial concentration allow one to examine more closely the differences between the B-1 and the commercial aircraft programs. What is required is that each state be considered as one firm and that the percentage of subcontracts in a state be analytically equivalent to that firm's market share. The concentration ratio (Cn) is the percentage of work done (here the equivalent to market share) in the n largest states (firms), with larger values indicating more concentration. N can be any number, but the most common values are four, eight and ten: C4, or the ratio for the four largest states, is 0.662 for the B-1 and 0.799 and 0.890 for commercial programs A and B, respectively.

The concentration ratio is an imperfect measure of dispersion, though, since it ignores size differences among firms and is insensitive to the total number of firms in an industry.[101] A different indicator, called the Herfindahl index (H), attempts to correct for this. H is simply the sum of

Table 6-2
B-1A Bomber vs. Commercial Aircraft

	B-1A Bomber[a]			Commercial Program A			Commercial Program B	
State	% Tot	Cum %	State	% Tot	Cum %	State	% Tot	Cum %
CA	28.5%	28.5%	1	43.5%	43.5%	1	56.6%	56.6%
OH	18.5	47.0	2	13.8	57.3	2	13.4	70.0
WA	10.1	57.1	3	11.9	69.2	3	9.9	79.9
NY	9.1	66.2	4	10.7	79.9	4	9.1	89.0
NJ	4.3	70.5	5	5.8	85.7	5	3.6	92.6
OK	3.7	74.2	6	3.7	89.4	6	1.0	93.6
MD	3.5	77.7	7	2.0	91.4	7	0.9	94.5
KA	3.4	81.1	8	1.8	93.2	8	0.8	95.3
TN	2.8	83.9	9	1.3	94.5	9	0.6	95.9
TX	2.6	86.5	10	1.0	95.5	10	0.5	96.4
GA	2.2	88.7	11	0.8	96.3	11	0.5	96.9
MA	2.0	90.7	12	0.7	97.0	12	0.5	97.4
IL	1.5	92.2	13	0.5	97.5	13	0.5	97.9
FL	1.4	93.6	14	0.5	98.0	14	0.4	98.3
CT	1.1	94.7	15	0.5	98.5	15	0.4	98.7
MI	0.9	95.6	16	0.4	98.9	16	0.4	99.1
AZ	0.9	96.5	17	0.3	99.2	17	0.2	99.3
PA	0.6	97.1	18	0.3	99.5	18	0.2	99.5

Table 6-2
(continued)

	B-1A Bomber[a]			Commercial Program A			Commercial Program B	
State	**% Tot**	**Cum %**	**State**	**% Tot**	**Cum %**	**State**	**% Tot**	**Cum %**
IN	0.4	97.5	19	0.2	99.7	19	0.2	99.7
VT	0.4	97.9	20	0.1	99.8	20	0.1	99.8
UT	0.3	98.2	21	0.1	99.9	21	0.1	99.9
WI	0.3	98.5	22	0.1	100.0	22	0.1	100.0
OR	0.2	98.7	23	0.1	100.0			
CO	0.2	98.9						
IA	0.2	99.1			$H = 0.240$			$H = 0.358$
NH	0.2	99.3						
WV	0.1	99.4						
MI	0.1	99.5						
NM	0.1	99.6						
VA	0.1	99.7						
MN	0.1	99.8						
MO	0.1	99.9						
SD	0.1	100.0						
LA								
NC								
KY								

Table 6-2
(continued)

	B-1A Bomber[a]		Commercial Program A			Commercial Program B		
State	**% Tot**	**Cum %**	**State**	**% Tot**	**Cum %**	**State**	**% Tot**	**Cum %**
NE								
ID								
AL	Less than 0.1%							
HA								
RI								
NV								
DE								
MT								
AR								
SC								
ME								
ND								

$H = .143$

[a]Production only, excluding research and development.

the squares of the market share of every firm in an industry; it can take values between 1 (monopoly) and $1/n$ (n firms with identical market shares), with higher values again indicating more concentration. The Herfindal index values for the different programs show more clearly the dispersion of B-1 subcontracts: H for the B-1 program is 0.143, significantly smaller than the commercial program H's—0.240 for program A and 0.358 for program B.[102] Subcontracts for the B-1, then, are much more widely spread out than for the two commercial programs. Still, this does not prove that politics is driving the B-1's dispersion. The B-1 is obviously a more complicated system than even the most complex commercial aircraft. It has sophisticated equipment such as electronics jamming systems, air refueling equipment, and specialized avionics, none of which have any commercial analogue. The B-1 unit price is also substantially higher—about $280 million in 1987 dollars—than the most expensive commercial planes (the 747–400 costs approximately $125 million). The level of complexity, not political considerations, might be driving the spread of suppliers.

The argument that the B-1s' subcontract spread is due to the system's complexity is based on the simple and plausible assumption that complexity and geographic spread are related. As the following discussion shows, though, there is in fact very little evidence to support such a judgment. Most weapons systems are widely distributed over a large number of congressional districts and states regardless of how complex or expensive they are. The Apache and F-15, for example, are far less complicated in terms of engineering complexity, cost, and number of parts than a ninety-thousand-ton aircraft carrier. Yet the distribution of suppliers is similar for the three systems. Aircraft carrier suppliers are located in 310 congressional districts, 30 percent more districts than F-15 subcontractors (237), and 13 percent more districts than Apache subcontractors (274). Bear in mind that the unit cost of a carrier is approximately $3.5 billion, two orders of magnitude greater than either of the other two systems. Differences in complexity cannot explain such geographic spreading.

The B-1 is much more widely dispersed than even the B-2 bomber, a system more analogous than commercial aircraft. Although the B-2 is spread out over nearly as many states (forty-six) as the B-1, suppliers are much more concentrated in several key states: California, Washington (where major prime Boeing works on the wing), Texas (location of major prime LTV), and Ohio. The Herfindahl value for the B-2 is 0.409, which indicates that nothing inherent in building military bombers requires a low concentration of suppliers. On the B-1 program, something other than technical necessity is driving geographic dispersion. Rockwell, with either active assistance or tacit approval from the air force, purposely spread the work to give as many areas of the country as possible a stake in the program. A similar strategy was probably used on the B-2 as well: $32 billion in subcontracts will go to California, which probably had suppliers capable of producing whatever the air force bought for $200,000 or less in Kentucky, Mississippi, Nebraska, Nevada, and West Virginia.

The relationship between complexity and the number of states involved for nine weapons systems, ranging from the relatively simple TADS/PNVS (about $1.5 million each) to the monstrously complex B-2 bomber (program unit cost of $568 million, assuming the original 132-unit buy), is shown in figure 6–1.[103] Here, unit cost is used as an indicator of complexity. While the simpler systems are spread out over fewer states than the most complex, the differences are relatively small. The B-2 is spread out over forty-six states, fewer states than the F-14 fighter, the V-22 Osprey, the F-15, and the B-1. Fitting a least-squares regression line—the solid line in figure 6–1—shows that the number of states involved in a program shoots upward rapidly and flattens after unit costs reach about $30 million. Even the tiniest defense program, if these data are representative, would be widely spread: according to this simple model, an item worth $1 million would have suppliers in more than thirty states.

The state subcontracting totals for five of the systems analyzed in this chapter are shown in table 6–3. All fifty states are involved in one capacity or another on the programs, even though some states receive very little work (North Dakota received only about $13,000 total from all five). Subcontract spreading strategies have effectively distributed the economic benefits of defense work across the entire country. There can be little doubt that these wide distributions are intentional. The state distribution of subcontracts shows that most systems have a long tail; that is, a few states do most of the work, and a large number of states receive relatively small awards. One explanation for this is that prime contrac-

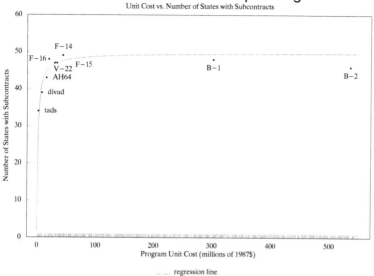

6-1

State Distribution of Defense Subcontracts

tors have only limited flexibility in choosing subcontractors for major systems. Only two companies, Hughes Aircraft Company and Westinghouse, for example, are capable of building aircraft radar systems; they face no competition from companies in Wyoming or South Carolina. Landing gear, flight control systems, castings, and other complex systems are similarly available from only a small number of companies that are probably located near major centers of defense contracting: southern California, New York, Seattle, San Francisco.

One explanation for the tail of states doing small amounts of work is that prime contractors spread smaller subcontracts as much as possible. Since these subcontracts will consist of work on the simpler parts of major programs, more firms will be capable of doing the work and the prime will have more discretion over whom to choose. At the smallest level of work, thousands of firms might be available, including some located in areas not already covered by the larger subcontractors.

Some support for this thesis comes from the detailed subcontracting data for the Apache helicopter. Martin Marietta Orlando Aerospace

Table 6-3
State Subcontract Totals—State Listing/Subcontracts Only (thousand $)

State	AH-64A	Carrier	F-15[a]	B-1A[b]	B-2[c]
Alabama	$9,382	$800	$43,290	$1,110	$4,000
Alaska					
Arizona	$60,112	$4,132	$278,982	$203,000	$206,500
Arkansas	$18,522		$1,295	$38	$1,400
Calif.	$1,304,860	$460,384	$2,381,533	$7,317,000	$32,100,000
Colo.	$1,249	$13,248	$7,769	$45,000	$204,300
Conn.	$230,000	$86,168	$119,972	$251,000	$182,000
Delaware	$4,071	$2,060	$19	$76	$5,800
Florida	$463,563	$15,488	$11,506	$319,000	$60,500
Georgia	$54,955	$2,818	$24,021	$489,000	$25,300
Hawaii		$54		$1,095	
Idaho		$4	$0[d]	$1,330	$3,200
Illinois	$140,298	$95,054	$128,859	$343,000	$670,600
Indiana	$111,167	$38,427	$20,425	$89,000	$6,300
Iowa	$48,140	$5,246	$72,168	$41,000	$159,300
Kansas	$1,675	$6	$17,737	$759,000	$22,400
Kentucky	$12,927	$2,224	$25	$1,714	$100
Louisiana		$4,486	$4,101	$2,685	$1,200
Maine	$161	$80		$8	$3,900

Table 6-3
(continued)

State	AH-64A	Carrier	F-15[a]	B-1A[b]	B-2[c]
Maryland	$6,953	$79,208	$6,845	$793,000	$51,700
Mass.	$331,004	$169,799	$257,591	$446,000	$233,900
Michigan	$36,874	$55,094	$147,174	$215,000	$58,800
Minn.	$113,997	$21,959	$277,955	$26,000	$330,500
Miss.	$5,462	$1,555	$8	$35,000	$200
Missouri	$1,514	$5,997	$96,403	$17,000	$31,700
Montana			$1	$46	$4,000
Nebraska	$977	$56	$510	$1,361	$200
Nevada	$12	$1	$47	$114	$200
N.H.	$11,758	$1,225	$4,071	$36,000	$3,400
New Jersey	$222,686	$93,115	$490,877	$972,000	$198,600
New Mexico	$83,695	$9	$33	$31,000	$279,500
New York	$105,414	$273,082	$539,806	$2,040,000	$1,100,000
N. Carolina	$3,677	$5,103	$7,754	$2,474	$4,700
N. Dakota			$5	$8	
Ohio	$119,721	$339,544	$630,135	$4,421,000	$904,300
Oklahoma	$2,702	$4,032	$11,365	$830,000	$700
Oregon	$36,221	$461	$8,123	$57,000	$26,000
Penn.	$68,206	$670,257	$34,588	$139,000	$45,000

Table 6-3
(continued)

State	AH-64A	Carrier	F-15[a]	B-1A[b]	B-2[c]
Rhode I.	$6,309	$1,119	$125	$1,025	$500
S. Carolina	$431	$5,056	$29	$23	$4,100
S. Dakota	$336		$10	$5,166	$300
Tennessee	$7,836	$148,017	$26,465	$642,000	$6,200
Texas	$26,388	$16,624	$121,944	$599,000	$5,300,000
Utah	$22,946	$1,567	$37	$64,000	$16,900
Vermont	$3,540	$1,725	$104,211	$82,000	$3,200
Virginia	$11,965	$487,415	$11,070	$29,000	$140,500
Washington	$9,329	$9,679	$23,912	$2,279,000	$11,600,000
Wash. DC		$463	$12	$198	$300
W. Virginia	$3,391	$2,254	$2,682	$34,000	$20
Wisconsin	$42,678	$30,621	$17,665	$60,000	$54,100
Wyoming			$15		
TOTAL	$3,747,104	$3,155,716	$5,941,776	$23,721,469	$54,056,320
H Value	0.159	0.118	0.204	0.154	0.409

[a]1981 buy only, converted to 1987 dollars.
[b]Entire program, including research and development; totals in 1976 dollars.
[c]Estimates for 132-unit buy.
[d]Total is $71.

builds the TADS/PNVS system and subcontracted to hundreds of firms throughout the country for parts and subcomponents. To manage the supplier network, Martin created a loose confederation of companies that it called Martin Marietta Subtier Suppliers (MMSS); the Apache subcontractor report lists award levels to each congressional district involved in the TADS/PNVS program: they range from $77 million to firms in the Orlando area to $2,000 in Maine's second congressional district. Martin awarded a total of $335 million to its suppliers, assuming a program buy of 593 Apaches.

The geographic spread of TADS/PNVS suppliers is astonishing. Martin Marietta awarded second-tier subcontracts to MMSS offices in 175 congressional districts in 34 states. More important, in 54 of those districts, the award was the district's only involvement in the Apache program; no other subcontracts were awarded. One-fifth of the Apache's overall distribution is due to these single-award districts, which increased the program's coverage from 220 to 274 congressional districts.

The average TADS/PNVS subcontract was $1.9 million, which suggests that the work involved was simple. There is little reason to suspect that only a few companies were capable of doing the work or that the subcontracts would have to go to a specific company or location. These awards might be used to locate work in areas not already involved in the Apache program, thus expanding the number of congressional districts with an economic stake. In fact, the single-award districts received an average of $1.2 million, or about one-half the $2.2 million awarded to districts that received both TADS and other Apache subcontracts. Many of the single-award districts are in states and areas not normally associated with defense contracts: Alabama, Georgia, Kansas, Missouri, Oklahoma, to give a few examples. These districts tended to receive the less complicated subcontracts, those that involved routine work requiring fewer specialized skills and that hence were more easily spread out.

Prime contractors, then, use less complex work to drive the number of states and congressional districts involved in any program higher. Once the major subcontractors have been chosen for avionics, landing gear, computers, and other critical systems, the prime has much more leeway in selecting suppliers for simple electrical components, connectors, standard military hardware, and other small and inexpensive items. Surely the prime could as easily have bought these parts in southern

California as in Oklahoma or Iowa. The political value of doing so, however, is marginal. A $1 million subcontract in a district otherwise uninvolved in a weapons program is more noticeable than the same award in a district with twenty other subcontractors already doing $500 million in business with the prime.

Congress exercises substantial influence over the defense contracting process but not in the ways most people suspect. Members cannot force the Pentagon to manipulate the source selection process to benefit particular firms, even though they often pretend they can. Funding advocacy is far more common and effective; members can channel money to specific programs and firms simply by adding more money to the budget than DOD requested. An even more effective way of protecting local interests is to insert restrictive language into the annual authorization bill, a technique most often designed to prevent the Pentagon from taking action—for example, second sourcing or investigating alternative ways of accomplishing the same mission—that would jeopardize existing interests.

Yet to characterize all such instances of congressional action as parochially motivated would be a mistake. No doubt those concerns are important to some legislators, but as the F-14 and M-1 examples demonstrated, nonparochial concerns often overshadow the economic effects. Many defense decisions, especially those on larger programs, would have been the same even if no economic benefits had been involved.

More important, identifying Congress as the sole culprit in allowing politics to intrude into contracting decisions is misleading. As chapter 3 showed, much of what occurs in DOD is political in the sense that competing interests fight for limited resources. The procurement decisions that emerge—what weapons to buy, how many to buy—do not form a rational list of priorities that Congress proceeds to contaminate with its own parochial concerns. What Congress does, and what DOD and prime contractors do in anticipation thereof, merely continues the process started when a military service initiates a program.

The wide geographic spread of work on weapons systems is no accident. Even though political subcontract targeting strategies are not foolproof—they could not save DIVAD and probably will be unable to preserve the B-2—contractors believe they are effective: strategic spreading makes it easier both to mobilize support from around the country and to gain access to legislators' attention and time. Given the huge stakes involved, contractors will seek any means available to protect their projects from the vicissitudes of congressional whim. Even if the results are not guaranteed, the strategy is inexpensive (both politically and economically) and easily implemented. Defense contractors do not like to take chances.

Do subcontract targeting strategies affect the quality of weapons? Probably not. No prime will purposely sacrifice quality in order to increase a program's geographic spread. If a weapon system does not work, the prime contractor will be criticized regardless of how many congressional districts have subcontracts. Program spreading more usually involves choices among several firms, each equally capable of producing less complicated components. Yet the B-1 example shows that contractors are willing, apparently, to sacrifice economic efficiency for political gain. There is simply no evidence that the program had to be spread out as widely as it was; this, combined with allegations that Rockwell subcontracted parts of the plane it could have built itself, at least raises the possibility that problems with the aircraft were related not to technology but to program management decisions made on the basis of politics.

Subcontract spreading is closely related to a new phenomenon in defense contracting called teaming. On many new programs such as the ATF, two or more prime contractors work together as team partners. Teaming is usually done for technical reasons when programs like the ATF involve large technical and financial risks that a single contractor might be unwilling to take on its own. On the ATF program, for example, the competing teams will spend hundreds of millions of dollars of their own money in building prototypes; a single firm would be unable to make such an investment. But teaming has several desirable political consequences. First, it allows fewer programs to sustain more companies, which in turn enables the Pentagon to preserve the industrial base when there are fewer major programs available. Second, it can increase a program's odds of political survivability, since cancellation would involve multiple major primes instead of one, and possibly multiple supplier networks. This increased economic and political visibility is unlikely to go unnoticed in Congress: "A single company . . . can already exert tremendous pressure on the U.S. Congress to keep its program alive. But when two or three giants work together on a program, such as Lockheed, Boeing, and General Dynamics on ATF, the lobbying power is likely to be awesome."[104]

CHAPTER 6. CONGRESSIONAL INFLUENCE IN DEFENSE CONTRACTING

1. U.S. Congress, Committee on Government Operations, Report of the Permanent Subcommittee on Investigations, *TFX Contract Investigation,* 1970.

2. Robert J. Art, *The TFX Decision: McNamara and the Military* (Boston: Little, Brown, 1968).

3. Interviews conducted by the author. Also, Terry J. Miller, "The Interaction between the Private, Public, and Third Sector in the Defense Contract Award Process: Lobbying for Defense Contracts in Los Angeles County 1951–1972" (Ph.D. diss., University of Southern California, 1980), 180.

4. Richard Stubbing, *The Defense Game* (New York: Harper and Row, 1986), 169.

5. Miller, "Lobbying for Defense Contracts in Los Angeles County," 105–06.

6. Merton J. Peck and Frederick M. Scherer, *The Weapons Acquisition Process: An Economic Analysis* (Boston: Division of Research, Graduate School of Business Administration, Harvard University,, 1962), and Frederick M. Scherer, *The Weapons Acquisition Process: Economic Incentives* (Boston: Division of Research, Graduate School of Business Administration, Harvard University, 1964).

7. Peck and Scherer, *The Weapons Acquisition Process,* 114.

8. Ibid., 382.

9. J. Ronald Fox, *Arming America: How the U.S. Buys Weapons* (Boston Division of Research, Graduate School of Business Administration, Harvard University, 1974).

10. Ibid., 281.

11. The GAO publishes a guide on how to protest contract awards. See General Accounting Office, *Bid Protests at GAO: A Descriptive Guide,* 2d ed., 1985.

12. Contractors do avail themselves of their protest rights. In FY 1987 the GAO reported that 1,783 protests were lodged with the GAO bid protest office by contractors doing business with DOD. Of these, 1,276 were either withdrawn or dismissed prior to adjudication. Of the remaining 487 cases, 57 were sustained in favor of the contractor (General Accounting Office, *Bid Protest Report,* OGC/B-158766, January 31, 1987).

13. "Ill Wind," *Aviation Week Space Technology,* September 18, 1989, 19.

14. Fox, *Arming America,* 269.

15. Ibid., 266.

16. Miller, "Lobbying for Defense Contracts in Los Angeles County," 149.

17. Peck and Scherer, *The Weapons Acquisition Process,* 383.

18. Craig Liske and Barry Rundquist, *The Politics of Weapons Procurement: The Role of Congress* (Denver: University of Denver Social Science Foundation and Graduate School of International Studies, Monograph Series in World Affairs, vol. 12, no. 1, 1974–75), 83.

19. R. Douglas Arnold, *Congress and the Bureaucracy* (New Haven: Yale University Press, 1979), 108–09.

20. James M. Perry, "Full Speed Ahead: Budget Deficit or No, Navy Builds a Port for Every Battleship," *Wall Street Journal,* June 15, 1989, 1.

21. Michael Weisskopf, "Navy Port Proliferation Criticized as Politics, Not Strategy," *Washington Post,* August 12, 1985, A7.

22. Ibid.

23. Charlotte Twight, "Institutional Underpinnings of Parochialism: The Case of Military Base Closures," *Cato Journal* 9, no. 1 (Spring/Summer 1989): 83.

24. Quoted in Twight, "Institutional Underpinnings of Parochialism," 86.

25. Fred Kaplan, "Weinberger Lists Three Facilities to Shut," *Boston Globe,* February 13, 1986, 3.

26. Ibid.

27. Helen Dewar, "Hill Sees Political Harm in Base Closings," *Washington Post,* January 31, 1990, A8.

28. Democratic Study Group, *The Great Base Closing Ploy,* Report No. 101–29, March 24, 1990, Appendix, table 3.

29. Ibid., 10.

30. Dewar, "Hill Sees Political Harm in Base Closings," A8.

31. Twight, "Institutional Underpinnings of Parochialism," 78.

32. See General Accounting Office, *Military Bases: An Analysis of the Commission's Realignment and Closure Recommendations* (GAO/NSIAD-90–42), November 1989.

33. Don Phillips, "86 Military Facilities To Be Shut," *Washington Post,* April 19, 1989, 1.

34. Matthew Purdy, "Congress Votes Cuts at Fort Dix," *Philadelphia Inquirer,* April 19, 1989, 1.

35. Peck and Scherer, *The Weapons Acquisition Process,* 113.

36. Quoted in J. Ronald Fox, *The Defense Management Challenge: Weapons Acquistion* (Boston: Harvard Business School Press, 1988), 93.

37. *Congressional Record,* August 3, 1970, 26960.

38. Interview conducted by the author.

39. Interviews conducted by the author. Also, Fox, *Arming America,* 281.

40. Clarence Danhof, *Government Contracting and Technological Change* (Washington, D.C.: Brookings Institution, 1968), 216.

41. Peck and Scherer, *The Weapons Acquisition Process,* 381.

42. John Fauber and James Rowen, "The Aspin Institute: Politics of Defense," *Milwaukee Journal,* December 4, 1988, 1.

43. Miller, "Lobbying for Defense Contracts in Los Angeles County," 141.

44. Robert Higgs, "Hard Coals Make Bad Laws: Congressional Parochialism vs. National Defense," *Cato Journal* 8, no. 1 (Spring/Summer 1988).

45. Ibid., 80.

46. Walter S. Mossberg, "Pork Barrel Politics: Some Congressmen Treat Military Budget as a Source for Patronage," *Wall Street Journal,* April 15, 1983, 22.

47. Interview conducted by the author.

48. Patrick J. Sloyan, "Les Aspin Brings Home Bacon to Wisconsin," *Minneapolis Star-Tribune,* June 19, 1989, 2; Les Aspin, "Why Doesn't Bush Want Trucks?" *Milwaukee Sentinel,* November 2, 1988, 18.

49. Mossberg, "Pork Barrel Politics," 22, emphasis added.

50. Rone Tempest, "U.S. Defense Establishment Wields a Pervasive Power," *Los Angeles Times,* July 10, 1983, part IV, p. 1, and Mossberg, "Pork Barrel Politics," 1.

51. Statement of Richard Stubbing, Office of Management and Budget, in U.S. Congress, Committee on the Budget, *Review of Defense Acquisition and Management,* 98th Congress, 1st Session, 1983, 564.

52. *Congressional Record,* July 20, 1983, H-5302.

53. Brooks Jackson, "Avco Corp. Makes Judicious Use of Gifts to U.S. Congressmen," *Wall Street Journal,* October 13, 1983, 1.

54. *Washington Post,* August 10, 1983, A21.

55. Dan Daniel and William L. Dickinson, "The Great Tank Engine War of 1983," *Armed Forces Journal International* (September 1983): 30.

56. Ibid., 31. Also see U.S. Congress, House Committee on Armed Services, *Department of Defense Authorization of Appropriations for Fiscal Year 1984,* part 3, 1661–62.

57. Testimony of Justin P. White, Jr., in U.S. Congress, House Committee on Armed Services, *Department of Defense Authorization of Appropriations for Fiscal Year 1985,* part 2, 939.

58. Daniel and Dickinson, "The Great Tank Engine War of 1983," 38.

59. Charles W. Stevens, "Grumman Vows Dogfight in Bid to Save F-14 Output, Slated by Pentagon to End," *Wall Street Journal,* 21 April 1989, A3.

60. James Bernstein, "F-14 Cut From Budget," *Long Island Newsday,* April 26, 1989, 5.

61. See "Porky Politics," *Air Force Times,* July 17, 1989, 21.

62. Mike Mills, "Hill Friends Fighting to Save Endangered Fighter Jet," *Congressional Quarterly Weekly Report,* May 27, 1989, 1268.

63. Department of Defense, *Department of Defense Budget for Fiscal Years 1990 and 1991, Procurement Programs (P-1),* January 9, 1989, p. N-3.

64. "Funding for New F-14s Preserves Grumman Option for Tomcat 21," *Defense Daily,* June 7, 1989, 25.

65. David C. Morrison, "Warning Shot," *National Journal,* October 10, 1989, 2449.

66. See "US ATF Problems," *Armed Forces Journal International* (March 1989): 24; James W. Rawles, "ATF Program Faces Tough Challenges," *Defense Electronics* (September 1987); General Accounting Office, *Aircraft Development: The Advanced Tactical Fighter's Cost, Schedule, and Performance Goals* (GAO/NSIAD-88–76), January 1988.

67. "Navy ATF to Show Only 60% Commonality with AF Version," *Navy News and Undersea Technology,* June 26, 1989, 1.

68. On the navy's attitude toward joint aircraft programs, see Art, *The TFX Decision,* 39–44.

69. See G. Philip Hughes, "Congressional Influence in Weapons Procurement: The Case of Lightweight Fighter Commonality," *Public Policy* 28, no. 4 (Fall 1980).

70. "Navy ATF to Show Only 60% Commonality with AF Version," 1.

71. David S. Steigman, "Advanced AF Fighter Needs Major Changes for Navy," *Navy Times,* June 11, 1990, 27.

72. See G. K. Smith et al., *The Use of Prototypes in Weapon System Development,* (Santa Monica: RAND Corporation, R-2345-AF, March 1981).

73. The ten-thousand-pound estimate is from Morrison, "Warning Shot," 2452; the GAO puts the additional weight at four thousand pounds. See Steigman, "Advanced AF Fighter Needs Major Changes for Navy," 27.

74. Morrison, "Warning Shot," 2452.

75. Nick Cook, "Tomcat 21 Fights for Survival," *Jane's Defence Weekly,* July 15, 1989, 83.

76. Stephanie Saul, "F-14 Surplus Predicted," *Long Island Newsday,* May 7, 1989, 3.

77. "Secret Long-Range Aviation Plan Undermines F-14 Lobbying Effort," *Inside the Navy,* May 8, 1989, 2.

78. Mills, "Hill Friends Fighting to Save Endangered Fighter Jet," 1271.

79. Robert Holzer, "A-12 Woes Prompt New Look at Intruder," *Defense News,* July 23, 1990, 1; John D. Morocco, "Navy Weighs Alternatives after Cheney Kills A-12," *Aviation Week & Space Technology,* January 14, 1991, 20.

80. Anthony L. Velocci, "A-12 Cancellation Could Bring Bonus Contract for Grumman F-14," *Aviation Week & Space Technology,* January 14, 1991, 22.

81. Interview conducted by the author.

82. "New York Legislators Ask for Fairchild Reprieve," *Aviation Week & Space Technology,* September 9, 1985, 18.

83. Rowan Scarborough, "Trainer's Fans Switch Strategies," *Defense Week,* June 16, 1986, 16.

84. "Senate Votes to Scrap T-46," *New York Times*, May 19, 1986, D5.

85. John R. Cushman Jr., "Panel Acts to Revive Air Force Jet Produced on L.I.," *New York Times,* June 26, 1986, A24, and Jonathan Fuerbringer, "House Moves to Retain Trainer Jet Made on L.I.," *New York Times,* August 12, 1986, A21.

86. David C. Morrison, "Chaos on Capitol Hill," *National Journal,* September 27, 1986, 2305.

87. Twight, "Institutional Underpinnings of Parochialism," 92.

88. See David Mayhew, *Congress: The Electoral Connection* (New Haven: Yale University Press, 1974).

89. Michael R. Gordon, "Are Military Contractors Part of the Problem or Part of the Solution?" *National Journal,* July 11, 1981, 1234. Also interviews conducted by the author.

90. Interview conducted by the author.

91. Les Aspin, "The Defense Budget and Foreign Policy: The Role of Congress," *Daedalus* 104, no. 3 (Summer 1975): 156.

92. Liske and Rundquist, *The Politics of Weapons Procurement,* 82.

93. Jacques Gansler, *The Defense Industry* (Cambridge: MIT Press, 1980), 150.

94. Kotz, *Wild Blue Yonder*; Bill Keller, "In Bull Market for Arms, Weapons Industry Lobbyists Push Products, Not Policy," *Congressional Quarterly,* October 25, 1980, 3206.

95. Liske and Rundquist, *The Politics of Weapons Procurement,* 82.

96. Kotz, *Wild Blue Yonder: Money, Politics, and the B-1 Bomber* (New York: Pantheon Books, 1988), 128–29.

97. The report is reprinted in *Congressional Record,* May 17, 1976, 14141–44.

97. The report is reprinted in *Congressional Record,* May 17, 1976, pp. 14141–44.

98. Interviews with industry personnel revealed at least one instance in which a major commercial manufacturer was pressured by state political authorities to buy parts from particular firms. The request was ignored because the company did not have to worry about the political ramifications of its decisions.

99. Data for the commercial programs were provided on the condition that neither the manufacturers nor the programs be identified. State names are coded to prevent identification of the manufacturers' main plant location.

100. For these smaller states, the dollar total was calculated by (1) regressing total expenditures on development expenditures (which were provided for all states) and (2) multiplying development expenditures by the resulting regression coefficient for the small dollar states. This calculation did not appreciably change the overall distribution percentages.

101. See Stephen Davies, "Choosing between Concentration Indices: The Iso-Concentration Curve," *Economica* 46 (February 1979): 67.

102. The Herfindahl index is not without its detractors, and there is a lively debate about how best to measure industrial concentration. For the purposes here, though, even approximate indices will suffice. See ibid. and Stephen Davies, "Measuring Industrial Concentration: An Alternative Approach," *Review of Economics and Statistics* 62, no. 2 (May 1980): 306–09.

103. State and cost data are from the following sources: TADS (thirty-seven states, $1.5 million unit cost) and Apache (forty-four states, $11.5 million), McDonnell Douglas cost data; DIVAD (thirty-nine states, $6.7 million), unpublished map devised by Westinghouse Corporation, shown in Project on Military Procurement, *Defense Procurement Papers, Campaign '88* (September 1988), 70, cost data from September 1983 Selected Acquistion Report estimate of $4.159 billion and 618 units; F-16 fighter (forty-eight states, $20 million), Simon, *Top Guns,* 33, and December 31, 1987, Selected Acquisition Report; V-22 (forty-seven states, $30 million), Richard H. P. Sia, "Determined Backers Fight to Get Endangered Osprey off Ground," *Baltimore Sun,* May 3, 1989, 3; F-15 (forty-seven states, $35 million), McDonnell Douglas data and December 31, 1987 SAR; F-14 (forty-nine states, $43.5 million), Pat Wechsler, "Grumman Facing Uphill Fight," *Long Island Newsday,* April 27, 1989, 7, cost data from September 1987 SAR and *DMS Market Intelligence Report* (1988); B-1 (forty-eight states, $300 million), see text, state allocation based on author's calculations, Kenneth R. Mayer, "The Politics and Economics of Defense Contracting," (Ph.D. diss., Yale University, 1989), 250; B-2 (forty-six states, $530 million), Northrop Corporation 1989 Annual Report, "B-2 Estimate Settles at $70 Billion Plus; Cheney Backs Program," *Aerospace Daily,* June 6, 1989, 380.

104. Greg Waskul, "Is Teaming Good for You?" *Interavia* (April 1987): 328.

Elections, the Economy, and Defense Contract Awards

I think we can use defense contracts to strengthen the economy as well as strengthen the country. . . . We will try to distribute defense contracts fairly so that it protects the United States and protects the economy.
—John F. Kennedy

The timing of defense contracts can be as important as their placement, particularly since DOD has more discretion in deciding when to award contracts than where they will go. By awarding contracts at politically opportune times, DOD can create goodwill in Congress, advance the political interests of incumbent presidents, and ease the consequences of economic downturns. Strategically timed contract awards are a manifestation of the political business cycle, which predicts that governments will time the allocation of government benefits or the specific application of economic policies to stimulate economic activity just before elections. To improve the economy's performance during election periods, government will, the theory predicts, dump transfer payments into the electorate, lower interest rates, and do anything else it can to provide jobs and put money into voters' pockets. Voters, the thinking goes, are unlikely to turn out such benefactors.

Defense contracts constitute an attractive instrument of such a strategy because of their economic consequences. Contracts mean jobs, and happily employed constituents are valuable to incumbents at election time. As tens of billions of dollars are involved, defense contracts can also serve the less immediate function of delaying recessions or counteracting high unemployment.

Electorally timed contracts generate noneconomic benefits as well. Contract award announcements are almost always followed by proclamations from legislators, who graciously and humbly accept responsibility for having made everything possible. Credit claiming is a prized side benefit, and its value rises in direct proportion to the closeness of election day.

Without question, there is an electoral cycle in U.S. defense contract awards, as the Pentagon awards between $2 and $6 billion additional prime contracts in the two months preceding presidential and congressional elections. There is less compelling support for the proposition that the government uses prime contracts as a countercyclical economic tool. Although countercyclical patterns are clear for the 1950–65 period, the growth since the mid-1960s of nondefense economic policy tools (primarily transfer payments and other social programs) has rendered defense spending less important as a way of responding to short-term economic conditions. Because a huge acceleration in contract awards would be needed to affect national economic conditions significantly, the value of aptly timed contract awards appears to be primarily political, with economic stimulation more of a subsidiary benefit. Thus contracts are less useful in counteracting economic downturns than they are in raising the political stock of incumbents.

Political-Business Cycles and Defense-Electoral Cycles

The question of politically timed defense contracts has two parts. One possibility is that the government uses contracts countercyclically to mitigate the effects of recessions and spur economic recovery. Another is that contracts are used as an explicitly electoral tool to make spending levels rise just before elections in order to stimulate the economy and improve incumbents' election-day prospects.

Previous research into these questions has attempted to tie changes in the annual defense budget to both changes in the macroeconomy and the timing of elections. The results are mixed. Some scholars detect evidence of electoral or economic cycles in annual U.S. defense spending levels, with budgets increasing in election years or when the economy is in recession. Others dispute the political argument[1] or find alternative explanations for the observed phenomena entirely adequate.[2] The broader question of whether there is, in fact, evidence of political-business cycles in any type of government economic or benefits policy is also in dispute. Although the theory that governments will tinker with economic policy is persuasive, the empirical results are ambiguous at best. Investigations of monetary policy, fiscal policy, transfer payments, and nearly every other possible candidate for manipulation have found little systematic evidence of electoral cycles.[3] And even when such cycles are detected, the conclusion is often that they make little difference. William Keech and Kyoungsan Pak studied electoral cycles in quarterly levels of veterans' benefit payments and concluded that "electoral cycles may exist in certain programs at certain times, but . . . such cycles are not an important general political phenomenon."[4]

The major problem with the political-business cycle literature is the difficulty in finding appropriate policy instruments. Such instruments, if they are to be used to manipulate the economy, must be controllable by incumbents and have swift and predictable economic effects. Major elements of fiscal policy are neither controllable nor swift: the budget cycle is cumbersome and colossally slow in showing demonstrable changes in the economy. Most transfer payments (welfare, retirement, and health care programs) are no longer controllable, as indexing has made both the size and the timing of increases automatic.[5] Monetary policy, which is controlled by the Federal Reserve Board, is insulated from day-to-day politics, and the board works hard to stay out of partisan skirmishes over its policies. "Even if presidents wish to use monetary policy to create a PBC [political business cycle]," Nathaniel Beck writes, "they are in no position to command the Fed to do anything."[6]

Most studies of the political-economic use of defense spending suffer from similar problems: research has yet to specify an instrument of defense spending that meets the criteria of control and quick, predictable effects. Furthermore, not all forms of defense spending are equivalent; some are more amenable to manipulation than others, and some are altogether uncontrollable. Budget authority, obligations, and outlays are not interchangeable, and neither are military pay and procurement accounts. They measure different quantities and are subject to varying degrees of timing discretion. This is a critical distinction because in devising a plausible model of how defense spending is used to political or electoral ends, one must show how such decisions can be implemented.

The contradictory results of research into whether there are in fact electoral cycles in defense spending are in large part due to an exclusive focus on annual levels of defense spending as the dependent variable. Although the yearly defense budget does change in response to long-term domestic economic and political trends, it cannot be manipulated quickly enough to produce the timely response required of electoral or Keynesian fiscal instruments. Three characteristics of the defense budget process make this clear.

First, the process is too long. Over two years elapse between the time the Joint Chiefs make their initial spending requests and final congressional action (assuming Congress approves the budget before the fiscal year begins, something it did only three times between 1953 and 1984).[7] Budget planning by DOD for FY 1988 (which began in October 1987) started in October 1985, sixteen months before the president formally submitted his total budget package in February 1987.

Even if the president could foresee future political or economic events that might call for budget tweaking, he could not be sure that the budget would ultimately reflect his own policy desires. Many different organizations and actors influence the final form of the defense budget; far from representing presidential fiat, the budget is the result of complicated bargaining among the individual services and various departments within OSD, OMB, Congress, and the White House itself. Some actors may share the president's political agenda, but there are no guarantees. Even within the Reagan administration, which was hardly hostile to the idea of increasing defense spending, DOD and OMB clashed over budget levels. Though OMB director David Stockman shared the goal of increasing spending levels, he began to worry about mounting deficits and as early as 1981 was pushing for defense budgets smaller than those Secretary of Defense Weinberger advocated.[8]

Congress's role in the budget procedure presents even greater obstacles. Since the mid-1970s, when Congress began picking over the budget in detail (as described in chapter 2), the president has generally been unable to get the budget through unscathed. Although Congress may share the president's desire to induce an electoral cycle (especially if the same party controls both branches), there is little reason to expect such movements to be consistent over time. Strategic concerns, moreover, play a larger role in determining the level of defense spending than many would like to admit: "Intended changes in military expenditures, and especially substantial changes, can only be explained by international developments and by foreign policy and strategic orientations or moods."[9]

Second, major parts of the defense budget are invulnerable to manipulation. Personnel expenditures, for example, are relatively uncontrollable; they are determined by the number of people in uniform, their distribution in rank, and salary levels, all of which are fairly stable from year to year (the pay budget and force levels alone are highly correlated, with $r = 0.92$). Manipulating this account would require changes in overall force levels or pay structure—an implausible instrument for short-term manipulation. Merely showing, as some have tried,[10] that aggregate personnel expenditures vary with elections means nothing unless these underlying factors change at the same time. If they do not, the relationships found must be spurious.

Third, the economic effects of one year's defense budget are delayed until well after the budget cycle for one year has concluded. Few jobs are created until money is actually obligated, a phase that may lag behind budget adoption by as much as five years.[11] Shipbuilding accounts, for example, which constitute a significant part of the budget—$10.8 billion in 1986 and $10.2 billion in 1987—normally experience a five-year lag.[12] Obligation rates for different categories of the defense budget are shown in table 7–1; the rates indicate that less than three-fourths of procurement funds are actually obligated in the year in which they are budgeted, and a sizable portion of that is obligated only during the last month of the fiscal year (see below). Outlays, or actual expenditures of

Table 7-1

Obligation and Outlay Rates, 1987–91, of Funds in the 1987 Defense Budget

Obligations	% Obligated in				
	FY87	FY88	FY89	FY90	FY91
All procurement	73	16	10	0.5	2
Shipbuilding	55	17	6	4	17
R&D	92	8			
Outlays	% Expended in				
	FY87	FY88	FY89	FY90	FY91
All procurement	15	30	27	14	1
Shipbuilding	6	17	20	21	15
Personnel	94	6			

Source: *Financial Summary Tables—Department of Defense Budget for Fiscal Years 1988 and 1989* (Washington, D.C.: Department of Defense, Office of the Assistant Secretary of Defense, Comptroller, Directorate for Program and Financial Control, January 1987), Tab O.

funds, lag even farther behind; less than one-fifth of the money budgeted each year for procurement accounts is actually spent in that year.

If political leaders want to effect short-term economic changes, manipulating the defense budget is a bad way to do it. Hence, the annual budget is the wrong place to look for electorally motivated manipulation of defense spending.

My analysis approaches the problem of defense budget tinkering from a different perspective, namely, by focusing on monthly prime contract awards to U.S. firms. The method has several important advantages. First, it can uncover month-to-month variations within years that annual analysis will overlook. Second, policymakers can easily control the level and timing of contract awards, something they cannot do with either the aggregate defense budget or other types of defense spending; this makes tinkering more likely. Third, prime contract obligations have by far the speediest economic effects of any kind of defense spending. Contract awards thus fulfill the requirements of an effective political-economic policy instrument: controllability and swift effects.

The Political Uses of Defense Spending

The major economic benefit of defense spending is jobs. Every $1 billion in defense expenditures creates between twenty-five thousand and fifty-five thousand jobs, depending on whether the calculation includes indirect employment effects.[13] Defense spending thus produces something of substantial potential usefulness to incumbents, whether in the White House or Congress. Members of Congress consistently work to protect defense-related jobs in their home districts, and presidential candidates take pains to stress their prodefense orientation to groups who rely on defense contracts for their livelihoods. During the presidential campaign of 1976, both Gerald Ford and Jimmy Carter took pro–B-1 positions in front of various groups involved in B-1 bomber production; Carter actually opposed the plane.[14] The political success of incumbent presidents and members of their political party is closely tied to their ability to avoid recessions and unemployment. One need not be a genius to detect the American electorate's tendency to be ruthless to presidents who are unfortunate enough to preside over periods of economic hardship.[15] Since Gerald Kramer's original contribution, evidence has continued to emerge that the electoral success of the president's party is strongly related to economic conditions.[16] Edward Tufte made the connection between economic conditions and incumbent behavior, finding evidence that presidents tinker with the economy before elections to improve their chances at the polls. Presidents, Tufte argues, pump up the economy through transfer payments, tax cuts, and other activities designed to better the electorate's financial condition as elections approach.[17]

The defense budget is a tempting candidate for this kind of manipulation. Increasing the budget before an election would inject money into the economy, create and preserve jobs, and protect against recessions. After the election, the budget could be cut back to guard against the onset of inflationary pressures. Presidents could also increase defense spending as a way of helping to bring the economy out of recessions, which are never good for presidential popularity. President Carter's handling of a major ship repair contract shows how careful timing can be useful in a campaign. In the fall of 1980, "Vice President Mondale sailed into a Philadelphia navy yard aboard the U.S.S. *Saratoga*, where the aircraft carrier began a $526 million overhaul that brought thousands of jobs and millions of dollars in contracts to Pennsylvania (27 electoral votes), Delaware (3), and New Jersey (17). At the time, Carter was running neck-and-neck with Reagan in Pennsylvania; Virginia, which lost the contract, seemed safely in Reagan's column."[18]

Prime Contract Awards

Incumbent politicians and officials are most likely to tinker with obligations, which for nonpay accounts occur when contracts are awarded. Incumbents can easily control the timing and level of contract awards and can quickly alter award patterns if political or economic circumstances warrant. Contract awards create jobs almost immediately, as defense contractors hire or retain engineering, manufacturing, and management personnel, issue subcontracts, and gear up production facilities as soon as a contract is awarded. Eric Greenberg's study demonstrated that the employment impact of a contract begins the same month the contract is awarded and reaches a maximum after one month. A $1 billion contract (in 1967 dollars, or about $3.6 billion in 1987) would create about thirty-five hundred jobs the month of the award and thirty-two thousand the next.[19]

The economic effects of contract obligations are unmatched by those of any other phase of defense spending, in part because of the way the government finances most defense contracting activity. Except for its smallest purchases, the Pentagon does not hand contractors a sack of money when it awards a contract. A defense contract represents a legally binding promise by the government to pay the contractor in return for specified goods and services. The contractor, knowing that the government is required to pay as promised, uses its own funds to begin work. Most large contracts are financed through progress payments, a procedure in which the contractor bills the government, usually monthly, for costs incurred throughout the life of the contract effort. The government pays a fixed percentage—now 80 percent—of those costs, with the balance of costs, plus profit, due upon final delivery of the product. Contract awards, or obligations, start this sequence of events.

Decision makers in the Pentagon have broad discretion in deciding when to award contracts. Apart from some statutory limits—funds must be obligated before they "expire" and certain awards must be listed in the Commerce Business Daily for thirty days before the actual date of the award—nothing prevents contracting agencies from accelerating or holding up contract award announcements as conditions dictate. Once money has been appropriated, DOD decides when to obligate it.[20]

This controllability manifests itself in different ways. The best example is the manner in which awards are accelerated before the end of each fiscal year as DOD tries to obligate all of its remaining funds in order to avoid having to return leftover money to the Treasury.[21] Since Congress views unobligated funds as a sign of mismanagement and excessive budget requests, any agencies with money left at year-end are likely to have their future budget requests slashed.[22] The military is not immune to this fate. In 1967, Congress "ordered a decrease in weapons procurement funds (primarily Navy) because the military services were maintaining excessively large carryover balances."[23]

To avoid this unpleasantness, agencies routinely rush to get money "out the door" during the closing days of the fiscal year. This yearly frenzy was once sanctioned. "Prior to 1971," Fox writes, "official notices were sent to all senior government personnel during April or May, reminding them to use all their funds before June 30."[24] The problem was noticed more than seventy years ago by the first Bureau of the Budget director, Charles M. Dawes: "It appears to have been the practice heretofore among some of the departments and establishments of the Government to enter into contracts and obligations involving large amounts during the month of June, with the possible purpose and inevitable result of there being no unobligated balance to their credit at the close of the fiscal year."[25]

Although many agencies now try to limit year-end accelerations, they have proved impossible to stop. The primary control involves prohibiting obligations after a specific date, say September 15, which simply moves the rush deadline back. Other laws have been no more effective. Since 1953, language in the defense authorization bill has prohibited DOD from obligating more than 20 percent of the available funds in the last two months of the fiscal year. However, the limitation applies only to about 30 percent of the defense budget and excludes all funds for procurement, research and development, and construction—which is to

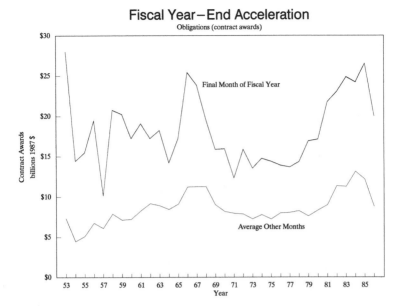

7-1

Fiscal Year-End Acceleration, 1953–1986, Obligations

say, nearly all contract awards.[26] The sheer size of the defense budget can propel the Pentagon spending fury to absurd heights. In 1983, the military obligated $4.5 billion on the last day of the fiscal year.[27] That is an annual rate exceeding $1.5 trillion, more than five times the 1983 budget. Other agencies are just as bad. In 1975, the Federal Maritime Administration awarded nearly three-quarters of its contracts during June and nearly half in the last two working days of the fiscal year.[28]

As shown in figure 7–1, 1983 was an unexceptional year for DOD. Between 1953 and 1986, contract award levels in the last month of the fiscal year have routinely been two to six times higher than the average award level for the other eleven months. Over the entire sample, 1953 to 1986, last-month obligations were 2.3 times larger than those of other months and were the year's biggest in every year except 1977, when the transition to the new fiscal year was made, and 1984, when awards peaked in November.

Outlays show no similar pattern (figure 7–2). The DOD fears no consequences if money is not actually expended by any deadline; once

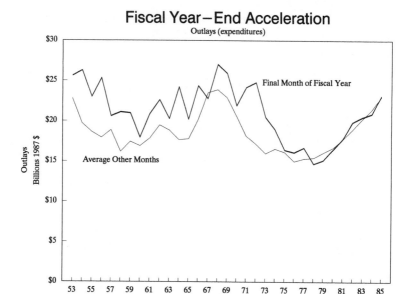

7-2

Fiscal Year-End Acceleration, 1953–1986, Outlays

the money is obligated, pressure disappears. Being less controllable, outlays are also difficult to manipulate for electoral purposes. The problems involved in controlling outlays were highlighted during hearings held to determine the impact the Gramm-Rudman balanced budget act would have on DOD.[29] Gramm-Rudman requires across-the-board cuts in outlays when deficits—also calculated on the basis of outlays—exceed prescribed levels. Thus DOD had to figure out how to manage its outlay rate, something Rudolph Penner, former director of CBO, thought nearly impossible: "Managing outlays would be difficult because of the decentralized nature of the defense finance and accounting system. Managing outlays would require fundamental changes in the way thousands of programs are pursued and in the business practices of equally numerous finance officers. One such difficulty stems from the fact that about a third of all defense outlays result from prior-year appropriations and contract commitments. Controlling these outlays would be difficult, because, as contractors make deliveries, they expect to be paid."[30]

Contract awards are the only phase of spending that decision makers can readily orchestrate. The fiscal year-end spending pattern shows that DOD can rapidly accelerate awards to meet an artificial deadline. Nothing inherent in the procurement sequence causes the fiscal year-end rush; the Pentagon is responding to a constraint imposed from outside. If the Pentagon can accelerate awards to meet one deadline, it can do so to meet others—elections, for example. The beauty of simply accelerating contracts is that it requires no increase in overall award levels. Those in power must only manipulate the timing of contracts that would eventually have been awarded in any case.

Other government agencies have used this tactic. Government grants in the Economic Development Administration and in Housing and Urban Development's sewer and water program went to key congressional districts during election years "among projects that would have been announced anyway"[31]—a bureaucratic strategy devised to protect budget levels and ward off congressional interference.[32] A GAO investigation in 1980 found the same pattern and concluded, "Grants that would have been awarded in the normal course of events were being timed and orchestrated to gain maximum political effect."[33]

The DOD could do the same thing by anticipating the electoral needs of the president or sympathetic legislators and by timing announcements to generate maximum political advantages for them. Alternatively, the government could speed up the awarding of contracts during times of economic hardship in an attempt to lower unemployment levels and insulate the defense industry from recessions.

THE POLITICAL-ECONOMIC MODEL

In order to generate political and economic effects, contract awards would have to be timed to respond to specific events, the most important of which are national elections. Specifying the appropriate economic trigger is more difficult, not only because the defense budget creates substantial economic effects on its own, but also because the level of spending appears, at least, to respond to a large number of economic variables. Those variables include corporate profits, unemployment, and inflation, according to the neo-Marxist model, and industrial productivity according to others. When political leaders speak of the economic benefits of defense spending, however, they almost always mean jobs: jobs in the defense industry, jobs created by large military installations, and the like. A reasonable hypothesis is that leaders will pay attention to the level of unemployment, an indicator closely related to public attitudes toward the economy and to the popularity of incumbents.

A political-economic model of defense spending predicts that contract awards should rise before elections and also accelerate when unemployment is high. Since the economic effects of contract awards kick in almost immediately, the accelerations should closely precede these events. To provide electoral benefits, contract awards must fall into a narrow window prior to election day, far enough in advance to maximize the preelection effects but proximate enough that credit claiming by incumbents is fresh in voters' minds.

One hypothesis is that awards should jump in September and October, when campaigns are in full swing and voters have time to notice economic stimulation and connect it with the candidates before election day in early November. If elections truly stimulate such accelerations, no pattern should appear in nonelection years. In response to high unemployment levels, contract awards should go up almost concurrently, especially during recessions. So, if there are economic and electoral cycles in defense contract awards, the following is one set of plausible expectations:

> Contract awards made in September and October of election years will be higher than award levels in the other months of election years and higher than award levels in September and October of nonelection years.

> Contract awards made in September and October of nonelection years will be no higher than awards made in the other months of those years.

> Contract awards will rise in response to high unemployment and will vary with the unemployment rate.

The data used to test these hypotheses are monthly DOD prime contract awards to U.S. firms between January 1951 and October 1986, with no seasonal adjustment. To simplify across-year comparisons and reduce the problem of autocorrelation, the series was converted to constant 1987 dollars through the use of a deflator calculated by DOD.[34] The analysis uses the seasonally unadjusted form because we are interested in the very types of seasonal variations that the adjustment removes.

Specification of the statistical model is straightforward. The equation

$$
\begin{aligned}
\text{Contract awards}_t &= b_0 + b_1 \text{LAGS} + b_2 \text{noncontract obligations} + b_3 \text{end of fiscal year} + b_4 \text{start of fiscal year} + b_5 \text{war} \\
&\quad + \text{Reagan Administration} \times (b_6 \text{time in office} + b_7 \text{end of fiscal year} + b_8 \text{start of fiscal year}) \\
&\quad + b_9 \text{calendar year} + b_{10} \text{election} + b_{11} \text{nonelection} + b_{12} \text{unemployment}_{t-1}
\end{aligned}
$$

where

Contract awards$_t$	= prime contract awards during month t
LAGS	= a set of variables encompassing a lag structure, which estimates the effect of previous contract award levels on current levels. This model includes 4 lags, Awards$_{t-1}$, Awards$_{t-3}$, Awards$_{t-6}$, and Awards$_{t-12}$
Noncontract obligations$_t$	= amount of money obligated in noncontract form (primarily military and civilian pay, housing assistance, etc.) in month t
End of fiscal year	= dummy variable, set to 1 if month t is last month of fiscal year = 0 otherwise
Start of fiscal year	= 1 if month t is first month of fiscal year = 0 otherwise
War	= 1 if the U.S. is involved in a war during month t = 0 otherwise
Reagan Administration	= 1 after January 1981, when Reagan assumed the presidency = 0 prior to that time
Time in office	= the number of months since January 1981
End of calendar year	= 1 if month t is December = 0 otherwise
Election	= 1 if month t is September or October of an election year = 0 otherwise
Nonelection	= 1 if month t is September or October of a nonelection year = 0 otherwise
Unemployment$_{t-1}$	= seasonally adjusted unemployment rate in previous month

The LAG variables take into account both seasonal variation and long-term trends. The lag structure was identified from the autocorrelations of contract award levels, which show that award levels are affected by levels in the previous month, as well as quarterly dependence at lags of 3, 6, and 12 months.

The dummy variables for the beginning and end of the fiscal year control for the spike during the last month of the year as well as for an expected trough during the first month of the following year. Noncontract obligations serve as an additional control.[35] The variables in the Reagan portion of the model estimate the impact of the post-1980 defense buildup; the awards data show that both the overall level and the fiscal year effect swings rise after Reagan's inauguration. Since obligations lag behind annual budget increases, the effects become more noticeable as Reagan's tenure lengthened (hence the Time in office variable).

The War dummy accounts for increased contracting activity during the Korean and Vietnam wars. Identifying the endpoints of the Korean War was simple: the North Koreans invaded in June 1950, and the armistice was signed in July 1953. Doing the same for the Vietnam War is more difficult, since U.S. involvement grew slowly and wound down gradually prior to complete disengagement in 1974. However, analysis of overall funding levels for the war effort shows that, as far as prime contracts go, the first jump occurred in 1965, when U.S. ground forces were introduced. Funding dropped after 1971 as part of the Vietnamization of the war. The variable War takes the value 1 starting in February 1965 and reverts to 0 after June 1971. This identification is somewhat arbitrary, but the model specification is surprisingly insensitive to war specification; changing the endpoints had no appreciable effect on the overall estimates.

The final control variable, the End of calendar year dummy, accounts for an expected rise in awards each December. Many contractors operate on a January–December fiscal year and thus push for December obligations to improve their year-end financial position. The military services frequently do the same, directing their procurement activities to obligate money by year-end to clean up accounts by an easily recognizable deadline. In December 1985, the Air Force Logistics Command (AFLC) instructed its network of offices around the country to obligate the $4.7 billion remaining in 1984 and 1985 funds by the end of the calendar year.

As a result, AFLC activities spent over $1 billion in the last twelve days of the year, including hundreds of millions of dollars in unpriced orders (that is, government-ordered goods for which the price is negotiated at a later date).[36]

The last three variables will detect political and economic cycles. The variable Election should be positive and significant, indicating that contract awards jump in the two months preceding both presidential and midterm congressional elections. The variable Nonelection estimates the rise in the same months of nonelection years; it should be small, indicating that no such acceleration occurs in nonelection years. The Unemployment rate coefficient will be positive if contracts are awarded in response to high unemployment levels.

The results for the entire series (1954–86) are shown in column 1 of table 7–2. They strongly confirm the model's hypothesis that contract awards accelerate in September and October of election years. Over the 1954–86 period, about $3 billion in contracts were heaped just before elections, roughly twice the increase in nonelection years. The coefficient for September/October of election years is 1459.9, which means that an additional $1.46 billion is awarded in each of the two months, for an overall acceleration of $2.92 billion. In all likelihood, no such acceleration occurs in nonelection years. The coefficient is small compared to its standard error, and has about a 10 percent chance of being 0 (the corresponding probability that the election year coefficient is actually 0 is less than 1 in 750).

The other coefficients show that contract awards rise by $6.7 billion at the end of the fiscal year. The use it or lose it phenomenon is substantial; $7 billion, Everett Dirksen would agree, is real money. No other factor has nearly as significant an effect. Activity during the final month is three times higher then during wartime months, although the level cannot be sustained for long. During the Reagan years, awards at the start of the fiscal year were over $4 billion lower than in other months, possibly because procurement personnel were exhausted.

Contract award levels rose in response to higher unemployment rates. Each 1 percent rise in unemployment led to $283 million dollars in awards the following month. That increase was sustained as long as unemployment stayed at the higher level, falling only in the month after

Table 7-2
Electoral Cycles, 1954–86 and 1954–76

Dependent Variable: Prime Contract Awards (million 1987 dollars)

Variable	**1954–86**	**1954–76**
Constant	3421.7	1664.3
Awards$_{t-1}$	0.143**	0.316***
	(3.11)	(6.23)
Awards$_{t-3}$	0.074*	0.145***
	(2.12)	(3.42)
Awards$_{t-6}$	0.116**	0.099
	(3.37)	(1.75)
Awards$_{t-9}$	0.037	0.082*
	(1.21)	(2.27)
Awards$_{t-12}$	0.247***	0.140**
	(5.73)	(2.79)
Noncontract obligations$_t$	−0.284***	−0.166**
	(6.21)	(3.19)
End of fiscal year	6721.2***	8100.1***
	(11.61)	(12.62)
Start of fiscal year	−339.0	−2247.6***
	(0.58)	(3.67)
End of calendar year	250.4	656.2
	(0.54)	(1.00)
War involvement	2111.8***	1222.9**
	(5.20)	(3.31)
Reagan time in office	66.0***	
	(5.63)	
Reagan*end of fiscal year	488.9	
	(0.44)	
Reagan*start of fiscal year	−4163.1***	
	(3.62)	
September/October election year	1459.9**	1393.0**
	(3.35)	(3.08)
September/October nonelection year	758.7	318.5
	(1.68)	(0.68)
Unemployment$_{t-1}$	283.2**	170.1
	(3.05)	(1.63)
Adjusted r^2	.72	.73

Table 7-2

(continued)

Dependent Variable: Prime Contract Awards (million 1987 dollars)		
Variable	**1954–86**	**1954–76**
Rho (est.)	.05	−.01
Std. Error	2124.0	1850.2
N	394	276

t-ratios in parentheses
*p < 0.05
**p < 0.01
***p < 0.001

unemployment declined. Although $283 million is not a great deal of money, when the increase continues over several months, total dollar amounts and the resulting economic impact begin to accumulate.

The model also reveals a strong negative relationship between non-contract obligations and contract awards. When noncontract obligations are cut by $1 billion, contract awards rise by $284 million; contract awards similarly fall by $284 million when noncontract obligations increase by $1 billion. One explanation for this is that the Pentagon persistently faces a stark trade-off between spending money in investment accounts (procurement, research and development) and spending it for day-to-day operations (personnel, operations, maintenance, and so forth). The military's reluctance to cut procurement spending is well known, and readiness accounts are the first to go during budget crunches.

The electoral accelerations observed in September and October might have been a spurious artifact of the fiscal year schedule. Since 1977, the fiscal year has run from October to September. As a result, use it or lose it accelerations will occur before every election (as well as in every off year). To eliminate the possibility that the September/October election year acceleration is an artifact of the post-1977 fiscal year, the model was reestimated for the 1954–76 period, when the fiscal year ended in June. The results, shown in column 2 of table 7–2, show clearly that the election year acceleration is real, with $2.8 billion heaped in September and October. Moreover, there is no evidence of similar accelerations in nonelection years. Election year accelerations in contracting activity have, apparently, been a fixture on the campaign scene. They cannot be attributed to the fiscal year-end effect.

The macroeconomic consequences of electoral and economic contract accelerations will be noticeable at the local level, even if the national effects are relatively small. When dumped into the economy immediately before an election, $2.9 billion in defense contracts produces between 72,000 and 160,000 jobs. Even if all of these jobs are new (which they probably are not), the totals will have only minor effects on either unemployment or national income accounts. At the November peak of the recession of 1982 (an election year), unemployment stood at 10.8 percent out of a total civilian labor force of 111 million. One hundred sixty thousand new jobs would comprise less than 0.14 percent of the labor force and would have reduced unemployment by less than 0.15 percent. Similarly, a 1 percent rise in unemployment means that about one million people have lost their jobs. The rise in contract awards—$283 million—creates about 16,000 jobs, an effect only 1.6 percent as large. Moreover, the extra few billions in contracts produced by either elections or recession would scarcely nick a Gross National Product measured in the trillions. This suggests that perhaps well-timed credit claiming, along with concern about economic conditions at the local level, is a major motivation for the electoral cycle in defense contracting.

Even though the political-economic accelerations are relatively small, they are significant when put into the context of overall national security policy. Since most studies of the defense budget find that defense spending responds most strongly to international events, we can, realistically, expect domestic factors to come into play only at the margins. Nevertheless, the fact that contract award timing does respond to domestic economic, political, and structural variables shows that defense spending has some important domestic functions unrelated to national security.

One way of distinguishing between the credit claiming and economic explanations for the accelerations is to see if award increases for congressional and presidential elections differ. Members of Congress are probably more concerned with credit claiming than with national economic conditions, presidents with economic stimulation. A major defense contract will have more impact on a congressional race than the national election; five thousand jobs can be decisive in an incumbent legislator's reelection quest but cannot realistically influence national outcomes.

Presidents also have more incentive than legislators to pump up the economy because their reelection success depends more heavily on national economic conditions. The same change in economic well-being, measured as change in per capita real disposable income, has more effect on presidential than congressional elections. Tufte found that a 1 percent increase in election year per capita disposable income caused a 1.3 percent increase in the popular vote for incumbent presidents but only a 0.6 percent increase in the national "midterm vote for the congressional candidates of the president's party."[37] A sitting president has more at stake in the national economy than do members of Congress, who may be able to mitigate the effects of national economic downturns by attending to local interests.

If national economic stimulation is the main motivation for the electoral contract award cycles, the preelection jumps should be larger in presidential election years than at midterm. To test this proposition, separate September/October effects were estimated for the two types of elections. The results, shown in table 7–3, indicate that the increases are about the same. Over the entire period, contract awards rose by $2.7 billion during midterm years and $3.1 billion during presidential election years. During the pre-1977 period, the respective increases were $2.9 billion and $2.7 billion. Given the variance of the estimates, the coefficients are indistinguishable, which means that the accelerations can be considered equal. This suggests election year accelerations serve mainly to give legislators the pleasant—and aptly timed—job of reminding constituents that they have a friend in Washington.

The size of the fiscal year-end acceleration points to a significant advantage of the current fiscal year structure. By shifting to an October–September fiscal year, Congress has guaranteed a huge acceleration before every election. That accelerations also occur in nonelection years is trivial, when billions of dollars in contracts spill into the economy every September. The size of these accelerations is shown in table 7–4, which gives coefficient estimates for the post-1977 period. This model requires a slightly different set of independent variables; the easiest way to separate the fiscal year effects from electoral effects is to estimate separate coefficients for September and October for presidential, mid-

Table 7-3

Cycles in Presidential and Midterm Election Years

Dependent Variable: Prime Contract Awards (million 1987 dollars)

Variable	1954–86	1954–76
Constant	3412.8	1666.3
Awards$_{t-1}$	0.140**	0.316***
	(3.10)	(6.22)
Awards$_{t-3}$	0.074*	0.145***
	(2.13)	(3.41)
Awards$_{t-6}$	0.116**	0.099
	(3.36)	(1.75)
Awards$_{t-9}$	0.036	0.082*
	(1.20)	(2.27)
Awards$_{t-12}$	0.248***	0.140**
	(5.73)	(2.79)
Noncontract obligations$_t$	−0.283***	−0.165**
	(6.20)	(3.17)
End of fiscal year	6722.6***	8099.7***
	(11.59)	(12.60)
Start of fiscal year	−337.6	−2252.1***
	(0.58)	(3.67)
End of calendar year	251.8	656.6
	(0.54)	(1.00)
War involvement	2116.9***	1215.9**
	(5.19)	(3.26)
Reagan time in office	66.0***	
	(5.62)	
Reagan*end of fiscal year	506.7	
	(0.46)	
Reagan*start of fiscal year	−4163.3***	
	(3.60)	
September/October midterm congressional election year	1366.9*	1456.7*
	(2.39)	(2.45)
September/October presidential election year	1557.0**	1330.6*
	(2.67)	(2.26)
September/October nonelection year	755.1	318.2
	(1.67)	(0.68)
Unemployment$_{t-1}$	284.3**	168.3
	(3.06)	(1.60)

Table 7-3
(continued)

Dependent Variable: Prime Contract Awards (million 1987 dollars)		
Variable	**1954–86**	**1954–76**
Adjusted r^2	.72	.73
Rho (est.)	.05	−.01
Std. Error	2126.7	1853.6
N	394	276

t-ratios in parentheses
*$p < 0.05$
**$p < 0.01$
***$p < 0.001$

term, and nonelection years. The estimated increase in nonelection years provides a baseline estimate of the fiscal year-end effect, which can then be compared to increases during election years. As shown in table 7–4, $8.9 billion in extra contracts are awarded in September and October of nonelection years, compared to an estimated $6.2 billion in midterm years and $3.9 billion in presidential election years. Although the accelerations are larger in nonelection years, the election year increases are two to three times larger than they were before 1977. Those in office will reap huge benefits from contract accelerations, even if elections no longer drive the process. That the fall spurts are now automatic does little to diminish their value.

Tufte's book *Political Control of the Economy* is in many ways a catalogue of the macroeconomic excesses of the Nixon administration, which was responsible for the most egregious examples of manipulating transfer payments. In October 1972, for example, almost twenty-five million social security checks were accompanied by an insert explaining how a 20 percent increase in benefits was "signed into law by President Richard Nixon."[38] Tufte goes on to note that the corresponding increase in social security taxes required to pay for the increased benefits was not assessed until after the election.[39] Nixon also purposely pumped up the economy through "deliberate planning and the mobilization of policy instruments producing acceleration in real disposable income growth."[40] That growth spurted in the last two quarters of 1972 and declined rapidly—for five straight quarters—immediately after the election.[41]

Table 7-4

Electoral Cycles, Post-1976

Dependent Variable: Prime Contract Awards (million 1987 dollars)	
Variable	**1977–86**
Constant	10455.1
Awards$_{t-1}$	−0.083
	(0.96)
Awards$_{t-3}$	−0.109
	(1.40)
Awards$_{t-6}$	−0.004
	(0.07)
Awards$_{t-9}$	−0.007
	(1.20)
Awards$_{t-12}$	0.289***
	(3.81)
Noncontract obligations$_t$	−0.570***
	(6.14)
End of calendar year	3016.7**
	(2.61)
Reagan time in office	143.6***
	(6.64)
September of midterm congressional election year	6218.8***
	(3.96)
September of presidential election year	3971.5*
	(2.07)
September of nonelection year	5872.6***
	(4.60)
October of midterm congressional election year	1833.8
	(1.07)
October of presidential election year	3510.2
	(1.80)
October of nonelection year	3074.9*
	(2.08)
Unemployment$_t$	369.7
	(1.80)
Adjusted r^2	.74
Rho (est.)	.06
Std. Error	2392.3

Table 7-4

(continued)

Dependent Variable: Prime Contract Awards (million 1987 dollars)

Variable	1977–86
N	118

t-ratios in parentheses
*p < 0.05
**p < 0.01
***p < 0.001

That manipulation was not confined to domestic policy. Column 2 in table 7–5 shows how contract awards peaked immediately before elections during the Nixon years, especially during presidential campaigns. The increases were much larger during this time than in any other pre-1977 period, jumping $4.2 billion in midterm years and $6.2 billion during presidential election years. Nixon presaged electorally motivated increases in defense spending as early as 1960, when he pressured Eisenhower's economic policy officials to help his campaign by raising defense spending.[42] There is little doubt that he resorted to the same strategy when his people were in power.

The military need not engage in "conspiracies" or violate contracting regulations to produce these effects. It need only speed up (or delay) the contract process to time the award appropriately. Legislators who support the military will presumably get this sort of favorable treatment (although there is no way to prove this with the available data). A former chief of staff to a prominent promilitary senator indicated that his office routinely requested that contract award announcements be timed to coincide as closely as possible to the senator's campaign schedule.[43] This practice, judging from the results shown here, may be widespread.

The importance of the credit-claiming function of award accelerations makes their countercyclical use less significant. The government can fight unemployment with more direct instruments without relying on defense contracts. Monetary policy and budget-wide fiscal policy (including tax policy) can do more for the economy than defense contract accelerations, and a wide array of social programs insulates the public from the worst effects of recessions. The relative contribution defense

Table 7-5
Electoral Cycles, 1954–64, and the Nixon Years

Dependent Variable: Prime Contract Awards (million 1987 dollars)

Variable	1954–64	1969–76
Constant	886.0	6657.8
Awards$_{t-1}$	0.285**	0.439***
	(4.02)	(4.68)
Awards$_{t-3}$	0.143*	−0.125
	(2.55)	(1.61)
Awards$_{t-6}$	0.187*	0.035
	(2.40)	(0.39)
Awards$_{t-9}$	0.110*	0.071
	(2.30)	(1.24)
Awards$_{t-12}$	−0.006	0.189*
	(0.09)	(2.00)
Noncontract obligations$_t$	−0.191*	−0.281**
	(2.28)	(3.00)
End of fiscal year	9694.8***	6603.3***
	(10.11)	(7.41)
Start of fiscal year	−370.1***	−1413.3
	(4.09)	(1.64)
End of calendar year	522.8	1190.3
	(0.52)	(1.57)
September/October election year	772.5	
	(1.25)	
War involvement		303.0
		(0.77)
September/October midterm congressional election year		2117.0**
		(2.75)
September/October presidential election year		3117.7***
		(4.31)
September/October nonelection year	56.4	999.1
	(0.08)	(1.57)
Unemployment$_{t-1}$	447.8*	−108.6
	(2.43)	(1.03)
Adjusted r^2	.74	.72
Rho (est.)	.04	−.10
Std. Error	1876.1	1307.5

Table 7-5

(continued)

Dependent Variable: Prime Contract Awards (million 1987 dollars)		
Variable	**1954–64**	**1969–76**
N	133	96

t-ratios in parentheses
*p < 0.05
**p < 0.01
***p < 0.001

contracts can make in this effort has thus declined, especially since the mid-1960s.

Support for this argument is found in column 1 of table 7–5, which estimates the model's parameters for the pre-1964 period. Then, defense contracts played a more important countercyclical role, with monthly contract award levels increasing $448 million for each 1 percent rise in unemployment. The coincidence between the timing of contract award accelerations and unemployment is shown in figure 7–3, which plots seasonally adjusted contract awards and the unemployment rate by quarter.[44] During the recessions of 1954, 1958, and 1961, contract awards grew along with unemployment, increasing by a total of about $10–$15 billion during the worst periods. When unemployment dropped, contract awards slowed. Tinkering with the timing of contract awards was a powerful way of affecting macroeconomic conditions.

Defense contracting activity increases immediately before elections, both to stimulate the economy and to advance the interests of incumbent legislators. Before the era of major social programs, defense contracts were also used to combat unemployment. The use of defense contracts to gain domestic political and economic advantages is no surprise, except for the fact that DOD claims, at least publicly, to be above all that. The patterns observed here show that in fact DOD is no different from any other agency, in that it has developed strategies designed to protect budgets, to attend to friends on Capitol Hill, and to advance the political interests of the administration. Until there are more data on where strategically timed contracts go, it is impossible to know whether Demo-

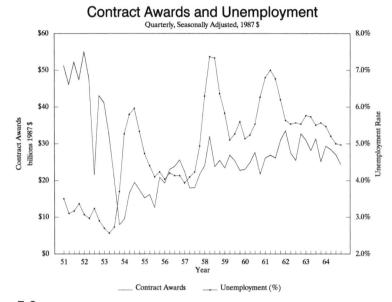

7-3

Contract Awards and Unemployment

crats benefit more than Republicans or Armed Services Committee members more than nonmembers; equally impossible is determining whether prodefense legislators get more cooperation from procurement agencies than military critics (all three are reasonable presumptions).

Neither is it possible to say what impact the accelerating or delaying of awards has on the quality of contracting decisions. Politically astute timing of announcements by itself will have little impact, since nearly all of the awards would have been made eventually. Procurement offices could conceivably be pressured into awarding a contract prematurely, perhaps by bypassing necessary management or engineering controls, but this is speculation.

The results of this analysis show how a major portion of defense spending—contract awards—fits into the broader picture of the American political economy. Far from being above politics, defense contracts are routinely—if not perniciously—used to political ends. Members of Congress gain from the biennial surge in electorally motivated contract awards because during their election campaigns (that is, when they can reap maximum political advantage) they can point to the jobs those contracts produce. Moreover, the government uses defense contracts to neutralize downward economic trends, at least at the margins. In these respects defense contracts are no different from any of the other macroeconomic tools that government actors manipulate to influence economic policy and assure their own political survival.

CHAPTER 7. ELECTIONS, THE ECONOMY, AND DEFENSE CONTRACT AWARDS

1. For arguments in favor of the political-business cycle approach, see Larry J. Griffin, Joel A. Devine, Michael Wallace, "Monopoly Capital, Organized Labor, and Military Expenditures in the United States, 1949–1976," in *Marxist Inquiries: Studies of Labor, Class, and States*, ed. Michael Burawoy and Theda Skocpol (Chicago: University of Chicago Press, 1982); Larry J. Griffin, Joel A. Devine, and Michael Wallace, "The Political Economy of Military Spending: Evidence from the United States," *Cambridge Journal of Economics* 6, no. 1 (1982); Alex Mintz and Alexander Hicks, "Military Keynesianism in the United States, 1949–1976; Disaggregating Military Expenditures and Their Determination," *American Journal of Sociology* 90, no. 2 (1984); and Miroslav Nincic and Thomas R. Cusack, "The Political Economy of U.S. Military Spending," *Journal of Peace Research* 16, no. 2 (1979). For arguments against, see Gert Krell, "Capitalism and Armaments: Business Cycles and Defense Spending in the United States, 1945–1979," *Journal of Peace Research* 18, no. 3 (1981).

2. Charles W. Ostrom, "A Reactive Linkage Model of the U.S. Defense Expenditure Policymaking Process," *American Political Science Review* 72, no. 3 (September 1978).

3. Nathaniel Beck, "Elections and the Fed: Is There a Political-Monetary Cycle?" *American Journal of Political Science* 31, no. 1 (February 1987); David Golden and James Poterba, "The Price of Popularity: The Political Business Cycle Reexamined," *American Journal of Political Science* 24, no. 4 (Fall 1980); Bennet T. McCallum, "The Political Business Cycle: An Empirical Test," *Southern Economic Journal* 44, no. 1 (January 1978).

4. William R. Keech and Kyoungsan Pak, "Electoral Cycles and Budgetary Growth in Veterans' Benefit Programs," *American Journal of Political Science* 33, no. 4 (November 1989): 909.

5. See Keech and Pak, "Electoral Cycles and Budgetary Growth," 910; R. Kent Weaver, *Automatic Government: The Politics of Indexation* (Washington, D.C.: Brookings Institution, 1988).

6. Beck, "Elections and the Fed" 198.

7. Jacques Gansler, *Affording Defense* (Cambridge: MIT Press, 1989), 115. Gansler notes that in FY 1983 Congress failed to approve six of the eleven categories of defense spending "by the end of the fiscal year" (115).

8. William Greider, *The Education of David Stockman* (New York: E. P. Dutton, 1982), 16–17; Stubbing, *The Defense Game*, 377.

9. Krell, "Capitalism and Armaments," 237.

10. See Nincic and Cusack, "The Political Economy of U.S. Military Spending."

11. Eric Greenberg, "Employment Impacts of Defense Expenditures and Obligations," *Review of Economics and Statistics* 49, no. 2 (1967); Lin Lee Maw, "Impact, Pattern and Duration of New Orders for Defense Products," *Econometrica* 38, no. 1 (1970).

12. U.S. Department of Defense. *Financial Summary Tables: Department of Defense Budget for Fiscal Year 1988 and 1989*, January 1987.

13. The lower figure is from Congressional Budget Office, *Defense Spending and the Economy* (Washington, D.C.: Government Printing Office, 1983). The larger figure is from Peter Ognibene, "The Air Force's Secret War on Unemployment," *Washington Monthly*, July-August 1975.

14. Kotz, *Wild Blue Yonder:* Money, Politics, and the B-1 Bomber (New York: Pantheon Books, 1988), 156–57.

15. Skeptics should see Samuel Kernell, "Explaining Presidential Popularity," *American Political Science Review* 72, no. 2 (June 1978).

16. Gerald Kramer, "Short-Term Fluctuations in American Voting Behavior, 1896–1964," *American Political Science Review* 72, no. 1 (March 1971); Donald Kinder, Gordon S. Adams, and Paul W. Gronke, "Economics and Politics in the 1984 American Presidential Election," *American Journal of Political Science* 33, no. 2 (May 1989); D. Roderick Kiewiet, *Macroeconomics and Micropolitics: The Electoral Effects of Economic Issues* (Chicago: University of Chicago Press, 1983); Steven Rosenstone, *Forecasting Presidential Elections* (New Haven: Yale University Press, 1983), esp. 139–42.

17. Edward R. Tufte, *Political Control of the Economy* (Princeton: Princeton University Press, 1978).

18. Rosenstone, *Forecasting Presidential Elections,* 61.

19. Greenberg, "Employment Impacts of Defense Expenditures and Obligations," 195.

20. Louis Fisher, *Presidential Spending Power* (Princeton: Princeton University Press, 1975), 123.

21. "When funds are made available for a specified period of time (either for one year or a multiple of years), any funds not obligated by that time will lapse." Fisher, *Presidential Spending Power,* 130.

22. J. Ronald Fox, *Arming America: How the U.S. Buys Weapons* (Boston: Division of Research, Graduate School of Business Administration, Harvard University, 1974), 134.

23. Fisher, *Presidential Spending Power,* 140.

24. Fox, *Arming America,* 134.

25. Treasury Department, Bureau of the Budget, Circular no. 28, September 1, 1921.

26. U.S. Congress, House Committee on Government Affairs, *Hurry Up Spending*, part 2, 1980, 280.

27. U.S. Congress, House Committee on the Budget, *Review of Defense Acquisition and Management*, 98th Cong., 1st Sess., 1983, 181.

28. General Accounting Office, *Federal Agencies' Contracting for Research and Development in the Private Profitmaking Sector* (PSAD-77–66), March 24, 1977, reprinted in *Hurry Up Spending*, part 1, 13.

29. Public Law 99–177, Balanced Budget and Emergency Deficit Control Act of 1985.

30. U.S. Congress, Senate Committee on Appropriations, Subcommittee on Defense, *Department of Defense Expenditure Rate and Outlay Management Control* 1986, 14.

31. Theodore J. Anagnoson, "Federal Grant Agencies and Congressional Election Campaigns," *American Journal of Political Science* 26, no. 3 (August 1982): 560.

32. Ibid., 549.

33. General Accounting Office, *Assessment of Whether the Federal Grant Process is Being Politicized During Election Years* (GCD-81–41), December 30, 1980, 3.

34. U.S. Department of Defense, Office of the Assistant Secretary of Defense, Comptroller, *National Defense Budget Estimates for FY 1988/1989* (Green Book), May 1987, 53.

35. This variable is calculated as the difference between total DOD obligations and DOD contract awards. Because of some retroactive adjustments made to the prime contract series during the Korean War, total obligations are recorded as being less than contract awards. Thus, it is necessary to begin the analysis in January 1955 to avoid this error in both the current and lagged independent variables.

36. "Air Force Santas Went Shopping," *Defense Week,* April 14, 1989, 7.

37. Tufte, *Political Control of the Economy,* 112.

38. Ibid., 31.

39. Ibid., 35.

40. Ibid., 45.

41. Ibid., 46.

42. See the discussion in ibid., 47–48, and Richard Nixon, *Six Crises* (New York: Doubleday, 1962), 310.

43. Kenneth R. Mayer, "The Politics and Economics of Defense Contracting" (Ph.D. diss., Yale University, 1988), 296.

44. Seasonal adjustment eliminates periodic fluctuations that may obscure other more interesting patterns (even election year accelerations are removed, since they occur at regular two-year intervals). Quarterly contract figures make visual inspection easier.

Conclusion: Politics, Pork, and Representation

This book tells a story of politics and defense, but not the one most people are accustomed to hearing. My main argument is that theories or explanations of defense spending that blame politics for budgets that are too big or too wasteful miss the mark. Put simply, congressional support of defense spending and of Pentagon contracting decisions is based less on pork barrel than is widely assumed. There is little systematic evidence that members vote against their policy preferences on weapon programs because of local economic impact; the Pentagon does not, indeed cannot, distribute defense contracts (as opposed to bases) for political purposes. Political explanations of contracting decisions describe neither process nor outcomes adequately and oversimplify a vastly complicated decision-making structure. Indeed, one reason pork barrel explanations are so attractive is that they are simple, parsimonious, and persuasive. They are also mostly wrong.

None of my arguments should be read to imply that congressional treatment of defense policy is unassailable or that members always place the national interest above those of their constituents. And they should not be interpreted as saying that Congress and the Pentagon make defense contract decisions in a political vacuum. They clearly do not. The major findings here suggest that decisions in certain phases of the process are indisputably political: prime contractors, without question, distribute subcontracts over as many states and congressional districts as they can, and contract awards are timed to provide maximum political benefit to legislators. However, these political strategies have very little substantive effect on defense policy, in terms either of how much the United States spends on defense or of which weapons it purchases.

Electorally timed contracts may run to the billions of dollars, which is a great deal of money. Yet the macroeconomic effects of that acceleration are virtually unnoticeable, and the overall level of defense spending neither rises nor falls as a result. Politically motivated subcontract distributions may be a political security blanket, but there is no evidence that they protect vulnerable programs from cancellation or that they play a significant role when Congress votes to keep programs alive. Money from PACs flows toward members who support defense programs in general, but contractors continue to fund members who vote against them, even on crucial issues. Contrary to popular belief, members of Congress do not instinctively respond, like so many Pavlovian dogs, to local subcontracts or campaign contributions by casting promilitary votes; the decision calculus is not so simple. Unquestionably, parts of the defense budget (especially military construction accounts) are sustained by pork barrel pressures, and members can always be expected to yelp when local programs are threatened. But even the most widely spread program will hit only three hundred or so districts with subcontracts, and legislators will normally be pulled in several different directions on any given defense issue. Members from districts in which a contractor faces a major program cancellation will surely fight to preserve it, but they will generally not succeed if the only argument they can muster is that jobs are at stake. There is, to be sure, a great deal of political activity surrounding defense contracting and spending decisions, but it has little direct effect on final decisions.

But why, if politics has less impact than is popularly believed, do most institutional actors in the process behave as though it is the central problem of defense policy? Members of Congress (and contractors) still complain about politically motivated contract decisions. The Pentagon and critics of Congress complain that members are too willing to push local pork at the expense of the public good or that they sell out the nation's defense in pursuit of PAC money. To use the old metaphor, it is difficult to believe there is no fire when there is so much smoke.

The political strategies highlighted here do serve two important functions: they help to define the congressional agenda and they help members in their credit claiming, or self-advertising, functions. By timing their campaign contributions carefully and letting subcontracts over a wide geographic area, contractors become more visible to members of Congress and thereby improve their chances of putting their program on the congressional agenda. As John Kingdon noted, members deal with a bewildering array of issues and problems, only a few of which can receive consideration. As a result, getting the member's attention is the first step toward obtaining relief; thus, a member's "conscious or unconscious choice about which matters will receive his attention is a decision of great moment."[1] Gaining access, either through campaign contributions, by having specific policy expertise, or by demonstrating that you represent a sizable coalition of constituents, is a crucial step. As one defense contractor lobbyist put it, "Money is not going to buy anyone. But you get their attention and you get the door open."[2] Contractors who face a service cancellation decision appeal to Congress for redress; their best bet for results is surely a member who represents the affected plant: he or she has a natural political constituency that demands some action. That member will raise the issue with colleagues and otherwise see to it that the issue makes the congressional agenda.

As I argued in chapter 6, however, success in this enterprise is not so much a function of the overall economic impact of the weapon system in question (as the pork barrel theory suggests) as of a series of admittedly political decisions about resource allocation, strategy, and alternatives. In this regard, it is true that whatever Congress does on any issue is political, as the action involves trade-offs among competing demands and interests: "The questions about what weapons are developed, where they are built, and how many and how fast they are produced, which firms go out of business—in short, the kind of questions policy makers must answer continually if they are to manage the acquisition process—are inevitably political as well as technical issues."[3] Yet it does not automatically follow that the process is by definition corrupt or otherwise ethically suspect.

The pretense that pork barrel politics drives defense policy also serves the credit-claiming needs of Congress. We have seen examples of members taking responsibility for contract awards, pretending to have some special pull with the Pentagon, when in fact they had no bearing at all on contracting decisions. As long as the public believes the political model of defense policy, such claims are believable, and they help members demonstrate their connection to local constituencies. At the same time, members on the wrong end of contracting decisions are quick to blame the same political process, asserting that their favored contractor lost because of politics, not merit. The ensuing calls for investigations, reports, and explanations give the impression that the member is making the Pentagon pay for its mistake and ensuring that it will not happen again.

In engaging in this sort of behavior, members are simply responding to constituents' expectations about the political process. Members who publicly support contracting decisions that go against local companies risk political retribution, or at least they believe they do. Indeed, we can hardly expect members of the House and Senate to turn their backs on their constituents when the latter's interests are threatened. Why should the New York delegation allow Secretary Cheney to cancel the F-14 without a fight, even if they agreed with him that the plane was too expensive? By doing so they would not only have risked political suicide, but also have ignored the devastating impact the decision would have had on the local communities they represent. While we may argue about the fairness of local groups insisting that the federal government bail them out, we should not be surprised when the affected groups appeal for relief. Those appeals will not always succeed. But, although the hardships may not worry legislators from other parts of the country, members of the New York delegation, acting within the bounds of their role as representatives, feel an obligation to promote and protect their constituents' interests. Representative Downey commented on this aspect of his job during an earlier battle over the A-6 attack aircraft, also built by Grumman (a battle he eventually lost): "When the A-6 Intruder was going to be killed, I'm the congressman from that district and I'm on the Armed Services Committee. It's my job, whether I think the A-6 is good or not, to support it."[4]

We are still left with the major question of why, in fact, politics matters less than most people believe. It is not enough to show that the political model is incomplete; we must craft an explanation of why it is so. One reason pork barrel politics is less of a factor in congressional decision making on defense contracts is that the spectrum of government activity in nondefense policy has widened considerably in the past twenty-five years. On the one hand, defense procurement comprises 70 percent of discretionary federal spending, defined as programs that Congress can change from year to year. Rep. Patricia Schroeder (D-Colo.) once argued that "the only place there is any money at all is the Armed Services Committee Bill."[5]

On the other hand, the fraction of the federal budget devoted to defense has dropped considerably from its postwar highs. In 1988, for example, only 10.5 percent of federal outlays was spent on procurement and research and development. In 1955, two years after the Korean War, the figure was 21.8 percent, more than twice as high.[6] Procurement and research and development as a percentage of GNP has dropped as well, from 3.7 percent in 1955 to 2.3 percent in 1988. The DOD now employs a smaller share of the federal government work force (61.5 percent) than it did during the entire period 1970–78 (the so-called decade of neglect).[7] Supporters of defense spending make these sorts of comparisons all the time, disingenuously arguing that the United States can surely afford to increase the defense budget to reflect these historical ratios.[8] My intent, however, is only to demonstrate that an increasing amount of government and economic activity has nothing to do with defense contracting.

Even those sectors that remain heavily dependent on defense contracts, especially aerospace, compose a smaller portion of the economy than they once did. According to industry figures, aerospace workers made up 6.7 percent of the total manufacturing work force in 1985. This ratio is higher than it was during the 1970s, when it hovered around 5 percent, yet it is slightly lower than comparable figures prior to 1970, when typically it was 7 percent or higher.[9] Although defense contracts clearly remain significant in absolute terms, their relative contribution to the overall level of economic activity has been shrinking. Former chairman of the Council of Economic Advisers Murray Weidenbaum summarized the major trends over the past fifty years: "Different ways of gauging resource use of the past half century yield the same point: defense outlays have accounted for a declining share of GNP; defense spending has been a declining portion of the federal budget; defense manpower has represented a declining fraction of the nation's work force; defense has received a diminishing portion of the nation's research and development funding."[10] In short, Weidenbaum concludes, "over a very significant time period, military activities have been a steadily smaller factor in the American Economy."[11]

As a result, legislators find themselves confronted with a range of issues, of which defense will be only one. Although members pay more attention to defense than they once did, the primary motivation for that increased attention is not that defense spending is more important economically, but rather that defense spending is more important politically. Even so, members may find their constituents more concerned about other issues, at least as those issues relate to local and national economic effects: "Acquisition issues relate to broad national goals as well as to local ones, and each member is likely to weigh these competing perspectives differently in different cases. . . . Even in the purely domestic political context, defense is likely to be only one of several issues of concern to constituents."[12] Although a few members may find themselves in a tight spot over a proposed cancellation that affects their constituents, the job of persuading their colleagues to see the issue as a dilemma becomes much harder.

A member's attention to defense issues, moreover, may have less to do with pork than with policy, at least on procurement issues. Past research on the constituency–committee membership connection, which I discussed in chapters 2 and 6, shows that members of the defense committees have no more defense contracts placed in their districts than nonmembers (although they do tend to represent districts with a large military base presence). More recent data show the same pattern. Only one member of the House military committees in FY 1986 represented a district in the top ten ranking of prime contract awards; two are from the top twenty, and only ten are in the top one hundred.[13] Subcontracting data follow this pattern, as chapter 6 demonstrated; committee members are no more likely to receive subcontracts for a particular system than members who are not on the committees.

The two most powerful congressional players in defense policy, Sam Nunn and Les Aspin, represent areas with small stakes in defense contracting. The first congressional district in Wisconsin, Aspin's base, was ranked by one source in 1986 number 280 out of 435 in defense contracts,[14] and by another 398th in total defense spending for 1987.[15] Aspin was unable to trade his influence over defense policy for support for other types of spending in his district: When a Washington consulting firm calculated the distribution of overall federal spending by congressional district in 1985, Aspin's district ranked 384th.[16] Nunn's state, Georgia, home to Lockheed, ranked 12th in the value of defense contracts in 1986 with $3.8 billion, which represented less than 3 percent of total contracts.[17] Georgia dropped to 19th place by 1988, with a contracting level one-half that of the 1986 total.[18] If a primary goal of legislators is simply to channel defense contract pork to their districts or states, both Nunn and Aspin—and indeed most members of the military committees—do a poor job.

Let us assume for the moment, however, that members are overly attentive to local benefits in the manner that is popularly expected. The overall political effect of the resulting battles would still be muted because members must increasingly compete head-to-head when trying to protect local programs. In 1989, Congress adopted a ceiling to the defense budget that required members who made additions to find the money by cutting elsewhere in the budget. Money to salvage the F-14 and V-22 Osprey in 1989 came from the B-2 account. Money slashed from SDI in later years went directly to other procurement programs. We are thus back at the point reached by Peck and Scherer nearly thirty years ago, namely, that "a further and perhaps more important factor that reduces the impact of political activity in source selection is that many of the political pressures cancel out."[19] McNaugher recognizes these crosspressures as well when he notes that even members who are concerned about protecting local benefits must recognize that "within the defense component there may be several kinds of contractors seeking federal business."[20]

We now add another assumption, which is that DOD obliges members who are obsessed with local benefits by in fact implementing a politicized distribution of prime contracts. In effect, we now permit the Pentagon to spread the wealth in the manner of prime contractors through their subcontracts. If that is the case, then DOD in fact performs poorly in its role of targeteer: fully two-thirds of prime contracts in FY 1986 were awarded in only ten states, and twenty-four states received less than $1 billion each.[21] The same top ten states received almost exactly the same cumulative share of contracts, 67 percent, in 1988.[22] Those top ten states represent 20 percent of the Senate and just under 44 percent of the House of Representatives. The Council on Economic Priorities argues that the Pentagon purposely spread contracts for SDI around the country in order to gain support in Congress but goes on to note that 78 percent of the SDI contract dollars spent between 1983 and 1986 went to only four states.[23] Yet aggregating at the state level obscures the often unequal distribution of contracts among states' congressional districts. One economic forecasting group calculated that defense spending is in fact a net economic drain on 321 congressional districts (meaning that the district's tax bite devoted to defense is greater than its share of defense spending) and that only 64 districts received more than $1 billion in total defense spending in 1985.[24] If the Pentagon's objective is to buy support by spreading contracts, this is hardly a recipe for success.

The same holds true for subcontract targeting, which is probably a better indicator of the degree to which support can be purchased because it focuses on individual weapons systems. The subcontracting data analyzed in this book show that only a handful of congressional districts receive a significant number of subcontracts on a given program. For the aircraft carriers, only 10 districts received more than $100 million (though one district received over $3.5 billion in prime contracts). Only 8 districts received over $100 million in subcontracts in 1981 for that year's buy of F-15 fighter aircraft; 11 for the Apache in 1987. In chapter 5 I demonstrated that even this high level of spending could not ensure support for the aircraft carriers, and there is little reason to believe that such a level would be persuasive on the other two programs. Defense spending is, in fact, concentrated in a relatively small number of congressional districts that contain the firms able to do the required work. That, not politics, is the driving factor.

Pork Barrel and Representation

Even though there is, in fact, little evidence that Congress as an institution routinely votes on defense issues solely because of pork barrel concerns, many are troubled by the level of activity that suggests a parochial imperative. Members do try to protect local contracts, and they are quite noisy about it. There are cases of congressional add-ons and extreme examples of how Congress treats military bases as political trophies. The most vocal congressional critics argue that any such behavior by legislators is unacceptable. Defense pork is not akin to agriculture pork or highway construction pork or irrigation project pork. Defense is different, they say, because it is sold to the polity as a public good. Defense spending is vital, we are told, because the physical security and interests of our nation are at risk from, by turns, the Soviet Union, the Warsaw Pact, Cuba, Nicaragua, North Korea, Colombian drug kings, and small radical nations soon to possess ballistic missiles. The entire country benefits from a large military presence that protects everyone from external harm; this argument might persuade otherwise recalcitrant people to spend money on defense when they would really prefer that the money go elsewhere. If the threat truly exists, protection is worth almost any price, and a $300 billion defense budget is simply an unpleasant, though necessary, burden.

But, argue those who accept the pork barrel explanation, the public should feel cheated if it turns out that the real reason the defense budget is so large—at the expense of other uses of the money—is that it advances the political interests of those in government and the economic interests of private actors. Robert Higgs, one of the harsher judges of Congress, frames the issue as a conspiracy: "A necessary condition for pork-barrel defense procurement is acceptance—by members of Congress and by the informed public—of what amounts to treachery. Members of Congress, with only a few exceptions, routinely betray our trust. In pursuit of their very private interest in reelection, they sell out the national defense of the United States. They know they are doing it; their colleagues know they are doing it; and the public, if it pays any attention at all, knows they are doing it. Yet everyone accepts it."[25] This is, though, an overstatement. Members achieve reelection by satisfying their constituents, and if the constituents support efforts to keep production lines open and forestall cancellations, that is surely their right. When a member fights to keep a fighter aircraft production line open, presumably his or her constituents support the effort, especially those who depend on defense contracts for their jobs. At the risk of sounding like a civics teacher, I think we must recognize that even if the situation is as bad as Higgs suggests, what he is describing is Democracy in action, warts and all: representatives will always have to balance competing national and local interests. The federal government was never designed to run efficiently but rather to mute the ubiquitous concerns of self-interested people into

something resembling a national good. The inefficiencies that remain—
and there certainly are some—are in a very real sense simply the cost of
doing business.

Herein lies one of the major problems in the pork barrel argument:
what to do about it. If pork barrel is the natural outgrowth of representative politics, of elected officials looking after the needs and interests of
their constituents, how can it be prevented? On this issue, pork barrel
opponents are of little help. Another critic of congressional activity, Nick
Kotz, recognizes the need for representation, but only within certain
limits. "It is legitimate," he writes, "for the Georgia legislator to look
out for workers at Lockheed and the California senator to look out for
those at Rockwell—that is, until those narrow interests begin to distort
the overall defense equation and the use of national resources."[26] Where
should those limits be set? It is unacceptable to conclude simply that
Congress is acting parochially whenever it votes to buy a weapon that
ultimately fails to meet expectations. And we cannot draw the line according to our own self-interest and then conclude that any congressional
decision that fails a personal test of worthiness or effectiveness indicates
that Congress has sacrificed the national good for local gain. One person's pork, as the saying goes, is another's steak.

At a deeper level, however, pork barrel criticism assumes that procurement decisions are clear-cut and based on information that nobody
could have failed to interpret correctly, save for the desire to protect a
parochial interest. Congress should have known better, the argument
goes. It is one thing to look at a completed program such as the B-1, for
example, and identify all the points at which something went seriously
awry. It is quite another to identify those problems beforehand. Information about the hugely expensive, fantastically complex weapons the
military buys is not easily understood, and neither is it always conclusive. Congressional vacillation over the purchase of a system normally
reflects confusion about the information it has rather than insidious
parochialism. Take away the pork barrel imperative, and the problems
would not go away. To suggest that Congress would find it easy to cancel
the MX if the system produced no economic benefits ignores the tremendous uncertainty surrounding the debate over the future of U.S. strategic
nuclear forces.

The major difficulty is that Congress does not, and in fact cannot, distinguish between grave difficulties that call into question the value of a new system and "teething pains," which are to be expected whenever the technical state of the art is being pushed far beyond existing limits. During development, when most of the important decisions are made, the information is usually inadequate. "It is easier to stop and start projects in their early stages," writes McNaugher, "but of course such choices are made on the basis of cost and performance information that is almost always wrong."[27] Making the wrong decision—either by buying a weapon that fails to perform as advertised or by not buying a weapon that would have eventually worked out—leads to an inefficient use of resources, but most would agree that the first type of error is preferable to the second. If Congress had voted to kill every weapon system that ever experienced cost or technical problems or all systems whose tactical rationale was controversial, the U.S. arsenal would be small indeed. Early problems do not necessarily mean a system will fail to perform. The F-111 fighter bomber would never have made it through the present process, since it exceeded its budget, faced substantial technical problems, and was generally ridiculed as a symbol of defense waste. Yet, "some twenty years after the controversy, it remains the most valued of all Air Force aircraft, always the first to be sent overseas in a crisis."[28] Conversely, notes Edward Luttwak, systems that sailed through the budget process have proven to be miserable operational failures: he cites the example of early radar-guided air-to-air missiles, which promised great performance but "turned out to be almost worthless when placed in service."[29]

Even so, many observers are harshly critical of continuing pressure by contractors to keep production open or to overturn a decision to cancel. Kotz takes the position that defense contractors should not be allowed to appeal such decisions: "Lobbying by interest groups is a legitimate form of representation, but it gets out of hand when an industry continues to press for a weapon that the nation's leaders have turned down."[30] To decide at the start that a defense contractor must categorically accept an early judgment that may be based on faulty or ambiguous information is surely an antidemocratic stance. Such an attitude assumes not only that national decision makers can get it right the first time, but also that defense contractors—or more properly, the people who run them and work for them—should sacrifice their political rights simply because they perform work for the government.

People who cry, "Pork barrel!" at every turn also implicitly assume that Congress is the primary problem, especially when it refuses to accept DOD judgments. The underlying position is that congressional supervision can act in only one direction: Congress is within its rights to refuse to give the Pentagon everything it wants (especially when it comes to the size of the defense budget) but it must never do the reverse, to insist when the Pentagon says it does not want something. Many of those whom Congress enraged when it demanded that the F-14 and V-22 programs continue would probably not object if the same institution canceled the B-2. Just as the Pentagon is not always right when it wants to buy something, it is not always right when it wants *not* to buy something.

Here, the case of the A-10 ground-attack aircraft provides some evidence. The A-10 is designed to attack ground targets in support of combat infantry. The air force has never been enthusiastic about the close air support (CAS) mission and would much rather spend its money on more glamorous fighters and strategic bombers. The A-10, unlike most other aircraft in the inventory, is slow, relatively unsophisticated, and unable to perform other missions, such as air-to-air combat. Although the air force refuses to give up the mission to the army, time and again it has resisted attempts by both the secretary of defense and the Congress to force it to purchase a dedicated CAS aircraft. Instead, the air force prefers to adapt its fighters to the ground-attack role. This makes army commanders nervous, since they fear that during a war the air force would hesitate to commit multimission aircraft to CAS.[31]

About the only time the air force shows any enthusiasm for CAS aircraft is when civilian leaders threaten to take the mission away from it. In the 1960s, McNamara allowed the army to develop the first generation of attack helicopters, the Cheyenne. Although the Cheyenne was never produced, McNamara was able to use it to thrust a CAS aircraft on the air force:

> By allowing the Army to begin developing the Cheyenne helicopter gunship, McNamara implicitly threatened to remove the close-air support mission from the Air Force's domain, something no service could accept however

little importance it attached to the mission. With this threat in place, McNamara used the Navy's A-7 project . . . aimed at producing a relatively cheap, slow aircraft strictly for supporting troops, as an alternative to the Air Force's desire to continue buying supersonic, multi-capable F-4s to perform the close-support mission. The effort succeeded: the Air Force bought the A-7.[32]

Virtually identical events occurred in the early 1970s, when, according to some accounts, Secretary of Defense James Schlesinger compelled the air force to buy the A-10 by threatening to give the CAS mission to the army. The air force gave in but purchased as few A-10s as it could (about seven hundred units) and almost immediately began transferring them to the reserves.[33] In addition, almost as soon as the last A-10 rolled off the assembly line in 1984, the air force started planning a follow-on, which turned out to be a modified version of the F-16. In this latest fight, the air force is resisting efforts within Congress and OSD to promote another dedicated CAS aircraft (dubbed the Mudfighter). Congress was especially unhappy about the air force's effort; the SASC in 1988 argued that "the Air Force has devoted insufficient attention to the area of modernizing close air support. The Air Force has programmed to spend some $13 billion to develop a new generation of air to air fighter, but has budgeted virtually nothing to develop a new generation replacement aircraft for close air support."[34]

In the early 1980s, Congress continued to fund A-10 production even after the air force said it wanted no more of the aircraft; some criticized it for funding a pork barrel project. The journalist Hedrick Smith called it "a case study in protecting pork for the home folks."[35] Yet, given the traditional air force opinion of CAS aircraft, others viewed it as a legitimate case of Congress stepping in to force the CAS issue with the air force. Congress was correct in insisting that the service buy more units of a plane that it needed but never really wanted in the first place. The presumption was that the air force, lukewarm to the A-10 from the beginning, canceled the program as soon as it could, irrespective of whether it had bought enough to meet requirements. Congress kept the program alive because the air force, for its own parochial reasons, chose to stop purchasing an effective and affordable system. Even critics like Richard Stubbing agree that the A-10 has "shown high operational reliability and an excellent armor-killing capability,"[36] and the aircraft performed well in the Persian Gulf War. Although the A-10 is not a "silver bullet" able to solve all of the military's CAS problems—its low speed makes it vulnerable, and it lacks the capability to attack targets at night or in bad weather—to argue that Congress had no business continuing production is unfair. What appears to one observer as pork looks to another like a legitimate policy dispute.

The Pentagon continually complains about congressional interference in the procurement process, arguing that capricious members cause a great deal of inefficiency and waste. However, even if those on the Hill behaved as perfect, rational actors or merely did the Pentagon's bidding, problems in the acquisition process would still exist. The Pentagon's claim that everything would be fine if Congress would simply leave it alone to do its job is nonsense. During the Cold War, the military services refused to make their own hard choices and benefited from a Congress content not to step in and do it for them. Now, though, fiscal realities and dramatic international political changes have forced the Pentagon's hand, and defense officials decry Congress's unwillingness to accept the secretary's decisions quietly. Those who criticize members who fight to protect local bases think nothing of the Pentagon's own fight to protect the defense budget from further cuts or of the services' effort to protect their own pet programs. A congressional focus implicitly assumes that politics intrudes only on the Hill, when in fact it penetrates in one way or another the entire acquisition and budget procedure.

Much of the preceding discussion assumes that Congress truly is driven by the parochial imperative in its dealing with the defense budget; in fact, my research has shown this to be untrue. Although the procurement process is almost by definition political, Congress does a tolerable job at not making major decisions on the basis of purely local considerations. Members do, however, strive to extract as much political advantage as they can from defense contracts because local constituencies do care about defense benefits. Political considerations may shape the manner in which issues are approached, but the institution as a whole pays more attention to national policy aspects than it is given credit for.

The political strategies that exist in Congress ultimately make very little difference in any case. More important, they will not stand in the way of major reductions in the defense budget. The end of the Cold War and the obsolescence of the assumptions that have driven U.S. defense policy have changed the way both the military and Congress must approach the defense budget. Political strategies—strategic subcontract distributions, well-placed PAC money, carefully timed contract awards—are an effective way of getting the institution's attention, and they may also cement preexisting support. They cannot, however, carry the full load themselves. Absent a public consensus in favor of more defense spending, the Pentagon and prodefense legislators will be less and less able to get their way. Their political tools are simply not that effective.

CHAPTER 8. POLITICS, PORK, AND REPRESENTATION

1. John W. Kingdon, *Congressmen's Voting Decisions* (New York: Harper and Row, 1973), 262.

2. Bill Keller, "In Bull Market for Arms, Weapons Industry Lobbyists Push Products, Not Policy," *Congressional Quarterly Weekly Reports,* October 25, 1980, 3024.

3. Thomas L. McNaugher, *New Weapons, Old Politics* (Washington, D.C.: Brookings Institution, 1989), 11.

4. Quoted in Richard Stubbing, *The Defense Game* (New York: Harper and Row, 1986), 91.

5. Both the 70 percent figure and Schroeder's comments are from David C. Morrison, "Chaos on Capitol Hill," *National Journal,* September 27, 1986, 2305.

6. See U.S. Department of Defense, Office of the Assistant Secretary of Defense, Comptroller, *National Defense Budget Estimates for FY 1991,* 103.

7. U.S. Department of Defense, *Annual Report to the President and Congress,* January 1990, Table A-4, p. 72.

8. See, for example, James R. Payne, "Wrong Numbers: Lies and Distortions about Defense Spending," *The National Interest* (Winter 1988/1989).

9. Aerospace Industries Association, *Aerospace Facts and Figures 1986–1987* (New York: Aviation Week & Space Technology, 1986), 150.

10. Murray Weidenbaum, "Why Defense Doesn't Matter," *The National Interest* (Summer 1989): 92.

11. Ibid., 93.

12. McNaugher, *New Weapons, Old Politics,* 10.

13. *Congress and Defense* (Palo Alto, Calif.: EW Communications, 1988), 141.

14. Ibid., 143.

15. James R. Anderson, *Bankrupting America: The Tax Burden and Expenditures of the Pentagon by Congressional District* (Lansing: Employment Research Associates, 1989), 9.

16. Cass Peterson, "Seniority Doesn't Unlock Pork Barrel," *Washington Post*, October 27, 1986, A6.

17. U.S. Department of Defense, *Prime Contract Awards by Region and State, Fiscal Years 1986, 1985, 1984* (Washington, D.C.: Directorate for Information, Operations, and Reports, 1986), 28.

18. *Defense Week*, March 27, 1989, 11.

19. Morton J. Peck and Frederick M. Scherer, *The Weapons Acquisition Process: An Economic Analysis* (Boston: Division of Research, Graduate School of Business Administration, Harvard University, 1962), 382.

20. McNaugher, *New Weapons, Old Politics*, 10.

21. *Congress and Defense*, 140.

22. *Defense Week*, March 27, 1989, 11.

23. Council on Economic Priorities, *Star Wars: The Economic Fallout* (Cambridge: Ballinger Publishing, 1988), 95.

24. Anderson, *Bankrupting America*, 1.

25. Robert Higgs, "Beware the Pork Hawk," *Reason* (June 1989): 34.

26. Kotz, *Wild Blue Yonder*, 236.

27. McNaugher, *New Weapons, Old Politics*, 123.

28. Edward Luttwak, *The Pentagon and the Art of War* (New York: Simon and Schuster, 1984), 131.

29. Ibid., 31.

30. Kotz, *Wild Blue Yonder:* Money, Politics, and the B-1 Bomber (New York: Pantheon Books, 1988), 237.

31. See David Morrison, "Pentagon Dogfighting," *National Journal*, October 8, 1988, 2527.

32. McNaugher, *New Weapons, Old Politics*, 55.

33. Stubbing, *The Defense Game*, 142.

34. Cited in General Accounting Office, *Close Air Support: Status of the Air Force's Efforts to Replace the A-10 Aircraft* (GAO/NSIAD-88–211), September 1988, 11.

35. Cited in Higgs, "Beware the Pork Hawk," 32.

36. Stubbing, *The Defense Game*, 142.